PUBLIC AFFAIRS AND POLICY ADMINISTRATION SERIES

System under Stress

THIRD EDITION

Other titles in the PUBLIC AFFAIRS AND POLICY ADMINISTRATION SERIES edited by Donald F. Kettl

PUBLIC AFFAIRS AND POLICY ADMINISTRATION SERIES

System under Stress

THE CHALLENGE TO 21st CENTURY GOVERNANCE

THIRD EDITION

DONALD F. KETTL

University of Maryland

Los Angeles | London | New Delhi
Singapore | Washington DC

Los Angeles | London | New Delhi
Singapore | Washington DC

FOR INFORMATION:

CQ Press

An Imprint of SAGE Publications, Inc.

2455 Teller Road

Thousand Oaks, California 91320

E-mail: order@sagepub.com

SAGE Publications Ltd.

1 Oliver's Yard

55 City Road

London, EC1Y 1SP

United Kingdom

SAGE Publications India Pvt. Ltd.

B 1/I 1 Mohan Cooperative Industrial Area

Mathura Road, New Delhi 110 044

India

SAGE Publications Asia-Pacific Pte. Ltd.

3 Church Street

#10-04 Samsung Hub

Singapore 049483

Printed in the United States of America

A catalog record of this book is available from the Library of Congress.

978-1-4522-3990-3

This book is printed on acid-free paper.

Acquisitions Editor: Charisse Kiino

Production Editor: Libby Larson

Copy Editor: Rachel Keith

Typesetter: C&M Digitals (P) Ltd.

Proofreader: Dennis W. Webb

Indexer: Michael Ferreira

Cover Designer: Rose Storey

Marketing Manager: Jonathan Mason

Permissions Editor: Karen Ehrmann

SUSTAINABLE FORESTRY INITIATIVE
Certified Chain of Custody
Promoting Sustainable Forestry
www.sfiprogram.org
SFI-01268
SFI label applies to text stock

13 14 15 16 17 10 9 8 7 6 5 4 3 2 1

Contents

Preface

One of the themes that echoes most in American politics is why big problems recur. Something important will happen—a terrorist attack, a major hurricane, a financial crisis. Citizens, reporters, and elected officials alike will demand an investigation about what happened and call for action to ensure it won't happen again. Top government officials pledge a firm response and launch new programs. Then, despite bold promises, the big problems happen again. Citizens, reporters, and elected officials alike are outraged. Public cynicism about government's ability to govern grows, and the big problems bounce onto the agenda yet again.

Why can't we do better? Is this the product of government managers who don't know how to manage, or of government leaders who don't know how to lead? Is it the result of problems that are simply too complex for anyone to solve? Or is it the inevitable outcome of deep and persistent pathologies in the American political system that create a movie that simply replays itself over and over again, with the same unhappy results?

These are puzzles that have deep meaning for anyone who cares about American politics. They are also questions that strike to the heart of our ability to govern ourselves. In this book, I look carefully at a series of mega-crises that swept over the system during a single decade. What do they tell us about the ability of American government to meet the challenges of twenty-first century governance?

In some ways, this book is deeply personal. Like all Americans, I was shaken by the horrific events of September 11, 2001. Not long after the towers fell, my wife and I visited Ground Zero in New York, where workers were painstakingly removing the debris, where the damp odor of the pulverized buildings was overpowering, and where recovery experts were still finding human remains. That experience led me to probe the attacks in the first edition of this book—to investigate how heroic first responders saved countless lives at the cost of their own and how "homeland security" came into regular parlance.

Everyone seemed determined to learn the lessons of September 11, to avoid repeating that awful day. Four years later, a new crisis occurred—a major hurricane that assaulted the Gulf Coast—and the strategies put in place to ensure we could respond far better to crises failed at their first test. Despite years of warnings that a big storm could inflict terrible damage on New Orleans, and despite the creation of a new federal department to ensure we could respond far better to the next attack, Hurricane Katrina caught all levels of government flatfooted. The devastation and the government's failure were captured live on international television. When my wife and I explored the city just a few months after the levees collapsed, I began to see parallels between the lessons of September 11 and the lessons taught again, painfully, in New Orleans. That story became the second edition of the book, which focused on two puzzles: why, despite repeated crises, it's so hard for the system to learn; and how seemingly different crises can underline the same lessons.

As I watched the 2008 financial crisis unfold, I was struck, yet again, by these same puzzles. Experts had warned that the interlocked system of mortgages, investments, and globally interconnected transactions had exposed the nation's—and the world's—financial system to tremendous stress. Like a series of dominoes, the problems cascaded until historic private institutions fell, millions of Americans lost uncounted billions of dollars in savings, other Americans lost their homes and jobs, and the nation fell into years of sluggish economic growth and high unemployment. Not only had the warnings gone unheeded, but many of the same basic problems with the nation's governance, so evident in the September 11 and Katrina cases, seemed to have spilled over into the completely different policy area of financial regulation. How did this happen? That puzzle drives the third edition of this book, which weaves in an analysis of the financial crisis and ends with an even sharper and more pointed examination of the challenges of American governance.

In preparing this new edition, I'm indebted to reviewers who provided invaluable guidance and suggestions: Pamela Brannon, Florida Atlantic University; Bryan Brophy-Baermann, Lesley University; Matthew Jones, Portland State University; and Charles Shipan, University of Michigan. Charisse Kiino and the entire staff at CQ Press, yet again, proved enormously supportive, and I'm grateful for their help. Rachel Keith's sure hand and careful eye were extremely helpful in copyediting the book, smoothing my prose and clarifying its meaning. I also want to thank my students and colleagues in the School of Public Policy at the University of Maryland, College Park.

My wife, Sue, has continued to prove a wonderful friend, with an unerring sense for the big questions and a compass for finding the truly fundamental values. She has been my companion in exploring the tales in this book, and together we have looked at the front-line challenges our government faces. I'm truly grateful for the unfailing support she's given me throughout the three editions of this book, and in the decades we've spent together.

This book is perhaps most a tale of the hard, often unseen work of so many Americans, dedicated to finding solutions to some of the most difficult problems we face. The cases in the book are stories of challenge. Our hope for solving them lies in the public service that these Americans—especially our public servants—perform, day in and day out. They deserve our thanks and our gratitude for tackling the issues on behalf of us all.

About the Author

Donald F. Kettl is the dean of the School of Public Policy at the University of Maryland. He is also a nonresident senior fellow at the Brookings Institution.

Kettl is the author or editor of more than 20 books and monographs, including *The Politics of the Administrative Process (2012) The Next Government of the United States: Why Our Institutions Fail Us and How to Fix Them* (2008) and *The Global Public Management Revolution* (2005). He has twice won the Louis Brownlow Book Award of the National Academy of Public Administration for the best book published in public administration. In 2008, Kettl won the American Political Science's John Gaus Award for a lifetime of exemplary scholarship in political science and public administration. He was awarded the Warner W. Stockberger Achievement Award of the International Public Management Association for Human Resources in 2007 for outstanding contributions in the field of public sector personnel management.

He was awarded a PhD in political science from Yale University. Prior to his appointment at the University of Maryland, he taught at the University of Pennsylvania, Columbia University, the University of Virginia, Vanderbilt University, and the University of Wisconsin-Madison. He is a fellow of Phi Beta Kappa and the National Academy of Public Administration.

Kettl has consulted broadly for government organizations at all levels, in the United States and abroad. He has appeared frequently in national media, including National Public Radio, *Good Morning America,* the *ABC World News Tonight,* the *CBS Evening News,* CNN's *"Anderson*

Cooper 360" and *"The Situation Room,"* the Fox News Channel, the Huffington Post, Al Jazeera, as well as public television's *News Hour* and the BBC. He is a regular columnist for *Governing* magazine, which is read by state and local government officials around the country. He chaired two gubernatorial blue-ribbon commissions for the Wisconsin state government, one on campaign finance reform and the other on government structure and finance. Kettl is also a shareholder of the Green Bay Packers.

Policy Lightning

ANYONE WHO PAYS CAREFUL ATTENTION TO AMERICAN public policy—in fact, policy anywhere in the world—is constantly struck by two big puzzles. First, does government work as well as it should? Jeffrey L. Pressman and Aaron Wildavsky provided a sharp answer in the clever subtitle to their 1973 classic, *Implementation*: "*How Great Expectations in Washington Are Dashed in Oakland; or, Why It's Amazing That Federal Programs Work at All, This Being a Saga of the Economic Development Administration as Told by Two Sympathetic Observers Who Seek to Build Morals on a Foundation of Ruined Hopes.*"[1] They poked carefully around a program for urban renewal in Oakland and concluded that the odds of success of government programs were small, and that the cynical views of so many Americans were well founded. Public confidence in governmental institutions is low and shrinking. Ruined hopes too often shape the public's expectations about whether government can deliver on their dreams.

And that leads to the second puzzle. Why, once we see government's problems, don't we fix them? Why do we seem doomed not only to ruin hopes but to ruin them repeatedly? When big crises spill into the news, "How did this happen?" is inevitably followed by "How can we make sure this never happens again?" All too often, however, it *does* happen again, and that only increases the public's cynicism. Why can't government learn better to avoid problems in the first place—and then, when problems do happen, to make sure they don't recur? Many citizens around the world complain about their governments, but Americans seem to complain more than almost anyone else. After all, we are a nation founded in revolution and we drove the British from the country (twice) at the muzzle of muskets. When failures are compounded by repeat offenses, more public cynicism is inevitable. Sniping among

Jamie Dimon—chairman, president, and chief executive officer of banking giant JPMorganChase—earned the reputation of one of the world's shrewdest financial managers in steering through the financial meltdown. Despite his legendary influence and tougher bank oversight, however, a rogue trader in the bank's London office lost more than $6 billion in trades that went bad.

elected officials is one thing. Failure to deliver on promises is quite another. And failing to learn painful lessons is even worse.

Consider, for example, the 2012 tale of Bruno Iksil, known as the "London whale" at JPMorgan Chase's enormous London operation. Over the course of many months, the London whale bet he could assemble super-complex financial deals designed to make money whether the economy improved or declined. Almost no one understood what he was doing, and no one, including the firm's top management in New York, properly supervised his activities. The whale made enormous mistakes in the deals, with losses rolling to $5 billion or more, upsetting the world's financial markets and creating new instability just as the shaky economy was struggling to recover from the ongoing recession.

It was bad enough that it happened at all. Members of Congress skewered Jamie Dimon, the much-respected head of JPMorgan Chase, for the multibillion-dollar loss. Adriana Vasquez, a janitor in the bank's giant Houston building, confronted Dimon to point out that the bank had made billions in profits and stood to lose billions more, but she was paid poorly as she worked to keep the bank running. "Why do you deny the people cleaning your buildings a living wage?" she asked.[2] But even worse was that the problem occurred following warnings generated by the 2008 economic collapse, when speculative bets by commercial banks had led the world's entire financial system to the point of collapse. In 2009, three years before the JPMorgan Chase mega-loss, former Federal Reserve Board chairman Paul A. Volcker had warned President Obama in a three-page letter about such activities, urging the president to take aggressive action. Obama was convinced, and the president's staff transformed the three-page letter into a ten-page proposal. By the time the proposed regulations for the "Volcker rule" were released, they had exploded into 298 pages of extraordinarily complex text. Even the best efforts of experts to boil down the proposal produced forty-one pages of not-quite-plain-English. Volcker himself was unhappy with the result. "I don't like it, but there it is," he told a reporter. "I'd like a much simpler bill. I'd love to see a four-page bill" banning banks from speculating with depositors' money. "And I'd have strong regulators. If the banks didn't comply with the spirit of the bill, they'd go after them."[3]

When the banks collapsed in 2008, experts concluded that it was too risky to have commercial banks, in which individuals trust their savings, making big speculative bets. Those bets had cost the banks untold billions and proved far too complicated for anyone to oversee properly. Volcker argued that such speculative transactions should be separated from the basic banking business, and the president agreed. But the rule got hung up in the regulatory process. Left unrestrained by government regulations and uncontrolled by superiors who struggled to divine what he was doing, the London whale cost his bank billions of dollars. In 2008, everyone had said things like that shouldn't be allowed to happen anymore. In 2012, it happened anyway. Why do big problems happen and, even worse, why do they recur when we all conclude they should never happen again?

This is a puzzle that stretches far beyond the financial crisis. A year before Hurricane Katrina devastated New Orleans in 2005, disaster planners conducted a drill that forecast, with eerie accuracy, the implications of a major storm hitting the city. In 1993, terrorists detonated a bomb in the garage of the World Trade Center's North Tower, killing six people and causing vast damage. Al-Qaeda returned to the building with its 2001 assault and brought both towers down, along with other buildings in the New York City complex. We get warnings but too often fail to react; we learn lessons from previous disasters but fail to prepare. Too often, we are hurt by quick-hitting thunderstorms. Unlike Benjamin Franklin, we haven't invented good lightning rods.

LENNON'S LESSON

This isn't just an American phenomenon. Governments everywhere increasingly face the challenge of mastering the unexpected. The Chinese government in Beijing carefully planned a high-level engagement with the United States only to find that a single dissident, warring with a provincial government out of sync with national policy, vastly complicated the strategy. European leaders met—and met—and met—to set plans for saving the Euro, only to have voters in Greece unexpectedly force a new strategy. London Olympics planners carefully scoped out every contingency to get athletes from Heathrow Airport to the Olympic Village only to have a bus driver get hopelessly lost on the very first day.

An inescapable problem for twenty-first-century leaders is the resounding message of the great twentieth-century philosopher, John Lennon, on the Beatles' *Double Fantasy* album: "Life is what happens to you while you're busy making other plans." Small problems have a way of quickly becoming big ones. No single organization can own the solution to any problem that matters. And, despite constant complaints about "big government," bold promises to cut the size of government often collide with the harsh realities of problems for which citizens—and voters—expect solutions. In fact, toward the end of the 2012 presidential campaign, Republican Mitt Romney had just that problem. In a 2011 primary debate, he said, "Every time you have an occasion to take something from the federal government and send it back to the states, that's the right direction." After Hurricane Sandy devastated parts of the East Coast, however, his campaign amended that position. States, a statement read, "are in the best position to aid affected individuals and communities." However, "this includes help from the federal government and FEMA."[4] It's one thing to campaign against big government. It's another to say that the government won't help people in trouble. That dilemma is emerging as one of the most fundamental puzzles, theoretically and pragmatically, for government in the twenty-first century.

Consider what happened in April 2010 when BP's Deepwater Horizon rig exploded in the Gulf of Mexico. As the magnitude of the disaster became clear, news cameras raced to the shoreline to watch the oil begin to roll in, and reporters asked what the government was going to do to solve the problem. Some analysts asked, "Will this be Obama's Katrina?" comparing the crisis to the Bush administration's bungled efforts to respond to the hurricane that swamped New Orleans. In fact, as every subsequent investigation showed, the BP spill was the product of private-sector failures. Government policy was that oil platforms shouldn't blow up, and that private industry was responsible for following carefully prescribed steps and installing sophisticated equipment to prevent that from happening. Nevertheless, this private failure almost immediately became a public concern, private problems defined the public agenda, demanding immediate results and bringing the threat of media punishment for failure. As problems anywhere become problems everywhere, John Lennon's lesson is a defining—and inescapable—challenge in leading and governing.

Tom Temin, host of *The Federal Drive*, an afternoon show on Washington's Federal News Radio, has coined a term for this: "policy lightning"—what happens when lightning-strike events blow policy off course. No leader wants to be surprised. Every leader wants to respond to important problems clearly, quickly, and effectively. But it's impossible to escape two conclusions: that policy lightning occurs with disturbing frequently, and that big changes are afoot that make such lightning strikes more damaging and more frequent.

In part, this is because of the uncertain nature of the problems the governance system faces. Former U.S. defense secretary Donald Rumsfeld famously captured the dilemma in a 2002 press conference about the war in Iraq: "As we know, there are known knowns; there are things we know we know. We also know there are known unknowns; that is to say we know there are some things we do not know. But there are also unknown unknowns—the ones we don't know we don't know. And if one looks throughout the history of our country and other free countries, it is the latter category that tend to be the difficult ones."[5]

Bureaucracies are created to deal with *known knowns*, which shape and define standard bureaucratic routines. While much maligned, bureaucracy is in fact a wonderful invention, allowing society to build the capacity to accomplish very complex things. The key to bureaucracy is specialization: identifying the basic mission, breaking it down into its component parts, developing expertise to efficiently accomplish each of those components, and doing so repeatedly and predictably. Most of government's routine is specifically designed to avoid policy lightning by breaking down complex missions into routine tasks. Moreover, government is very good at dealing with known knowns. Despite its financial difficulties, the U.S. Postal Service delivers mail quickly and with remarkable efficiency, yet "Mail Delivered Yet Again Today" is never a headline. The Social Security Administration accurately delivers monthly payments to almost everyone almost all the time, and its representatives answer calls to its toll-free information number in just—on average—180 seconds.[6] The Federal Aviation Administration's air-traffic controllers safely manage 51 million takeoffs and landings every year and serve more than 730 million passengers.[7] Bureaucracy is about doing routine things well, and the overwhelming evidence is that government bureaucracy does just that.

Effectively led bureaucracies can also deal with *known unknowns*. No one knows if or where severe thunderstorms will cause lightning, but we can prepare buildings for this known unknown by installing lightning rods. As Walter Isaacson describes in his brilliant biography of Benjamin Franklin, the inventor of the lightning rod installed a device on his Philadelphia home in the 1770s.[8] After returning from his long stay in Paris, Franklin disassembled part of the house to find that his invention had been struck by lightning but had saved his home from being destroyed. Nimble and resilient bureaucracies, nimbly and resiliently led, can build similar capacity for anticipating and mitigating serious public problems. In the 1990s, the Federal Emergency Management Agency (FEMA) discovered that a large proportion of hurricane damage came from roofs blowing off in fierce winds. FEMA could pay after the fact for the vast expenses resulting from ruined homes and contents—or it could work with builders, homeowners, and local governments to encourage the installation of tie-down straps around roof trusses to keep the roofs from blowing off to begin with. Bureaucracies can manage known unknowns both through *mitigation*—helping society take steps to prevent problems and reduce their cost, through strategies like the truss straps—and through *response*—providing effective help if problems occur. Mitigation is often (but not always) better than response; strong bureaucracies are good at both, and at balancing the relative investment. But the point is that good bureaucracies can deal well with both known knowns and known unknowns.

The policy lightning problem is most serious with *unknown unknowns*—troubles that are not, and perhaps cannot be, anticipated. The BP oil spill and the Euro crisis fit into this category, as do many other problematic twenty-first century events. Now, it's important to be careful with this category; it's easy to make it a catch-all explanation whenever government fails to solve big problems. It's tempting to automatically label all such calamities "policy lightning," the product of "unknown unknowns"; after all, if they had been anticipated they surely would have been prevented. Moreover, the problem of unknown unknowns certainly isn't a twenty-first century issue. For the earliest humans, life beyond the entrance to the cave was an enormous and frightening mystery. The Book of Exodus is a tale of the Israelites' journey into the unknown. Whole movie genres, from Westerns narrating settlers' unsteady journey into wild new territory to science fiction films forecasting an unpredictable future, are about epic battles with uncertainty. From the cave to Exodus to Westerns to science fiction, there are grave dangers, enormous risks, frightening turns—unknown unknowns that challenge every step. For the leaders of bureaucracies—from the chiefs of early human tribes to the heads of the tribes of Israel, the leaders of wagon trains, and the captains of space ships—the search for effective leadership of complex organizations becomes an effort to advance the frontiers of bureaucracy to embrace and solve new problems.

LIGHTNING STRIKES

Six months after Hurricane Katrina ravaged the Gulf Coast on August 29, 2005, I stood atop the temporary levee along the 17th Street Canal in New Orleans. It was a truly remarkable sight, on both sides. Where the water had burst through and flooded this once-picturesque neighborhood, the Army Corps of Engineers was busy driving steel pilings deep into the banks to provide a temporary patch. Behind the pilings, the corps had filled in the breach with soil. Nearby were unforgettable reminders of the flood. Katrina's fierce storm surge had ruptured the canal's levees along a two-block-long path. Shreds of the enormous sandbags that had been dropped by helicopters to plug the hole lay near the temporary repairs, as did piles of branches and other debris.

With my back to the canal, I saw unimaginable devastation. Directly in front of the breach, where charming town houses once stood, nothing remained. The water had obliterated everything. Half a block away was a house on which the owners had clearly lavished a great deal of care. The beautiful molding in the dining room was easy to see—the front wall was missing. Next door, patterns of green mold blossomed on walls that had soaked for weeks in storm water. Block upon block, the scene was the same, until I reached a large, open boulevard a hundred yards wide. Not long before, the area had held debris—trees, branches, shrubs, and parts of homes—piled five stories high. Now it lay vacant. But there was also profound irony, for directly across the canal everything was normal. The storm surge had breached only one wall of the canal.

Far more eerie was the drive through the city's famous Lower Ninth Ward, home to jazz legend Fats Domino and an important part of the city's historical culture. Another levee had failed there, and the scene was even more horrifying. Along the acres and acres of what once had been a lively neighborhood, there were only a few abandoned cars. Around what had once been homes, I saw nothing larger than two cinder blocks among tiny shreds of personal lives: the burner plate of a gas stove, the mangled remains of a bicycle, a few feet of fence flattened by the water's force. The neighborhood was simply gone.

A mile away from the breach, the debris came in larger pieces. A whole house was intact upon its concrete foundation, but the water had floated the house from its lot, foundation and all, and deposited it in the middle of the street. Another house had been pushed into the one next door. One house would be mostly intact; the next would be rubble. All the homes bore a high-water mark at the middle of the second floor, testifying to the floodwater the storm had left behind for three weeks. None of the homes had windows, and all of them had spray-painted marks left by the searchers who had scoured the neighborhood for the dead. Fats Domino had survived, despite early reports that he had died in the storm, but his house and his club next door lay ruined, as did much of the city he loved. When many New Orleans residents had returned, all they had discovered of their homes was the concrete slabs on which they had been built.

The news media had saturated their coverage of the storm with images of thousands of refugees at the New Orleans Superdome and of intrepid Coast Guard helicopter pilots plucking stranded victims from their rooftops, thus painting a human face on the tragedy. But what the news cameras never succeeded in capturing was the sheer size and scope of the damage and suffering. Even six months after the hurricane struck, it was possible to drive for more than half an hour and see only the first stirrings of a return to normal life: a car dealership just reopening here, a home supply superstore there. Most of the scene remained one of devastation: motels surrounded by chain-link fences, empty strip malls with the shelving from the stores piled in the middle of the parking lot, vacant garden apartment buildings with all their windows on the first two floors shattered. For mile upon mile, the scene was a grim reminder that the news cameras had caught only a small part of the story.

Reports from neighboring Mississippi and rural parts of the Louisiana Delta made clear that even these sprawling scenes of devastation were a tiny snapshot of the far larger disaster. One Native American chief had proudly negotiated with Wal-Mart to obtain plastic containers for refugees from her tribe to use in collecting their belongings. But when tribe members returned to their community after the waters receded, they emerged with empty containers, for there was simply nothing left. Fishermen scrambled to get back to work, but they couldn't bring their fish ashore because there were no working ice plants to keep the fish fresh. When their nets broke, there were no repair shops for hundreds of miles.

Just a few months later, I returned to the scene of the attacks on the World Trade Center in New York. It had been nearly five years since the terrible day in 2001 when terrorists hijacked jumbo jets and crashed them into the towers. The site was a construction project—seventy feet deep and stretching a fifth of a mile. As with Katrina's assault on the Gulf Coast, the one thing that the news cameras had not been able to capture was the sheer scale of the disaster. The towers had reached 110 stories into the sky and, when they collapsed, they left debris piled high across block after block of lower Manhattan.

The visit brought back memories of one of the truly awful summer jobs I had held while in college. I had helped repair frosted glass panels for recessed fluorescent light fixtures in office buildings. You have undoubtedly seen them—light tubes sit within a metal case recessed into the ceiling, and a textured glass panel flips up and locks into place to diffuse the light and camouflage the fixture. A different company had won a contract to build the fixtures we worked on, but when the thousands of glass panels arrived at the construction site, workers discovered that they were a fraction of an inch too wide for the fixtures. The glass could not be machined down, so the company contracted with a small business in my hometown to use air-powered screwdrivers to disassemble the frames, remove the old glass, insert a new piece of the correct size, and put the panels back together. The new panels were then shipped back to the construction site, and the thousands of defective glass panes were tossed into a dumpster and taken to the landfill.

Years later, when I started my academic career at Columbia University, I could admire my handiwork from my office window more than ten miles away. The panels, it turned out, had been made for several floors of the World Trade Center, and the lighted floors of the two 110-story towers were among the city's most recognizable landmarks. As I prepared to teach my classes, I always got a chuckle when I looked south toward the buildings, knowing that my summer work had produced a small—a very, very small—piece of those buildings.

I visited the site with my wife just a few months after the buildings collapsed. Plywood walls erected during the search and recovery process had been turned into memorials to the 343 firefighters and 60 police officers who had died in the attacks. The street was filled with other people who had quietly come, as we had, to pay their respects to the more than 2,800 people who had lost their lives there that September morning. Just the day before that visit, in fact, workers had discovered the remains of three more victims.

The site was emotionally moving. Poignant personal notes from family members, posted nearby on the makeshift walls around historic St. Paul's Chapel—which had served as a headquarters for rescue workers—bore testimony of the rich lives of those who had died. Dust was everywhere. In fact, the smell of wet dust (the removal teams had been spraying the debris with water for months to keep the dust from blowing around) was our first introduction to the site, even from blocks away. It was impossible to escape the sense that the dust was the pulverized remains of the buildings and everything within them, including, in a small and ridiculously insignificant way, the fluorescent light panels on which I had worked as the towers were being constructed.

The two Boeing 767 jets that flew into the World Trade Center towers caused the biggest loss of life, but they were only part of the terrorist assault that morning. In an attack that was both exquisitely designed and horribly delivered, a third hijacked plane, American Airlines Flight 77, flew into the Pentagon at such enormous speed that, according to engineering experts, the plane penetrated 310 feet of the building in less than a second.[9] The west side of the building collapsed, and the 64 people aboard the plane and 125 inside the Pentagon died. Among those who lost their lives were Georgetown University economist Leslie Whittington, her husband, and her two young daughters, who were on their way to Australia for a year-long sabbatical. Also killed was Lieutenant General Timothy Maude, the thirty-four-year army veteran who had developed the highly successful "Army of One" recruiting campaign.

On a fourth hijacked plane, which al-Qaeda terrorist leaders later claimed was bound for the Capitol in Washington, passengers learned through their cell phones that other planes had been hijacked and crashed in New York and Washington. Todd Beamer, a father of two from Cranbury, New Jersey, had called GTE Airfone operator Lisa Jefferson to tell her about the hijacking. "We're going to do something," Beamer told Jefferson, and he added simply, "I know I'm not going to get out of this." He asked the operator to pass along a message to his wife, Lisa: "Tell her I love her and the boys." Beamer asked Jefferson to recite the Lord's Prayer with him. When he had finished, Beamer asked a team of fellow passengers, "Are you guys ready?" He then said, "Let's roll." Listening intently, Jefferson heard screams, a struggle, and then she lost the connection.[10] Authorities later determined that Beamer and his colleagues had rushed the cockpit and struggled with the hijackers to prevent another catastrophic attack. The plane fell from the sky into a field in Shanksville, Pennsylvania, hundreds of miles short of its intended target, killing all forty-four passengers and crew members.

On the morning of September 12, 2001, editorial writers for the *New York Times* surveyed the crushing damage of the previous day's terrorist attacks. "It was, in fact, one of those moments in which history splits, and we define the world as 'before' and 'after,'" the editors wrote sadly. "We look back at sunrise yesterday through pillars of smoke and dust, down streets snowed under with the atomized debris of the skyline, and we understand that everything has changed."[11] Chris Patten, foreign affairs commissioner for the European Union, added, "This is one of the few days in life that one can actually say will change everything."[12]

There had been no lack of warning of such threats. In fact, in early 2001, FEMA had identified the three biggest disasters that might afflict the United States: a terrorist attack in New York, a strike by a major hurricane in New Orleans, and a major earthquake in San Francisco. One of these disasters hit within months of FEMA's predictions. A second hit within four years. But despite the clear warnings and the recurring drills to prepare the nation, both events caught the system flatfooted. Before September 11, the nation's intelligence services had collected numerous threads that, if woven together, might have helped prevent the attacks. Everyone knew an assault by a major hurricane on New Orleans, most of which is below sea level and all of which is protected by an extended string of vulnerable levees, could leave large parts of the city under water. Nevertheless, when the long-feared storm arrived, local, state, and federal officials were woefully unprepared. Nowhere were the problems worse than at FEMA, which had itself issued the warning.

THE RISE OF "HOMELAND SECURITY"

In the weeks that followed the September 11 terrorist attacks, President George W. Bush and his advisers devised a new strategy for "homeland security." The president appointed Pennsylvania Governor Tom Ridge to head a new White House Office of Homeland Security, and at Ridge's swearing-in ceremony Bush outlined his strategy. "We will take strong precautions aimed at preventing terrorist attacks and prepare to respond effectively if they might come again," he said. "We will defend our country; and while we do so, we will not sacrifice the freedoms that make our land unique."[13]

The "homeland security" label rankled some Americans. To some, it sounded Hitler-esque, an echo of the German dictator's plan to purify his homeland. Others thought it had an Orwellian "big brother" feel to it. In fact, according to *New York Times* columnist and wordsmith William Safire, *homeland* had begun to creep into the political lexicon during the early 1900s as Zionists worked to establish a Jewish homeland in Palestine. Fascists in Austria and Germany later picked up the term to refer to "homeland defense." Conservatives began using the word well before September 11 to refer to defense of the United States from a new variety of modern threats. At the same time, defense analysts began exploring the national implications of a spread of terrorism. It was not surprising, therefore, that when the Bush administration needed to respond quickly to September 11, it used concepts—and a name— already in play. There were alternatives, such as the less ponderous "domestic security," but that risked confusion about threats from abroad that might affect the nation's communities. So Washington policymakers reached for a term already in common (if narrow) use and built their new policy on it.

Bush faced several dilemmas. He pledged to prevent attacks, but he also promised to be ready to respond if they occurred. He pledged to defend the country but promised to defend liberty. He struggled with the central, inescapable trade-off at the core of "homeland security": achieving security against new, uncertain threats from terrorism inevitably meant giving up other things, including some freedoms. Just how much protection did the nation want? And how much sacrifice of civil rights and individual liberties would citizens tolerate in exchange for that protection?

That led administration officials to the central dilemma. They sought *prevention*: to do everything possible to ensure that those who might launch such attacks were stopped before they could try. But they also needed to strengthen *response*: to do everything possible, should an attack occur, to minimize injuries, loss of life, and damage to property. Administration officials knew that although any attack was unacceptable, total protection was impossible. The terrorists had proved that they were cunning strategists who worked hard to identify and exploit points of vulnerability. Officials were also aware that they needed to strengthen the system's response. But that would matter only if the prevention strategy failed, and they didn't want to talk publicly about that possibility. Officials thus needed to maximize their ability to respond while doing everything possible to prevent attacks in the first place.

For years, defense analysts had been warning that the nation needed a stronger strategy to prevent attacks. Just three months before the attacks, in fact, a coalition of defense think tanks had staged an exercise at Andrews Air Force Base, just outside Washington, to explore the potential effects of a smallpox attack on the United States. Called "Dark Winter," the exercise put experienced government officials into a hypothetical situation and tracked their decisions (former senator Sam Nunn, D-Ga., for example, played the president).[14] The exercise suggested that as many as a million Americans might die from such an attack. Analysts concluded that the nation's leaders were ill prepared for bioterrorism and that the health system did not have the capacity to deal with mass casualties.[15] As Nunn ominously told a congressional committee on July 23, 2001, following the "Dark Winter" exercise, "You often don't know what you don't know until you've been tested. And it's a lucky thing for the United States that—as the emergency broadcast network used to say: 'This is just a test, this is not a real emergency.' But Mr. Chairman, our lack of preparation is a real emergency."[16]

Indeed, earlier events had shown the need for a better national strategy to identify threats and prevent attacks, which were growing in number and destructiveness. The very same group of terrorists who launched the September 11 attacks had bombed the World Trade Center in 1993. Six people died in that attack and more than a thousand were injured. In Oklahoma City in 1995, an American, Timothy McVeigh, blew up the Murrah Federal Building and killed 168 people. In 2003 police arrested Eric Rudolph for the bombing of Atlanta's Centennial Park during the 1996 Summer Olympics. The bombing of the Yale Law School in May 2003, just days before graduation, hurt no one but made those attending the ceremonies very jittery.

Other nations have struggled for years with terrorist activity, from attacks in Israel during the Palestinian uprising to explosions staged by Northern Ireland partisans in London. A Japanese religious cult obsessed with a coming apocalypse released sarin, a nerve gas, into the Tokyo subway system in 1995. The attack miraculously killed only twelve, but it injured more than five thousand. In 1996 al-Qaeda killed nineteen American servicemen in an attack on the Khobar Towers military barracks in Saudi Arabia. In 1998 the group simultaneously bombed the American embassies in Nairobi and Dar es Salaam. More than three hundred persons, including twelve Americans, died in those two attacks.

Disaffected groups have increasingly relied on terrorism, especially since the end of the Cold War in the 1980s. Facing big and powerful military forces, these groups have realized that small, focused, continual attacks—especially attacks on civilians—can undermine governments and strengthen their own position. An unrelenting terror campaign drove Russian troops out of Afghanistan, and groups in the Middle East began plotting more such attacks against American might. Handfuls of terrorists could not directly take on the American military, so they plotted what military analysts call "asymmetric attacks," bypassing the main military forces to inflict terror and pain, gain publicity, and deliver a message that no head-on military attack ever could.[17]

America's long-stated policy against negotiating with terrorists helped shape the terrorists' strategy. American officials had determined never to be forced into bargaining with people who used violence to advance their goals. But if terrorists could not seize hostages and negotiate political deals, they found that they could use violence to promote their ideas and try to frighten nations that pursued policies they opposed.

Resorting to violence has also made terrorists more secretive, impeding the efforts of government intelligence services to identify threats and uproot terrorist cells.

Meanwhile, innovative technologies have opened new avenues to terrorists. Weapons have become smaller and more portable. The miniature nuclear bomb that fits into a suitcase is now the antiquated device of spy novels. Although such a weapon is not feasible, it has become possible to put a nuclear bomb in a container small enough to be easily transported in a van. Microscopic bits of anthrax could kill hundreds and radioactive materials could injure thousands, and other biological and radiological weapons are also highly portable. After September 11, investigators discovered that Osama bin Laden and his al-Qaeda terrorist cells communicated through highly sophisticated cellular phone networks and e-mail, even as bin Laden was hiding in primitive caves.

Small numbers of terrorists, armed with sophisticated weapons and even more sophisticated strategies, can stage bold attacks. America's massive military forces, which can defeat any army in the world, cannot guarantee protection against such tactics. The nation's homeland defense can be excellent, but 99.9-percent protection is not enough when terrorists can slip through tiny cracks in the system and inflict enormous damage. It took just nineteen terrorists, armed with weapons that passed through metal detectors in at least four different airports, to stage the September 11 attacks.

In the years after the September 11 attacks, the Bush administration focused squarely on terrorist risks. It would have been unthinkable to do otherwise. The attacks had killed more Americans on American soil than any belligerent act since Pearl Harbor, and al-Qaeda made clear that the assault was only the first in what it pledged would be a long campaign. In signaling their resolve to prevent a slide back into business as usual, Bush and members of Congress agreed to create a new cabinet department to bring together the related elements of the homeland security mission. Twenty-two agencies, from the Secret Service to the Immigration and Naturalization Service, joined in a new campaign to protect and defend the homeland.

One of the agencies incorporated into the Department of Homeland Security was FEMA, which had long been responsible for helping the nation recover from major disasters, natural or manmade. FEMA was the organizational child of the civil defense organization created to help the nation rebuild after a possible nuclear attack, and its homeland security roots run deep. After Hurricane Andrew forged a devastating path through southern Florida in 1992, however, the Clinton administration worked hard to significantly strengthen its capacity to help communities recover from natural disasters. Andrew, a Category 5 storm, had wiped whole neighborhoods off the map, and the scale of the devastation was almost unimaginable. FEMA's response, however, was poor and sluggish, and federal officials vowed that that they would learn Andrew's lesson and ensure that no community ever had to suffer in that way again.

But Katrina's swath through the Gulf Coast belied that promise. Yet again, Americans were in great peril and their government's response proved slow and ineffective. After forming in the Caribbean, Katrina had threaded its way between Florida and Cuba before blowing suddenly into a Category 5 storm. It weakened slightly before slamming into Louisiana and Mississippi but remained the third strongest hurricane ever to hit the United States, with winds of 125 miles per hour and monstrous storm surges. Damage was extensive from Texas to Florida, but New Orleans suffered the greatest damage. Levees designed to protect the city from an even larger storm failed as the water poured in.

It was the worst-case fear of longtime emergency planners—precisely the storm FEMA planners had worried about in 2001 and for which they had conducted major exercises just the year before. New Orleans is shaped like a bowl, with levees at the edges to hold back the Mississippi River and Lake Pontchartrain. The storm hit the city with a glancing blow; it was the back side of the storm that inflicted most of the damage. The retreating storm's winds pushed a wall of water across Pontchartrain and down the city's drainage canals. The levees, which had been designed to withstand a storm of the size Katrina had attained when it finally hit New Orleans, failed at several key points. Water poured through the gaps and quickly made most of the city impassable. Within hours, about 80 percent of the city was submerged, in some places to a depth of twenty feet.

Many residents who did not (or could not) evacuate in time were stranded inside their homes. As the water rose, they moved higher and higher until, trapped in their attics, they chopped through their roofs and frantically waved to Coast Guard helicopters flying rescue duty overhead. An estimated 25,000 refugees gathered at the Superdome, the city's sports arena, where they quickly ran out of the meager emergency supplies of food and water. The Superdome became rancid from a lack of air conditioning and toilet facilities. Another 20,000 evacuees gathered a few blocks away at the New Orleans Convention Center, where the facilities soon became just as bad.

In the steamy heat, elderly evacuees died without their medicine. Civil order broke down. Many of the city's police officers were victims themselves, and some simply walked off the job. Those working the streets found themselves without radio communications or gasoline for

Failure of the levee along the London Avenue Canal, along with breaches in the 17th Street and Industrial canals, led to widespread flooding in New Orleans. The back side of Hurricane Katrina's storm surge pushed water down the narrow canals. When the walls collapsed, water quickly covered 80 percent of the city.

their police cruisers. Ammunition ran short as rioters and looters ran wild. New Orleans Mayor Ray Nagin found himself isolated from most other city officials and resorted to communicating with the outside world through interviews with CNN. "I need everything," he pleaded. When help did not arrive quickly, he condemned federal officials. "They're thinking small, man. And this is a major, major, major deal. And I can't emphasize it enough, man. This is crazy." Federal officials told him that help was on the way. Nagin countered, "They're not here." Frustrated, he added, "Now get off your asses and do something, and let's fix the biggest goddamn crisis in the history of this country."[18] Louisiana Governor Kathleen Blanco phoned President Bush and asked for "all federal firepower." She continued, "I mean everything. Just send it. Give me planes, give me boats . . ."[19]

Their pleas for help seemed to go nowhere. News broadcasts from the scene showed hungry, thirsty, desperate, often angry people swarming the makeshift evacuation centers. Others waved the shirts off their backs to helicopters. Airboats poked along the flooded streets while the police and National Guard struggled to keep the city from drifting into anarchy. It was all broadcast live into the nation's living rooms. The images provided searing evidence of the tragedy, and they led to tough questions from many citizens. If CNN could get its cameras to the scene, why could the government not deliver food and water? If network broadcasters could use satellites to beam out their video, why were government officials having such a hard time talking with each other?

As the waters receded in New Orleans and across the Gulf Coast, the search for victims began. It quickly turned grim. Rescuers found thirty-four residents of St. Rita's Nursing Home who had drowned in the storm. Their searches found other victims, some floating in the tepid water and others trapped in their homes. In all, more than 1,800 people died in the storm. Property damage exceeded $75 billion, making Katrina one of the most costly natural disasters in the nation's history. But the consequences paled in comparison with the near meltdown in the nation's—indeed, the world's—financial system just three years later.

FINANCIAL COLLAPSE

On January 3, 2009, Michael Lewis and David Einhorn wrote a devastating column in the *New York Times*. Americans, they said, were entering the new year as "financial lunatics." For a long time, "even our harshest critics have been inclined to believe that we knew what we were doing." But then came the gargantuan financial collapse of late 2008. In just a few short weeks, one of the world's oldest and most respected investment banking firms, Lehman Brothers, declared bankruptcy. Since 1850, the firm, founded by two Bavarian immigrants, Henry and Emanuel Lehman, had helped arrange the financing for the growth of many of America's best-known companies, such as Macy's and BFGoodrich. When it came tumbling down, along with hundreds of community banks, the stock market plummeted, falling more than 22 percent at the beginning of October 2008. The nation's two largest funders of home mortgages, Freddie Mac and Fannie Mae, were taken over by the federal government. Housing prices continued the steep decline that had begun a year before, and many homeowners found they were "underwater," owing mortgages higher than their homes were worth. The crumbling of the home mortgage market, the stock market collapse, and deeper problems in the financial industry led many banks to close or to be acquired by others. Credit froze up, with few lenders being willing to lend money to anyone for anything until the markets stabilized. It was, Lewis and Einhorn said, "the end of the financial world as we knew it."[20]

Although big financial problems had been brewing for months, the bankruptcy of the giant investment banking firm Lehman Brothers catapulted the problems into a full-scale crisis, which soon spread across the globe.

The crisis staggered the financial system, producing a precipitous decline in home prices and driving unemployment to 10 percent (much higher in some especially hard-hit parts of the country) by October 2009. The Obama administration counterattacked with a $787-billion economic stimulus program, even though that drove the federal debt to astonishing heights. Recovery proved very slow and excruciatingly painful, and the battle over recovery of American jobs defined the central contest in the 2012 campaign between Obama and Republican challenger Mitt Romney.

At the bottom of this crisis, bigger than any the U.S. economy had suffered since the Great Depression of the 1930s, were simple questions: How did we allow this to happen? Didn't anyone see this coming? After all, private bond rating agencies like Moody's and Standard & Poor's had been paid to judge the safety of investments. The federal government had charged an alphabet soup of regulatory agencies—the Securities and Exchange Commission, the Federal Reserve, the Office of the Comptroller of the Currency, and a host of others—with overseeing the financial industry. But, in the end, neither private nor public regulators had proved up to the task. The simple questions, as it turned out, had simple answers: too many investors, from ordinary home buyers to masters of the financial universe, were leveraging their borrowing beyond their means. And far too many financial investments were too complicated for anyone to fully understand what they were selling or buying. One symptom of the problem was that many investment banking firms were aggressively recruiting astrophysicists.

Astrophysicists and investment banking? Astrophysics requires the ability to create complex models through advanced mathematical analysis and thus promised to be extremely helpful in designing intricate financial instruments that would make money no matter which way the markets moved. This approach serves very well to predict the behavior of stars and the motion of planets. When it was applied to the financial system by people who didn't understand the financial forces they were modeling, and when it was based on assumptions that could easily be proved wrong, the result was what one might expect: economic disaster.

Stung badly by the collapse, federal regulators sought to understand not only what had happened but also how to predict future weak spots in the system and keep rips in the financial fabric from producing a deeper collapse. In early 2012, the Federal Reserve conducted a special analysis of the nation's banking system, a "stress test" that subjected the banks to projections about their financial health under a variety of difficult economic circumstances, including a severe recession. The most severe test involved the following scenario: unemployment of 13 percent, a drop in housing prices of 21 percent, big shocks to the stock and financial markets, and economic recessions in both Asia and Europe. Compared with the high anxiety of 2008's economic crisis, the news was mostly good: fifteen of the nation's nineteen largest banks received a good grade. Even after such economic shocks, most of the banks would have adequate capital to stay in business and make good on their customers' deposits. Everyone—bankers and the stock markets—breathed a sigh of relief.

In the midst of the meltdown, the Fed and Treasury had taken historically aggressive action to shore up the banking system. In many banks, assets vaporized as complex instruments, including some modeled by the astrophysicists, lost value or simply could not be traded, since no one knew whether they were worth anything. This jeopardized the ability of the banks to stay in business. In addition, as many bankers put it, the credit markets "froze up": bankers didn't know who they could trust to repay loans, and they didn't know what collateral borrowers had put up to secure their loans. As a result, almost no one was lending anyone any money to do anything, and that increased the downward economic spiral to the point of near collapse of the international financial system.

Congress rushed through the Troubled Asset Relief Program (TARP) to put up $700 billion that the Treasury could use to buy the "troubled assets" of banks to keep them afloat. Under the program, any dividends the banks paid had to be approved by the federal government, to avoid a situation in which the government propped up the banks and the banks used their government-funded capital to reward private shareholders. Many of the banks had recovered to the point that the federal government authorized them to begin buying back their shares and to resume paying dividends to shareholders. To determine whether it was safe to go further, the Fed conducted its stress test, and most of the banks got high grades.

The executives of JPMorgan Chase were among those who celebrated the March 2012 announcement that their firm had scored well in the stress test. This meant not only that the bank had weathered the crisis but also that it was ready for a robust relaunch of its global operations. Before the 2008 crisis had shifted into high gear, the bank had been one of the strongest in the world. In March 2008, through weekend negotiations with the Fed, JPMorgan Chase had acquired Bear Stearns at a deeply discounted price. It emerged from the collapse not only as the nation's largest bank but with the reputation of being an exceptionally well-managed bank. Jamie Dimon, the bank's president, chairman of the board, and chief executive officer, was widely seen as one of the very best bank officers anywhere. He championed Wall Street's efforts to fight off even more governmental control. Following the 2008 debacle, Dimon took a straightforward approach to restoring the banking industry's reputation. "You do the right thing every day, or try to. There will be mistakes—you correct them," he said. That approach won him the reputation of "America's least-hated banker," as a *New York Times* headline put it.[21] Dimon and JPMorgan Chase celebrated the strong stress test scores by announcing a 20-percent increase in the bank's dividends, saying that it would buy back $15 billion of its stock from the federal government. Clearly they intended to lead the charge back from the financial precipice.

But just months later came the reports that the London whale had engaged in rogue trading. At first, Dimon dismissed the news as "a complete tempest in the teapot," which his London colleagues would recognize as a twist on the British idiom "storm in a teacup."[22] But Dimon had this one wrong. Initial estimates that the loss would be $2 billion soon doubled and then tripled. JPMorgan Chase had to postpone its stock buyback, an embarrassment to the bank's efforts to rebuild itself and lead the financial industry to success.

Even more fundamental, though, were a series of stunning questions: How did such a powerful global institution find itself entrapped in the international financial meltdown? How, once it managed its way through the collapse and received stellar grades from the stress test, did it yet again find itself derailed by activities its top executives did not understand and had not approved? To return to our core puzzles, why don't government's policy systems work better? And why, once we see problems, can't we fix them?

ADMINISTERING THE STRESS TEST

The stress test label, of course, comes from medicine. For the uninitiated, this is a test doctors give to check how well a person's heart works. The doctor wires the patient to a heart monitor and the patient hops onto a treadmill. The doctor starts the treadmill and gradually increases the speed and slope to see how well the heart responds—and how long the patient can last. The cardiologist is very, very careful, but he always has a faint smile as he makes his patients sweat.

The test is extremely valuable. It checks how well the heart supplies blood to the body, including to its most important muscle, the heart itself. It can also reveal any underlying problems, like abnormal rhythms, that could prove dangerous or fatal if the heart had to respond to unusual stress. This is important for people who have cardiovascular disease so that their physician can determine how best to treat the illness. And it can prove a lifesaver for people who don't yet know they have circulatory problems. Doctors have developed a remarkable array of treatments to help people with cardiovascular problems live long and happy lives. But to do so, they need to diagnose simmering problems before they rear up, because sudden heart attacks are often life threatening—and sometimes fatal.

If serious problems show up in one stress test, the cardiologist will usually recommend strong treatment for the patient—perhaps some medication, a change in diet and exercise, and sometimes a surgical procedure to diagnose and treat the trouble. If two stress tests in short succession show serious problems, the cardiologist will be very worried. These results will almost always bring quick and powerful treatment, because physicians know that these problems never get better on their own—and they often get worse. Cardiologists never tell patients they "failed" a stress test. They don't want to be judgmental. But back-to-back tests showing continuing problems will induce any cardiologist to exchange her warm bedside manner for a stern lecture on the need for more exercise and a better diet.

American government had three stress tests in seven years—the 2001 terrorist attacks, the 2005 hurricane, and the 2008 financial collapse.

Any cardiologist whose patient showed those symptoms would act aggressively and immediately. Of course, government officials did likewise. In each case officials pledged aggressive action to ensure that the problems would not recur, promising to rebuild bigger and better than ever. The nation's emergency preparedness and response system has clearly improved. Indeed, a whole new federal department and a vastly expanded field of study, both christened "homeland security," have come to center stage. Financial regulation is now unquestionably stronger. But despite these efforts, there are disturbing signs that government officials have not put into practice what the two disasters so painfully taught us. Even though the experiences of September 11 offered obvious lessons, we suffered from many of the same problems when Katrina struck. And the 2012 fiasco resulting from the London whale's activities occurred despite promises that the system had been fixed—and despite the clean bill of health the Fed's own stress test had provided.

These three stress tests are a powerful diagnostic tool, for they provide strong insights into what government does well—and what it doesn't. A careful look at how these crises have affected the system not only can assist us in determining how best to improve policy, but also can give us powerful clues into the inner workings of American government—the analytic insight that can help us see what often remains hidden in the government's daily operations.

POLICY LIGHTNING AND PUBLIC POLICY

Citizens rely on government to manage the country's defense and foreign affairs, to help communities recover in times of need, to safeguard their banking system and protect their savings. The very nature of these issues, however, requires citizens to play central roles themselves. No matter how good a homeland security system the nation builds, it cannot be foolproof, and terrorists can find a way to exploit any vulnerability. Citizens anywhere may find themselves at risk from natural disasters, and they might have to rely on their own wits for safety. And investors who sink their money into things they don't understand and who spend beyond their means are courting big trouble.

Citizens want strong leaders who can help them understand the threats they face and what they can do about them. When problems happen, they want a government that can respond, quickly and effectively. Moreover, they have little patience for problems that recur after everyone, especially government officials, had full warning. After September 11, analysts and media pundits pointed endlessly to the "connecting-the-dots" lapse in dealing with problems that, in hindsight, seemed to have been in full public view but for which diagnosis and prevention beforehand and effective response afterward seemed hamstrung by a lack of vision and coordination.

In the days after September 11, the news media were full of stories posing the question, "Why do they hate us?" Reporters tried to fathom why the terrorists would willingly give their lives to kill and injure Americans they had never met, and why other foreigners would dig deep into their pockets to finance the operation. Understanding that the terrorists came from "failed societies that breed anger," as *Newsweek* put it, helped a bit.[23] But Americans were looking for more than just an intellectual explanation. As parents struggled to convince nervous children that they were safe, the nation's citizens wanted—and needed—reassurance that the government was doing everything it could to prevent similar attacks in the future. President Bush's resolute speeches fueled a bump in his public approval rating to more than 90 percent. But as memories of the September 11 attack faded, his ratings fell back. Even at the height of Bush's popularity, however, analysts and observers on all fronts worried about whether the attacks demonstrated a fundamental failure of American government. The criticism extended to state and local governments, which found themselves financially stretched and administratively challenged in coping with new security demands. Many governors and mayors, used to responding to floods and fires, suddenly found themselves worried about terrorists—and the need to reassure citizens they were safe in their homes.

Four years later, Katrina only reinforced this debate. When the news cameras showed horrific scenes of Americans stranded without food or drink or focused on bodies floating in tepid water, the outrage was loud and inescapable. Many Americans demanded to know how the government could have so failed its citizens. Some observers countered that some of the victims had ignored the warnings to evacuate, but many New Orleans residents simply had not been able to leave. Some were old or ill. Others had no cars and little money for tickets on the last planes and buses out of town. "It's like being in a Third World country," one hospital manager said sadly in struggling to deal with the storm's consequences.[24] Why did the government not respond better to citizens' obvious needs? The recurring question seemed to have no satisfactory answer.

Then came the financial meltdown, as many citizens saw the value of their homes plummet and their retirement savings dissolve. Giant institutions, whose history and stability had helped provide reassurance through financial storms, evaporated overnight. A psychology of panic swept over many investors. As Hyun Song Shin, an economics professor at Princeton, explained, "It's like having a fire in a cinema," because "everybody is rushing to the door. You are rushing to the door because everyone is rushing to the door. Clearly, as a collective action, it is a disaster."[25] The headlines were tales of unrelenting disaster, with one financial crisis tumbling to the next, and with problems in one investment bank quickly infecting the rest of the nation's—and then the world's—economy. The sense of unease was palpable. The aura of anxiety was inescapable. But worst of all, according to the official government commission created to investigate the crisis, "this financial crisis was avoidable." In fact, the report concluded, "the captains of finance and the public stewards of our financial system ignored warnings and failed to question, understand, and manage evolving risks within a system essential to the well-being of the American public. Theirs was a big miss, not a stumble. While the business cycle cannot be repealed, a crisis of this magnitude need not have occurred. To paraphrase Shakespeare, the fault lies not in the stars, but in us."[26]

This, in fact, is a theme—perhaps even a frequent indictment—of American democracy. Just as Cassius pleaded with Brutus in Shakespeare's *Julius Caesar*, we have to confront this basic question: does the human condition, coupled with the workings of the American system, make such crises inevitable? The stress tests of these crises provide important clues about what happens, why it keeps happening, and what we can do about it.

C h a p t e r

2

Coordination Dilemmas

THE MAINE COAST CREATES A PICTURESQUE BACKDROP for the Portland International Jetport. Inside the modern terminal, airport security officials long ago installed x-ray machines and hidden surveillance cameras. For travelers trying to avoid the traffic congestion around Boston's Logan Airport, it proves a convenient spot for connecting to other flights.

On the morning of September 11, the surveillance cameras caught two young travelers carrying lightweight bags. The bags passed x-ray inspection and the two hurried to their plane for the short hop to Boston. Once at Logan, they had to rush to catch their connecting flight, American Airlines Flight 11 to Los Angeles. Their connection was tight. They made it to their seats near the front of the plane, but their luggage was left behind on the tarmac. Inside these bags, detectives would later find a will and other papers suggesting the impending death of Mohammed Atta, who soon after takeoff led a team of five hijackers in taking over the two-aisle Boeing 767 aircraft.

Flight controllers overheard a mysterious message from the jet. "We have some planes," said a voice over the open radio. "Just stay quiet and you will be OK. We are returning to the airport." The transmission continued, "If you try to make any moves, you'll endanger yourself and the airplane." Inside the cockpit, the voice warned, "Just stay quiet." Flight attendant Betty Ong grabbed her cell phone and called the American Airlines operations center. She told Craig Marquis, the manager on duty, that hijackers had seized the plane, killed one flight attendant, seriously wounded another, and slit a passenger's throat before storming the cockpit. Another flight attendant, Mary Amy Sweeney, was able to reach Michael Woodward, an American Airlines manager back at Boston's Logan Airport. Sweeney told Woodward that the hijackers were armed with sharp instruments, perhaps box cutters. (The box cutter, sold in hardware stores, is a shirt-pocket-size metal sheath holding a razor blade that slides out to open packing boxes.)

Controllers frantically tried to raise the crew on the radio but heard nothing. Anxious to figure out what was happening, Woodward asked Sweeney where the plane was. Sweeney craned her head to look out the window and reported that she saw water and buildings. Radar tracks later showed that the plane had made a sudden turn to the south over Albany, New York, and picked up speed as it flew down the Hudson River toward Manhattan. Woodward heard Sweeney say, "Oh my God— oh my God," and then the plane, piloted by Mohammed Atta, crashed at enormous speed into the World Trade Center's North Tower.[1]

United Airlines Flight 175, another Boeing 767, had taken off from Boston just fourteen minutes after American Airlines Flight 11. Soon after the plane left the ground, the pilot noticed something wrong in the radio traffic from another plane. "We heard a suspicious transmission on our departure," the pilot radioed in. "Sounds like someone keyed the mike and said, 'Everyone stay in your seats.'"[2] Minutes later, the pilot found his cockpit overwhelmed by the same tactics that had hijacked American Airlines Flight 11. Just as Atta had done, the hijackers cut off the radio and disconnected the transponder, the device that automatically broadcasts the plane's location, direction, and speed. To the horror of Americans all over the country watching the North Tower inferno live on television, the hijacker at the controls, believed to be Atta's cousin Marwan Al-Shehri, took the plane on a looping turn and flew it into the South Tower of the World Trade Center.

The crew and passengers of two Boeing 757s—smaller, single-aisle planes—found themselves hijacked as well. American Airlines Flight 77 took off from Washington's Dulles Airport, bound for Los Angeles. Authorities suspect that the hijackers used sharp blades to disable the crew, take control of the plane, and fly it into the Pentagon. A fourth team of hijackers at Newark, New Jersey, seized United Airlines Flight 93 and turned it toward Washington; investigators suspected they were aiming for the Capitol. Air traffic congestion had delayed the plane's takeoff, giving its passengers time to use their cell phones to learn the fate of the other planes. They were determined that their plane would not be used as a bomb and gave their lives in a frenzied rush to the cockpit. It was the only plane that did not reach the terrorists' intended target that morning.

In the days and weeks that followed, investigators struggled to determine what had happened—and how it had happened. There was a powerful sense that the nation's airport security system had broken down. Somehow dangerous individuals had gotten dangerous weapons

Early on the morning of September 11, two men, later identified by authorities as Mohammed Atta (right) and Abdulaziz Alomari (center), passed through security screening at Portland International Jetport. Minutes later, they took a commuter flight to Boston, where they boarded American Airlines Flight 11. Soon after takeoff, they joined with three other hijackers to take over the plane and crash it into the World Trade Center's North Tower. This ghostly image of the two men coasting through security would later come to represent the apparent ease with which the hijackers exploited the gaps in airline security.

aboard the planes and had turned the planes themselves into weapons. Somehow the intelligence services that were supposed to alert officials to threats had not detected the hijack plan. Somehow the hijackers had discovered and exploited holes in America's security, to disastrous effect. The system had failed, and cries arose across the country begging for it to be fixed to ensure that such a horrific attack would never recur.

The hijackers had passed through the security systems at four different airports. If the weapons in fact had been box cutters (analysts remain uncertain what weapons the hijackers used) and if the screeners had discovered them (and there was no evidence that they did), they would have been powerless to confiscate them. Under Federal Aviation Administration (FAA) regulations, in place since a spate of hijackings involving pistols in the early 1970s, passengers were forbidden to carry "deadly" or "dangerous" weapons onto airplanes. However, knives with blades less than four inches long were legal. Box cutters contain razor blades less than half that length. Why was four inches the standard? Many travelers carried pocketknives, especially the popular Swiss army knives, and FAA regulations seemed to recognize that practice. But the head of aviation policy for the Government Accountability Office (GAO), Congress's investigative organization, said that the rule about knives "was always a puzzle to me." As Gerald Dillingham said a few days after the hijackings, "I couldn't find an explanation of why 4 inches was acceptable. I'm still trying to find it."[3]

As investigators tracked the movements of the hijackers in the period before the attacks, they determined that several of them had taken previous flights to test the airlines' routines. They knew that they could sneak small blades onto aircraft. They had carefully studied boarding procedures, routes and landmarks, and when flight attendants began their meal service. They had checked the security of the cockpits and found that the doors could easily be forced open. They had found that morning flights were far more likely to be on time than evening flights and that Tuesday flights, especially after the end of summer vacations, were often less crowded, which meant fewer passengers would have to be controlled. So the hijackers decided to act on the morning of the second Tuesday in September to make it easier to synchronize their attacks. To maximize the explosions they were planning, they chose large planes fully fueled for transcontinental trips.

Within a few hours after the attacks, federal investigators identified the September 11 hijackers and linked them to al-Qaeda, an international terrorist ring responsible for the 1993 truck bombing of the World Trade Center. Having failed to cause sufficient damage in that first attack, al-Qaeda's leader, Osama bin Laden, and his chief lieutenants determined to try again, this time with a more sophisticated plan and larger weapons targeted at the major symbols of New York's financial power and Washington's political and military centers. The collapse of the two World Trade Center towers and other buildings in the area proved the most destructive attack on American soil since Pearl Harbor.

Fearing that yet more planes might be hijacked and turned into bombs, the FAA, for the first time in history, ordered all planes to land immediately at the nearest available airport. Passengers on transcontinental flights found themselves at small midwestern airports, and planes scheduled for transatlantic flights crowded small Canadian airports. In St. John's, Newfoundland, where the airport typically saw just one small passenger plane land each day, twenty-seven jumbo jets containing a total of 4,300 people arrived within a very short time. Tiny Gander, a Newfoundland town of 10,000 people, almost doubled its population within hours with thirty-nine jets on the ground. The Canadians proved to be generous hosts, despite the overwhelming crowds that strained their capacity to house and feed everyone. Grateful Americans later set up special scholarship funds for the children of those who had helped them.

The skies remained eerily empty for two days. For the first time in generations, no aircraft—except military fighters on patrol—were in the air over the United States. Air operations gradually returned, but not to normal. Travelers faced tough new restrictions, from extra identification checks while boarding to additional screening of their luggage. Waits in security lines, which had lasted only minutes, now stretched into hours. Ronald Reagan National Airport, just across the Potomac River from Washington and within sight of the Capitol, stayed closed for three weeks. When it reopened, the FAA restricted it to many fewer flights on highly restricted flight paths. Many Americans were afraid to fly. Airline traffic remained depressed for years following the attacks, and the airline industry suffered an enormous financial blow.

Everyone agreed that air travel security needed to be tighter. In fact, the long lines at airport checkpoints provoked surprisingly few complaints. Some frequent fliers ridiculed the new regulations. They discovered, for example, that they could fly with nail clippers but not the tiny nail files attached to them. Security officials countered that terrorists could use the pointed files as terrorist weapons. Security officials forbade passengers from using metal forks and knives with their on-board meals. First-class fliers complained about trying to eat with plasticware, but that proved to be a short-lived problem. In response to the airlines' financial crises, meals served on board were dramatically scaled back, so there was little food to cut.

Members of Congress love Ronald Reagan National Airport, which they can reach from the Capitol in just ten minutes. But security officials have long known that the White House lies nearly straight off the northern end of the main runway. The Capitol is only seconds away from planes landing and taking off. Security officials recognized that they had virtually no chance of stopping a plane that suddenly veered off course. But when the airport was closed, members of Congress had to travel more than an hour to one of the area's two other airports.

The extra security also proved inconvenient, expensive, and crippling to businesses. Powerful pressures began building across the country to ensure that the emphasis on security did not choke business and deny freedom. Everything had changed, but some changes could not be permanent. No one wanted to chance another hijacking. However, Ronald Reagan National Airport could not close. Were nail files really dangerous enough to ban? Could parents carry baby bottles on board for their infants? How would government set the balance?

The attacks presented a stunning challenge to the American system. A well-functioning bureaucracy coordinates complex activities into seamless services. If the system's designers fail to anticipate possible loopholes, or if the system's operations fail to close them, serious problems can develop. For the vast array of routine government programs, from mailing Social Security checks to putting out fires, experience usually makes the system work smoothly. But the September 11 attacks presented the system with new tests that officials had not anticipated, and these tests revealed deep fissures, ranging from failure to detect and prevent the attacks to state and local officials' inability to adequately respond to them. They caused difficulty in dealing with an unexpected wave of anthrax attacks and with yet another threat from a terrorist with a bomb hidden in his shoes. Designing and managing an effective homeland security system poses many difficulties, and the consequences of failure can be dire. Like any good stress test, these issues help chart the system's manifest strengths as well as its points of vulnerability.

CONNECTING THE DOTS

The spotlight quickly focused on the nation's intelligence services. Who were these hijackers, and how could the intelligence agencies have failed to detect their plot? In fact, investigators learned that many clues had emerged in the months before the attacks. Other clues lay undiscovered. Even worse, the intelligence agencies had failed to piece together the clues they did have. One question became a common refrain: why had the intelligence agencies failed to connect the dots?

Investigators first focused on determining who the hijackers were, as that would give them a clue to where the attacks had come from. Aboard one of the planes, a flight attendant had managed to identify the seat numbers where some of the hijackers had been sitting. A check against the boarding manifest gave investigators the hijackers' names to add to the fragmentary intelligence they had collected before the attacks and the telephone communications intercepted later that day. In relatively short order, they identified the likely hijackers, and just as quickly they determined that the men were members of al-Qaeda.

In Mohammed Atta's luggage, investigators found his will. In several cars rented by the hijackers, handwritten lists of rules, including "Be calm" and "You are carrying out an action God loves," were found. Atta and other hijackers had wired thousands of dollars back to the United Arab Emirates in the days before the attacks, and Atta had visited an

ATM machine, a gas station, and a Wal-Mart the night before. Atta and a fellow hijacker on the American Airlines flight had slept at a Portland Comfort Inn. The cleaning staff reported later that the hijackers had slept on top of the sheets—and left behind a bathroom floor full of body hair. Investigators believed this was part of their preparation: a smooth body would facilitate easier passage into the afterlife.[4]

In a disquieting near miss just two days before the attacks, a Maryland state policeman had pulled over Ziad Jarrah on Interstate 95 near the Delaware border. Jarrah was doing ninety in a sixty-five-mile-per-hour zone, and State Police trooper Joseph M. Cadalano issued him a $270 ticket. Investigators later found the ticket in the car's glove compartment at the Newark airport and a fragment of Jarrah's passport in the Shanksville wreckage. They believe that Jarrah was the pilot of the fourth plane and that the plane was bound for the Capitol.[5]

Even more startling, investigators discovered that several of the hijackers had received flight training in the months before the attacks. According to their instructors, none was an especially good pilot. Atta had once simply walked away from a plane at a Miami airport instead of parking it properly. Hani Hanjour, one of the hijackers who crashed the American Airlines jet into the Pentagon, claimed to have had six hundred hours of flight experience, but his Maryland flight instructors found that he flew so poorly that they wouldn't let him fly solo.[6] In Scottsdale, Arizona, a flight instructor said that Hanjour had missed flights and skipped homework assignments.

As investigators uncovered the trails of the hijackers, they began to build evidence about who they were, how they'd been trained, and where they'd gotten their money. They discovered a common link to earlier al-Qaeda operations, including Ramzi Yousef's role in the 1993 World Trade Center bombing and in a complex plan to blow up twelve American jetliners simultaneously over the Pacific—a plan that eerily came back to life in 2006 with plans by England-based hijackers to blow up planes over the Atlantic. Yousef, intelligence officials knew, had also received flight training in the United States, and they knew that he had considered flying a hijacked plane into the headquarters of the Central Intelligence Agency (CIA). Intelligence had uncovered previous al-Qaeda operations, as well as plans to turn planes into bombs. They knew that some terrorists had received flight training, and they suspected that more attacks might be in the works. But they failed to collect enough information about the September 11 operation in time to prevent it.

Some Federal Bureau of Investigation (FBI) field agents, in fact, had worried that al-Qaeda operatives were getting flying lessons and might be preparing new attacks. Two months before the September 11 hijackings, Phoenix FBI agent Kenneth Williams warned his superiors that Middle Eastern students at a nearby flight school might be members of al-Qaeda preparing for hijackings. Agents in Minneapolis warned their superiors that Zacarias Moussaoui, a French citizen, was taking flight lessons.[7] Later, congressional investigators were stunned to learn that the FBI had identified two suspicious flight training programs but had not acted. There was no evidence that top FBI officials had learned of all these warnings until after the September 11 attacks. Lower-level officials had been sorting out competing leads, and the Phoenix and Minneapolis warnings did not receive serious attention until after the attacks. That concerned Senator Charles Grassley (R-Iowa), who pointedly asked, "What will it take to 'connect the dots' necessary to piece together obscure clues and pursue leads to prevent another September 11 from devastating America all over again?"[8] Led by Grassley and Senator Bob Graham (D-Fla.), members of Congress asked out loud why federal officials had not assembled the clues in a way that would have helped them detect and prevent the attacks.

The deeper they dug, the more evidence congressional investigators found that terrorists had long been considering the use of airplanes for staging terrorist attacks. As early as 1994, intelligence experts had learned that terrorists planned to crash an Air France jet into the Eiffel Tower. Four years later, in August 1998, intelligence officials uncovered evidence that Arab terrorists were planning to fly an explosives-laden plane into the World Trade Center and that Osama bin Laden was actively considering terrorist strikes in the United States, possibly in New York and Washington. But the intelligence agencies did not produce any analysis on how much of a threat bin Laden might be or the risk that the nation faced from the use of airplanes as flying bombs. A 2002 congressional investigation concluded that "there [had been] apparently little, if any, effort by Intelligence Community analysts to produce any strategic assessments of terrorists using aircraft as weapons." But intelligence officers also had mountains of other suspicious activities to assess, including threats to public buildings that proved groundless. So despite some information to the contrary, the FBI—after sorting through all the intelligence less than a year before the September 11 attacks—had estimated the risk of attack through civil aviation to be low.[9]

Congressional investigators found that, despite mounting evidence collected by the intelligence agencies, the agencies had failed to share the information they had with each other. No agency had the whole picture, but the pieces collected before September 11 painted an interesting, albeit inconclusive, picture. The FBI did not share what it had with the Central Intelligence Agency (CIA), and neither adequately shared information with the State Department, whose consular offices could have prevented the terrorists from entering the country if they had been warned. The National Security Agency (NSA) had other information, but the agency was not linked adequately to the FBI, CIA, and State Department. "It is a colossal intelligence failure," Mary Ryan, head of the State Department's Bureau of Consular Affairs, said a month after the attacks. For example, the State Department had issued Atta a visa to enter the country in May 2000, even though other intelligence officials had collected evidence that he had met with key al-Qaeda officials five months earlier.[10] In their 2002 report, congressional investigators pointedly asked why the agencies had not shared information with each other.

The investigators also found that immigration officials had lost track of the hijackers after they entered the country and that the terrorist teams had assembled an impressive array of identification cards. On the morning of September 11, three of the hijackers had expired visas and thus were in the country illegally, but airline ticket agents had no way of knowing this. Investigators later concluded that the nineteen hijackers held a total of sixty-three driver's licenses.[11]

The congressional investigation also found that the super-secret NSA, which intercepts electronic communications, had in 1999 listened in on conversations between two future hijackers and discovered that they were linked to a suspected al-Qaeda facility. The NSA did not share this information with other intelligence agencies. Meanwhile, the CIA independently learned of the men's al-Qaeda connections, but it did not share the information with immigration officials, who could have prevented them from entering the country. The FBI had developed an informant who lived with two of the future hijackers, but the bureau's officials did not learn of what the CIA knew until after September 11. Had the agencies linked what they knew, it is possible that these hijackers could have been kept out of the United States, that the FBI could have used its informant to learn more about the developing plot, or at least that the intelligence agencies could have investigated further.

The post–September 11 investigations revealed that although government agencies kept a dozen different "watch lists" of suspicious individuals, officials had not coordinated the information they contained. The GAO found that the watch lists "include[d] overlapping but not identical sets of data, and different policies and procedures govern[ed] whether and how these data [were] shared with others."[12] The government had collected vast quantities of data on possible threats, but the agencies simply had not cooperated to piece together a coherent picture from the fragments collected.

In short, as Senators Grassley and Graham pointed out, the problem lay in "connecting the dots," a phrase that became burned into the policy dialogue. Investigators did not find any clear evidence that senior officials had known enough about the plans for the September 11 attacks to be able to prevent them. But the investigators did find a large number of tantalizing clues that, if connected, would have provided evidence of the need to take decisive action. In surveying the information they collected, investigators also determined that the United States remained highly vulnerable to further attacks. Osama bin Laden, among others, was vowing more strikes.

The conclusion was that unless the government did a far better job of coordinating efforts, the nation risked further catastrophes. With better preparedness, officials might be able to prevent the attacks or, at the very least, greatly reduce the damage resulting from them. Senator Graham summed up the findings: "If there had been more cooperation and sharing of information, if there had been more creativity, and some luck, this plot could have been discovered well before it resulted in September the 11th."[13] The system broke down not so much because the government had not collected the information but because its agencies had failed to share and digest the information they had. Sad and infuriated, congressional investigators turned "connecting the dots"—the need to coordinate intelligence—into a national watchword.

MYSTERIOUS POWDER

Americans had barely caught their breath when, three weeks after the September 11 hijackings, sixty-three-year-old Florida photo editor Robert Stevens died from inhaling anthrax. Anthrax is a natural bacterium that often occurs on farms and is rarely harmful to people in its natural state, although it has caused widespread death among livestock. Government weapons experts have long known that the spores can be grown in a laboratory, purified and concentrated, and separated into tiny microscopic dust just one twenty-fifth the thickness of a piece of toilet paper. The dust can then be made into an aerosol that hangs in the air and can be easily inhaled. In the early stages of infection, anthrax affects the lungs as a common cold would, and antibiotics can treat it effectively. But once the toxin spreads, the lungs fill with suffocating fluid and the body goes into shock; the disease is fatal 90 percent of the time.

Investigators at first suspected that Stevens had contracted anthrax from a natural source. Florida officials reported that there was no cause for alarm and that this was probably an isolated case, saying that they were carefully examining the circumstances but were not treating the event as a criminal incident. All that changed dramatically when investigators discovered that a letter passing through Stevens's company's mailroom contained anthrax and that his work area was contaminated. They found more anthrax in a nearby postal facility. In Stevens's building a second worker, Ernesto Blanco, came down with anthrax. Doctors caught Blanco's infection early and treated him with heavy doses of Cipro, an antibiotic highly effective against anthrax. Blanco survived.

Soon, cases of anthrax began popping up across the East Coast. An assistant to Tom Brokaw, anchor for the *NBC Nightly News*, contracted the skin-based version of anthrax. The substance had entered the newsroom in an envelope, and three other people who handled the envelope contracted anthrax as well. At ABC, the seven-month-old son of a news producer came down with the skin-based form. So did an assistant to CBS anchor Dan Rather and an employee at the *New York Post*. Anthrax turned up in the New York City office of Governor George Pataki and in four sorting machines in Manhattan's largest mail distribution center. A hospital worker was admitted on October 29 with what authorities suspected was inhalation anthrax. She died two days later.

The cases spread to Washington, DC, where twenty staffers in the office of Senate Majority Leader Tom Daschle (D-S.D.) tested positive for anthrax. At the Brentwood mail processing facility, which processes most of the mail for the Washington area—including the Capitol—two postal workers died. The contamination forced the closure of the facility until late 2003 and the rerouting of hundreds of thousands of pieces of mail. More anthrax turned up at the State Department, the Supreme Court's off-site mailroom, the Department of Health and Human Services (HHS), and in a letter addressed to Senator Patrick Leahy (D-Vt.). Additional cases appeared in New Jersey, and a few weeks later, a ninety-four-year-old Connecticut widow, whose mail had apparently gone through the sorting machines at about the same time as other anthrax-laced mail, died.

In all, the anthrax attacks killed five people and sickened seventeen. With major New York news organizations and Washington politicians as targets, the attacks seemed to have been planned to maximize publicity. The Postal Service posted tips about how to handle suspicious mail.[14] Officials warned schools to establish policies in case a worrisome package arrived, and many businesses put similar policies into place. The September 11 bombings had targeted prominent entities, but the seeming randomness of the anthrax infections—a photo editor working at his desk, a widow reading her mail, a baby visiting an office—terrified already shaken Americans.

Emergency officials across the country found themselves swamped with calls about suspicious powders. A bit of vanilla pudding prompted the evacuation of a building in Albuquerque. Monterey, California, police discovered that a suspicious substance outside a hotel was spilled mango juice. Another turned out to be bird droppings on a driveway. A worried New Jersey resident called 911 because a piece of Halloween candy had burned his tongue. A state police trooper carefully collected the suspicious candy and sent it to the state police laboratory for careful analysis, where laboratory workers found that it was, in fact, Halloween candy. New Jersey state police officers responded to more than 3,500 false alarms in the months immediately following the first attacks. Most came from citizens who worried they might be next. Some were deliberate hoaxes. More than two hundred family planning and abortion clinics received envelopes signed by the "Army of God," containing suspicious white powder, and bearing the message, "This is anthrax. Now you die."[15]

Officials and intelligence analysts had feared a second wave of attacks, but they didn't know what form such attacks might take. When anthrax arrived on the scene, they didn't know whether it came from al-Qaeda or some other source. Officials discovered that Mohammed Atta had taken flight training a short distance from the photo editor's office and that the terrorists had explored the use of crop dusters to spread harmful chemical or biological agents. It was hard to believe that the timing of the anthrax attacks was coincidental. Moreover, the focus on Washington officials and New York media stars matched al-Qaeda's operating style. Analysts determined that the anthrax was of high quality, which suggested that whoever had spread the spores was highly skilled and had access to sophisticated equipment. Yet after years of exhaustive laboratory and field work, which included draining a pond near a suspect's home, they were unable to determine who had spread the anthrax. They couldn't ascertain whether the anthrax had come from foreign or domestic sources, whether it had been supplied by a hostile nation such as Iraq or had come from a disgruntled worker at a federal institution. They believed that only a handful of people—or governments—were capable of producing the kind of spores they'd found. But they couldn't determine who had mailed the powder.

Despite their failure to identify the source of the anthrax, officials knew that the attacks underlined the bigger message—everything was different now. Analysts worried that the threats had changed but the government's capacity had not. In particular, they were concerned that the attacks revealed new and serious problems of coordination. Across the country, fire and police officials found themselves swamped with false alarms. When a few cases proved genuine, the system was slow to respond, and some infected victims didn't get Cipro treatment in time. It was clear that without better coordination, future attacks might bring more devastating casualties.

Before September 11, intelligence analysts well understood the possibility and risks of biological and chemical attacks. The Japanese terrorist group Aum Shinrikyo had already conducted a sarin attack and another attack in which it sprayed anthrax from a rooftop and a van. American experts had conducted exercises on the impact such attacks might have in the United States. In October 1999, ABC's *Nightline* aired a five-part series on the implications of an attack on the Washington subway. Its "Biowar" investigation began with the hypothetical smashing of a jar of anthrax on the subway's tracks. Within eight days, the show's consultants concluded, the death toll might well reach fifty thousand and the region's health care system would be overwhelmed.[16] Local officials had studied the problem as well. In August 2001, officials in Madison, Wisconsin, planned an exercise to test the local response to an anthrax attack. The exercise, scheduled for October, was canceled when officials were overwhelmed by hundreds of calls from worried residents who were finding suspicious powder.

Given the potential of anthrax to kill thousands, officials quietly breathed a sigh of relief that the October attacks had been limited to five deaths. They'd found that an effective anthrax attack was hard to stage and, if victims were treated quickly with antibiotics, easy to stop. But they'd also found that the biological attack, coupled with the extra security put in place after September 11, badly strained state and local governments. As Mayor John DiStefano of New Haven, Connecticut, explained a year later, "in an environment where 40-odd states are experiencing budget deficits and oftentimes solving those deficits, in part, on the backs of cities and towns, you're getting communities that are stressed by the increased demand to provide security services." The strain was wearing on cities, said Steve Charvat, emergency management director of Washington, DC. "They're lucky if they can do the bread-and-butter type disaster plans, much less everything that's been thrown on their plate since 9/11."[17]

State and local agencies were discovering their own connect-the-dots problems. The terrorist attacks had posed new challenges for state and local officials, who had to put their police and fire departments on overtime. They also had to devise new strategies for coping with hypothetical problems, since those scenarios might one day become reality. And they quickly realized that they needed to do far more to coordinate local emergency workers into integrated teams. No longer was terrorism the concern of just a handful of big cities. Officials around the country had to face the possibility that the mail could bring terrorism to their doorsteps and that, in any event, worried citizens might swamp their emergency services with false alarms. They discovered that they needed to connect their own dots and to find new ways of paying for vastly more difficult and complex services.

WORRIES SPREAD

Nervous travelers became even edgier on December 22, 2001, only days before Christmas. On American Airlines Flight 63 from Paris to Miami, passengers were just finishing lunch when a terrified woman's shriek broke the calm. A passenger in a window seat, Richard Reid, was lighting matches and holding them to a fuse protruding from his sneaker. Two flight attendants struggled with Reid and other passengers jumped up to stop him, some contributing their belts to restrain him. The crew sedated Reid with drugs from the first-aid kit, and a basketball player towered over him for the rest of the flight to ensure that he didn't move from his seat. No one was sure that Reid did not have accomplices on board—after all, the September 11 hijackers had traveled in groups. Accompanied by military jets, the plane diverted to Boston, where it landed safely and was quickly evacuated.[18]

The FBI took Reid into custody and examined his sneakers. They discovered that the shoes were packed with enough explosives to blast a large hole in the plane's fuselage and probably blow it out of the sky. Investigators found no accomplices, but they did find links between Reid and al-Qaeda. They found that Reid had received training in bin Laden's Afghan camps and that al-Qaeda had developed shoe bombs some time earlier. The bomb was sophisticated, and the FBI found hair and palm prints on the shoe that didn't belong to Reid. They concluded that he had to have had help, and thus it was likely that he was part of a larger terrorist network. They also worried that Reid's name had not appeared in earlier terrorist investigations and that, if he had succeeded, the 767 jetliner might simply have dropped into the ocean, leaving behind few clues. Even though the United States had attacked Afghanistan in October 2001 and quickly toppled the Taliban regime there, top officials realized that al-Qaeda had trained many terrorists who had scattered around the world. Destroying the central headquarters would not destroy the rest of the network.

At that point, in late 2001, aviation security officials dramatically increased the screening of passengers and their carry-on luggage and strengthened background checks of airline employees and before-flight computer checks of passengers. With the new worry that terrorists might use suicide shoe bombs, passengers were asked to remove their shoes and put them through security screening. Passengers complained about the continued inconvenience. As a Seattle Internet consultant grumbled, "The other night, they had everybody taking off their shoes—grandmothers surrendering their wooden clogs and teenagers taking off their Chuck Taylors."[19]

In early 2002, Americans learned they also needed to worry about "dirty bombs." Attorney General John Ashcroft announced the arrest of Abdullah Al Mujahir, an American citizen and a member of a Chicago street gang, as he entered the United States. Ashcroft said Al Mujahir was suspected of being involved in a plan to detonate a "dirty bomb," a conventional explosive mixed with radioactive materials. It was not a nuclear weapon, but if it exploded it could spread radioactivity throughout a neighborhood. Such a bomb, experts estimated, could kill thousands, sicken thousands more, and contaminate the neighborhood for a long time. Indeed, American officials suspected that the contamination and fear factor might well prove to be such a bomb's biggest impacts. As *Time* magazine correspondent Mark Thompson explained, "any bomb that killed people and set off Geiger counters would terrify a whole city. It's ultimately a pure terror weapon."[20] American officials believed that any plot was in its earliest stages. They transferred Al Mujahir to a naval base and held him in custody as an "enemy combatant."

American intelligence officials knew that al-Qaeda and other terrorists had been working for some time to obtain radioactive materials. Obtaining such material would be much easier than buying actual nuclear weapons, although officials worried that the collapse of the Soviet Union might have made a few nuclear bombs available to terrorists. A dirty bomb did not require much sophisticated equipment. A wide variety of nuclear materials, from old power plants or for medical use, could be coupled with truck bombs like the ones al-Qaeda had used against the World Trade Center in 1993 and Timothy McVeigh had used in 1995 in Oklahoma City, to kill large numbers of people and spread radioactivity. Officials later concluded that the dirty bomb plot had not advanced past the discussion stage and that no attack was imminent. But Al Mujahir's arrest added one more dimension to the mosaic of homeland defense problems confronting American governments at all levels.

In fact, the very complexity of the problem and the range of possible threats proved daunting. New problems were emerging at a dizzying rate. The public did not know which things to worry about most or, indeed, how much to worry. Officials were concerned about dangerous gaps both in preventing and responding to attacks. Because the terrorists were relying on "asymmetric" attacks, in which small numbers of terrorists could inflict great devastation, the problem loomed even larger. Attacks could come anywhere, at any time, through any of a wide variety of routes. Terrorists had targeted civilians as well as symbols in ways guaranteed to attract the broadest possible public attention and to make citizens fearful for their security—to induce terror, in short. Intelligence officials learned that al-Qaeda operatives believed that the United States was contaminating Islamic culture and supporting governments (such as Saudi Arabia's) that were subverting the core of the Islamic religion. By inflicting damage on American territory, the terrorists hoped to drive the United States out of the Middle East and to undermine the American way of life. The attacks were as large a shock as the United States had suffered since the Japanese attack on Pearl Harbor in 1941. They also foreshadowed a change in the policies and processes of American government—and American life—that would be even bigger.

New threats had emerged, and citizens were understandably more anxious. They had to find new ways of coping with threats that were both unpredictable and frightening. The government's intelligence operations had to devise new methods to prevent attacks. State and local agencies had discovered serious problems in responding to attacks once they occurred—and to citizens' fears from false alarms. State and local officials complained that federal officials were not providing enough information. Federal officials worried that state and local officials were not sufficiently coordinated to provide an effective response. They were concerned that police officers were not working closely enough with firefighters, that firefighters were not closely linked to emergency medical technicians, that public health workers expert in biological threats were not called in soon enough—that, in short, there were too many gaps in the system through which too many people might be hurt or killed.

POLICY PROBLEMS AS COORDINATION PROBLEMS

Homeland security, at its core, is about coordination. It is not only about developing new tools, but also—more fundamentally—about far more effectively weaving together the nation's existing experts and resources. It is a matter of doing some new things, many old things much better, and some old things differently, all in an environment that can punish any mistakes severely.

At the same time, none of the nation's other goals and aspirations have evaporated. Citizens still expect good local schools, quality colleges and universities, regular delivery of Social Security checks, and high environmental quality. They expect good roads, effective snow removal, and regular trash pickup. They want safe streets, quick emergency care in case of an accident, and a fire department that will promptly extinguish flames. They want national parks to preserve beauty, and they want a safe food supply. With the rise of homeland security as a concern, none of the old policy imperatives has disappeared. It's just that new ones have been added.

The country can spend almost limitless amounts of money and incur extraordinary costs and still not prevent a clever terrorist from finding a crack in the system. At the same time, a streamlined, well-designed system can frustrate most terrorist schemes. The key to an effective homeland security system is, in fact, connecting the dots—ensuring strong coordination among those responsible for prevention and those charged with response. No single agency, no single level of government—indeed, no government itself, without the active partnership of its citizens—can hope to forestall attack. Should an attack occur, no single agency, level of government, or government can adequately respond. At its core, homeland security is a problem of coordination.

As political scientist Harold Seidman points out, coordination is the "philosopher's stone" of government's work. Medieval alchemists believed that if they could find this magic stone, they would find the answers to human problems. Coordination, Seidman argues, has the same appeal for public officials today. "If only we can find the right formula for coordination," he writes, "we can reconcile the irreconcilable, harmonize competing and wholly divergent interests, overcome irrationalities in our government structures, and make hard policy choices to which no one will disagree."[21]

"Coordination" is a diagnosis of the homeland security problem. Terrorists work by trying to identify and exploit gaps in the system. It is also a diagnosis of the solution: improved homeland security is a matter of strengthening coordination in both preventing and responding to attacks. In each case, identify the dots that must be connected and the problems will be solved.

This applies not just to detecting and preventing terrorist attacks, but also to ensuring an effective local response to terrorist events. When such events occur, they place big demands on local first responders—police officers, firefighters, emergency medical technicians, public health workers, and others—who arrive on the scene. Big terrorist events, like the attacks on the World Trade Center and the Pentagon, require extraordinary levels of coordination. Even smaller-scale events, however, like the tragic crash of United Airlines Flight 93 into a Pennsylvania field, require response from several neighboring communities. Such events are not simply fires, crime scenes, or places with injured people. They can happen all at once and can swamp the ability of any agency or any jurisdiction to respond. Hence, the effectiveness of a community's response to a terrorist event depends on the level of coordination it can marshal. And since terrorist events, almost by definition, are sudden shocks, such coordination depends on putting response plans into place long before the event.

That was just the case in Arlington County, Virginia, where local first responders confronted the crash of American Airlines Flight 77 into the Pentagon. At 9:37 A.M., Capt. Steve McCoy and his crew aboard Engine 101 were traveling to a training session on Interstate 395 near the Pentagon, talking as they went about the tragedy at the World Trade Center. Suddenly they saw a jetliner in a steep dive bank sharply before disappearing in a thunderous explosion. From their location, McCoy and his crew could not determine where the plane had crashed, but another team of firefighters already on duty at the Pentagon barely escaped the explosion and radioed in the location. The plane had been traveling close to its maximum speed and had penetrated the first three of the building's five rings. Soon McCoy and his crew, along with hundreds of other first responders from the area, were at the scene.

Within minutes, well-practiced emergency plans went into effect. Fire and rescue units from nearby Ronald Reagan Washington National Airport sped to the scene, as did other units from across Arlington County. The FBI's Washington field office dispatched its response team. The first units arrived on the scene within two minutes of the attack. Fire department commanders established their headquarters within four minutes, and the FBI's field commanders arrived within five. The area's hospitals were ready to receive the injured within twelve minutes.[22] The fire chief of neighboring Alexandria sent a battalion chief to the Arlington command post to say, simply, "Anything you need, you've got."[23] For the next ten days, the county's emergency operations staff remained on the scene to conduct search and rescue operations.

A few months later, the county asked a private consultant to evaluate its performance. The consultant's report found the response exemplary—"ordinary men and women performing in extraordinary fashion."[24] Coordination efforts proved to be "a model that every metropolitan area should emulate." The county responded so well—and its coordination with the FBI and neighboring governments worked so effectively—because of the leadership the county's emergency services officials had shown in the years leading up to the attacks. "Leadership isn't learned in a day," the consultants argued, "it is learned every day."[25]

Among other things, Arlington County officials had carefully framed an emergency response plan built on an integrated command structure, mutual aid agreements with surrounding communities, a solid emergency team, an assistance program to back up employees amid the stress of their work, and constant drilling over several years. The response, the consultants said, "was successful by any measure." Loss of life was minimized, and "had it not been for the heroic actions of the response force and the military and civilian occupants of the Pentagon, clearly the number of victims would have been much higher."[26]

The coordination extended to the region's health authorities. Many of the most badly injured victims had suffered severe burns, and the area's hospitals soon ran short of skin grafts. The usual procedure would have been to fly in the replacement skin from another location, but because of the attacks all flights in the nation were grounded. Medical officials created a nonstop relay of drivers to transport seventy square feet of skin from Texas to Washington. Local police officers in jurisdictions along the way provided escorts to speed the emergency supplies along, itself an extraordinary feat of coordination.[27]

By contrast, the attacks on the World Trade Center produced staggering coordination problems.[28] Commanders in the lobbies of the two towers lacked reliable information about what was happening above them or outside the buildings. In fact, horrified television viewers around the country had better information on the spread of the fires than the lobby commanders, who had no access to the television broadcasts. Radio communications were sporadic throughout the towers. A New York City Police Department (NYPD) helicopter circled overhead, but the fire chiefs had no link to police information. There were no senior NYPD personnel at the fire department's command posts—and vice versa. Desperate to help their comrades, some firefighters raced up the stairs without waiting for orders, but that made it impossible for New York City Fire Department (FDNY) officers to track who was at the scene.

The FDNY had no established process for securing mutual aid from surrounding communities. Both Nassau and Westchester counties supplied ad hoc assistance, but the FDNY had no procedure for integrating reinforcements into its own efforts. With half of the FDNY force at the World Trade Center, and without an established mutual aid agreement with neighboring communities, the rest of the city was left with perilously thin protection. Almost all the city's special operations units, such as hazardous materials and rescue teams, were at the World Trade Center, leaving few resources to respond should another major event have occurred.

New York City's consultant found that although the FDNY had previously considered many strategies to enhance coordination, it had "never fully brought them to fruition." The consultant pointedly concluded, "Success will be predicated on managers, civilian and uniformed, who are committed to bringing about profound change, are capable of leading all personnel by example and are eager to embrace full accountability for their own performance."[29] The consultant warned that even after the attacks, there were few signs that the department's leaders had taken the steps necessary to improve coordination, especially with the police department.

First responders raced into burning buildings without regard to their own safety, but the scale of the New York attacks swamped the system. After the attacks, however, investigators found that deep-seated rivalries, especially between the NYPD and the FDNY, had prevented the two departments from sharing critical information on the morning of the attack. Coordination problems within the departments, especially the FDNY, may have increased the death toll among firefighters. The local response systems had proved just as susceptible to bureaucratic competition and coordination problems as the intelligence community had in dealing with the disconnected early clues it received about the hijackers' activities.

It must be said, in fairness, that the situations in Washington and New York were very different. The New York attacks involved two buildings, not one. The buildings' collapse and the resulting fires involved sixteen city blocks, destroyed all seven buildings in the World Trade Center complex, and seriously damaged many more. A forty-story skyscraper across the street from the South Tower, owned by Deutsche Bank, was so badly damaged that officials later decided to demolish it. The fires were fueled by the tanks of planes far larger than the one that crashed into the Pentagon, and the tall, thin World Trade Center towers created a far more difficult evacuation problem than the broad, low Pentagon building. Any emergency system would have struggled with the sheer scale of the New York attacks, and in the view of many experts, New York's emergency system is perhaps the best in the world.

Public officials—especially in the White House—concluded that they had to do something to prevent further attacks and, should any occur, to improve local response. The September 11 attacks thus not only provided a stress test for the way the nation's homeland defense systems operated, but also created a case for testing how political institutions—especially the presidency and Congress—respond to sudden shocks to the political and policy systems. The stress test revealed critical problems in the nation's homeland security system. The intelligence community proved too fragmented and disjointed to assemble and digest the evidence it had

Just four days after the World Trade Center fell, President Bush joined firefighter Bob Beckwith atop a burned fire truck to address a crowd of rescuers still searching for survivors. Bush's actions that day rallied public support and helped spark a sense of determination that continued to build in the weeks following the attacks.

collected. The intelligence system had not only collected information about many of the attacks' elements, including flight training by suspicious individuals, but had also discovered that top al-Qaeda officials were traveling broadly. Intercepted "chatter" warned of some impending event. The bureaucratic barriers between the intelligence organizations— the FBI, the CIA, and the NSA, in particular—prevented the needed coordination. First responders stunned everyone with their bravery, but the systems in which they worked revealed other problems of coordination. Each new event, from anthrax to the shoe bomber, turned up unexpected weaknesses that, in turn, required further attention.

The shocks strained the system and revealed its vulnerabilities. The September 11 attacks, coupled with the anthrax attacks, demonstrated that the costs of failing to identify and solve the coordination problems in the nation's homeland defense could be extremely serious. To a degree never before seen in American politics, elected officials at all levels called for better coordination among all terrorism prevention and response units. But as we shall see in the next chapter, the first step— improving coordination among the bureaucratic agencies—proved a large hurdle indeed.

3

Reshaping the Bureaucracy

IN THE AFTERMATH OF THE SEPTEMBER 11 ATTACKS, federal officials urgently debated how to respond. Everyone agreed that the attacks revealed deep and fundamental problems with the federal bureaucracy, and everyone agreed they had to be fixed. The independent 9/11 Commission uncovered multiple failures: imagination, policy, capabilities, and management.[1] Everyone agreed that the fix had to begin with fundamental changes in the homeland security bureaucracy.

At the same time, however, experienced Washington hands knew that transforming the bureaucracy requires uncommon patience and great skill. Bureaucratic change has frequently seemed a case of an irresistible force meeting an immovable object, and "reform" has often proved to be the impossible dream. Even with the impetus provided by the unparalleled shock of the terrorist attacks, no one knew quite how the bureaucratic landscape would change.

The first steps came in President Bush's address to a joint session of Congress just nine days after the attacks. It was an evening of both profound solemnity and great celebration. For the first time since the attacks, all the branches of government gathered under one roof—the justices of the Supreme Court, both houses of Congress, and President Bush. Conspicuously absent was Vice President Dick Cheney, carefully hidden at a "secure undisclosed location" away from Washington in case the terrorists struck again. To thunderous applause, cheers, and whistles, Bush's wife, Laura, came into the chamber, followed by New York Governor George E. Pataki, New York City Mayor Rudolph W. Giuliani, a New York City police officer, and a New York fire chief. Bush's speech proved to be one of his best ever. The audience interrupted him thirty-two times with applause. "We will rebuild New York City," he pledged.[2]

At the end of his speech, Bush held up the shield of police officer George Howard, who died trying to rescue people trapped in the World

Trade Center. The president spoke solemnly: "It is my reminder of lives that ended and a task that does not end."[3] He pledged a multifront campaign against terrorism and demanded that the government of Afghanistan, where al-Qaeda was based, hand over the group's leaders. He also announced the creation of a new White House office devoted to homeland security and headed by Pennsylvania Governor Tom Ridge. Bush had known Ridge for years and had seriously considered naming him as his vice presidential running mate. Ridge had military experience and was one of the nation's most respected Republican governors. Bush pledged to bring him into the White House and create a new homeland defense strategy. Ridge's job, according to one homeland security expert, was to find "someone who can connect those dots."[4]

Bush had quickly sorted through competing options. Everyone agreed on the need for better coordination of the nation's homeland security functions, but there was wide disagreement on how best to do it. In the face of the coordination problems that the September 11 attacks revealed, some members of Congress pressed the president to create a new cabinet department devoted to homeland security. Such a department, they believed, should bring together all the government's agencies devoted to homeland security. In particular, they said, the government needed the new department to consolidate its intelligence operations, which had failed to detect the terrorists' plot. Bush, however, resisted. Having run for office as a conservative dedicated to restraining the growth of government, he didn't want to create a new entity that would undoubtedly become one of the government's largest organizations. He argued instead for a more limited new organization: a White House office, headed by Ridge and supported by a small staff, that would coordinate the government's existing agencies. That, the president hoped, would help strengthen the government's capacity without compromising his small-government principles.

ORGANIZATIONAL CHALLENGE

For years before the attacks, experts had been studying the risks of terrorism, and they had repeatedly identified the government's great difficulty in coordinating the many agencies related to homeland security. For decades, different agencies had managed different parts of the intelligence function. The FBI dealt with domestic threats, the CIA with foreign threats. The National Security Agency (NSA) gathered electronic intelligence from spy satellites and intercepted cell phone calls. The Defense Department had a separate intelligence operation, and each branch of the armed forces ran its own intelligence shop. The State Department and the Secret Service had related operations. The president's National Security Council (NSC) was ultimately responsible for digesting all the information and presenting it to the president, but sometimes the agencies didn't share sufficient information with the NSC or with each other to allow analysts to clearly identify possible threats. Each agency resisted meddling from others and sought to defend its own turf. That made it hard for a clear, integrated picture of possible threats to emerge, and gaps often developed in intelligence gathering and analysis.

Still other federal agencies were responsible for safeguarding the nation's borders. The Coast Guard was in charge of guarding the waters off the U.S. coastline. The Immigration and Naturalization Service (INS)—a part of the Justice Department, although much of its work abroad was done through State Department consulates—was responsible for keeping dangerous people out of the country, and the Customs Service (in the Transportation Department) was responsible for keeping out dangerous goods. The Department of Agriculture's Food and Safety Inspection Service and Animal and Plant Health Inspection Service were charged with protecting the nation from the importation of harmful food, plants, and animals. The National Park Service kept an eye on the land and coastal territory that was part of national parks and sea-shores. Within the Department of Health and Human Services (HHS), the Centers for Disease Control and Prevention (CDC) monitored possible risks from disease and bioterrorism. The Nuclear Regulatory Commission monitored the security of nuclear power plants, but the Department of Energy safeguarded former nuclear weapons production facilities and the nation's stockpiles of weapons and weapons-grade plutonium.

Multiple agencies were responsible for providing aid in case of a terrorist attack. HHS housed several agencies charged with responding to public health emergencies, including the CDC, the Public Health Service (PHS), and the National Institutes of Health (NIH). The Federal Emergency Management Agency (FEMA) responded to natural disasters, such as hurricanes, tornadoes, and floods. But its workers also were trained—and in turn trained state and local officials—to deal with terrorism-related disasters such as building collapses and chemical threats. The Department of Transportation's Federal Highway Administration (FHA) and Federal Aviation Administration (FAA) had highly trained crews ready in case of damage to critical infrastructure. The Environmental Protection Agency (EPA) had specialists on radiological and chemical threats.

In sum, the federal government had extraordinary expertise, but that expertise was highly fragmented and compartmentalized. Threats, however—especially terrorism threats—demanded carefully integrated intelligence and response. As the September 11 attacks (and later the response to Hurricane Katrina) showed, such coordination proved lacking at the most critical moments. Coordination is the central element of all bureaucracies, and problems of coordination are their most persistent pathology. Management expert Chester I. Barnard put it best: "Organization, simple or complex, is always an impersonal system of coordinated human efforts."[5] The September 11 attacks showed how difficult it is to pull expertise together and create a secure system or seamless response. As one reporter explained,

> To get an idea of the number of federal agencies potentially involved in counterterror efforts, just trace what the terrorists were doing in the days before the attack of September 11. As they set out for America months before the attacks, the CIA presumably was trying to recruit some of their Al Qaeda comrades as informants; the State Department, to persuade Arab governments to arrest them; the Treasury, to freeze their bank accounts; the military, to plan a raid on their Afghan training camps. As they came into the country, Customs checked their baggage; Immigration checked their names against a watch list. As they lived among us, the FBI tried to track them down. As they boarded their chosen planes, the Federal Aviation Administration was trying to keep airport and airline security up to date on the latest threats.
> They still got through.[6]

Complexity and Coordination

Better coordination, experts agreed, was what the government most needed to prevent future attacks and to improve the nation's ability to respond should attacks occur. But the staggering range and number of agencies involved raised tough questions for the policy planners. How should the dots best be connected? Which agencies should be linked? How? Homeland security involves so many different agencies performing so many different functions that drawing clear lines is difficult. Figuring out how to make all the agencies work together is far harder. As journalist Sydney J. Freedberg Jr. observed, "The U.S. government was just not designed with terrorists in mind."[7]

Bureaucratic Autonomy

The bureaucratic players are numerous and varied, and each has its own ideas about what ought to be done and how to do it. Political scientist Herbert Emmerich argued long ago that "there is a persistent, universal drive in the executive establishment for freedom from managerial control and policy direction." In fact, "the desire for autonomy characterizes the operating administrations and bureaus."[8] Managers, like most other people, want flexibility in how they do their jobs. Over time, most of the federal government's managers have come to know far more about their work than almost anyone else. As a result, they believe strongly that they know best how to accomplish their respective missions. Bureaucrats tend to have a strong self-interest in promoting their autonomy and frequently fight off any efforts that smell of control. In the meantime, many of these same bureaucrats have a strong professional and personal interest in working hard to respond to policymakers.[9] It's one thing for the government to build strong bureaucracies possessing great expertise; it's quite another for each of these bureaucracies to peer past its own boundaries for ways to cooperate with others.

The intricacy of homeland security, however, leaves government officials little choice but to rely heavily on government bureaucrats. Unfortunately, these mixed desires make it difficult for policymakers to manage the conflicting incentives of bureaucratic autonomy and responsiveness. Every effort at cooperation inevitably requires each side to give a bit and, most important, to surrender a bit of the very autonomy that managers fight so hard to protect. In truth, cooperation is risky. It requires managers to step out of their relatively protected enclaves. It can put individual programs, prerogatives, and budgets at risk. Managers often find it easier and safer to retreat from complex problems, burrow into their agencies behind tall barriers of rules and procedures, and shrink away from ties with other organizations. Before September 11, such forces made it hard for the intelligence agencies to share what information they had collected about possible threats. No single agency had a full picture, but their individual pieces, if carefully assembled, would have given senior government officials intriguing hints about the disaster that al-Qaeda operatives had planned.

Mission Conflicts

The long history of different, sometimes conflicting, missions among the various intelligence agencies added to the difficulties of sharing information. In the years leading up to the September 11 attacks, both the CIA and the FBI assembled information on al-Qaeda operatives. The CIA tracked them, along with many other threats, in foreign countries. The FBI identified possible al-Qaeda members inside the United States, but at the same time its agents remained focused on the bureau's traditional mission of tracking and capturing criminals such as bank robbers. Each agency had other missions in addition to the detection and prevention of terrorist threats. As former attorney general Dick Thornburgh testified before a congressional committee, "The FBI can't connect all the dots if it doesn't have all the dots in the first place."[10]

The same conditions characterized other areas. In border security, for example, the INS tracked persons entering and leaving the country, but the Customs Service reviewed materials coming in. One agency monitored plants; another scrutinized food products. As securing the safety of the food supply became more important after September 11, this fragmentation created numerous hurdles.

Individual agencies pursued what they viewed as the most important issues. These competing and conflicting missions often did not overlap. Agencies did not see things the same way. Intelligence, as a result, slipped through the cracks. "It's no surprise that the FBI and CIA don't cooperate. We haven't wanted them to—until now," explained homeland security specialist Gregory F. Treverton.[11]

Each agency had a core mission separate from the core missions of the other agencies; none focused solely on homeland security. Each had other important missions for which it was responsible. To bend the mission to accommodate the coordination demands of homeland security risked undermining an agency's other—and, in the minds of many agency managers, more important—missions. No one wanted to put the nation at risk, but everyone wanted to make sure that they accomplished their core tasks as well.

Indeed, homeland security was not a mission created to replace old ones; it was a new mission added to existing ones. No one suggested that government agencies should do any less of what they had previously been doing. A vast array of them faced the new and often fuzzy problems of homeland security. Worries about new terrorist attacks caused senior Coast Guard commanders to shift many of their assets—fast cutters, small patrol boats, and a substantial number of forces—to homeland security duties. But no one suggested for a moment that the Coast Guard should not respond, just as quickly and effectively, to boaters in trouble or to oil spills in harbors. Nor did anyone suggest curtailing the war on drugs, in which the Coast Guard also plays a major role. Keeping up with these crosscutting responsibilities strained the agency's resources. For instance, in Pittsburgh, where the Coast Guard helps control traffic on the busy Ohio River, homeland security activities grew from 10 percent to 50 percent of the agency's workload after the September 11 attacks.[12] Meanwhile, the Coast Guard spent 60 percent less time on drug interdiction in 2002 than it had in 1998. Time invested in preventing foreign encroachment on American fishing territory and enforcing fishing laws shrank 38 percent. As the Government Accountability Office (GAO) concluded, "The Coast Guard faces fundamental challenges in being able to accomplish all of its new homeland security responsibilities, while rebuilding capacity in other missions to pre–September 11th levels."[13]

Different Cultures

More than just meshing different agency missions, coordination also requires integrating the very different organizational cultures of these agencies. Although some analysts have questioned whether "organizational culture" is anything more than a mushy term with uncertain meaning, anyone who has spent any time working in an organization knows that each one is different. Every organization has its own unwritten rules, including a common understanding of who really makes the key decisions, how to dress, how best to spin a new idea to win approval, and whether new ideas are even welcomed. Workers at Disney theme parks go through intensive training to learn how to treat all visitors as "guests." Some state departments of motor vehicles have tried to train their employees to look on citizens as "customers." Of course, in some organizations, the "service" offices provide nothing like service. In every organization, as political scientist Anne M. Khademian contends in her insightful book *Working with Culture*, the people working there share understandings about how things get done, and those common understandings define an organization's culture.[14]

Meshing organizations with different cultures can pose vast challenges. Different cultures cause people to think differently about how to do their jobs and even about what jobs are most important to do. It's one thing to try to integrate border security; it's quite another to link Coast Guard members, who are part of a uniformed military service, with immigration control officials, who work at desks and in airport terminals. And either group would be difficult to meld with the Animal and Plant Health Inspection Service, which employs a "Beagle Brigade"— dogs with green vests who search for contraband plant products by sniffing piles of luggage arriving on international flights.

Existing cultures can also blind employees to homeland security issues and make it difficult to incorporate homeland security into existing missions. The FBI, for example, faced a massive task in working homeland security into its traditional missions, such as combating organized crime, tracking white-collar criminals, and protecting civil rights. Not only did the FBI live by the watchword "We always get our man [or woman]," but its agents also received intensive training in how to carefully and deliberately build a case before arresting a suspect and then collect evidence to ensure a conviction. FBI officials were convinced that no law enforcement agency in the world was better. It had long been charged with investigating crimes on American soil, and the CIA was forbidden from conducting operations inside the United States. So the FBI concluded that terrorism on U.S. territory was its turf.

This cultural mindset created barriers to collaborating with other agencies, especially the CIA. Terrorism specialist Michael O'Hanlon put it like this:

> Suppose that the CIA generates information from its deep intelligence sources, such as infiltrators, for example. The FBI might want to acquire the information and to use it to arrest potential terrorists. Later, it might then want to use that information in a court to convict the terrorists. If the CIA shares the information, however, it might put its sources at risk; it might lose an infiltrator who took years to burrow into a terrorist organization and gain the trust of its leaders. A public trial in court might also reveal capabilities, electronic and human, that the terrorists did not know the United States had. Thus, the CIA's sharing of information with the FBI might jeopardize its ability to collect intelligence and perhaps track down terrorist ringleaders. On the other hand, the CIA's penchant for secrecy could make it harder for the FBI to convict terrorists and put them behind bars. Each agency had long had strong incentives to do its own business in its own way. These fundamental differences in organizational culture undermined the ability of analysts to connect the dots in the days before the September 11 attacks, and afterward they still proved extremely difficult to bridge.[15]

The FBI's culture was part cop and part lawyer. Terrorism presented a stark challenge to its traditional culture. For this agency, homeland security was more about detecting and preventing terrorist attacks than about finding and arresting the perpetrators. It put far more focus on quick actions in advance than methodical actions after the fact. The CIA's culture was part research and part intrigue. The two cultures did not mesh well. An official at the Customs Service, founded in 1789 to catch people trying to bring goods into the country illegally to avoid paying the import duty, put it bluntly: "You don't throw away centuries of culture and history overnight."[16]

Gaps: Distance and Technology

Even when agencies and their leaders want to coordinate closely, physical barriers may intervene. FBI headquarters is on Pennsylvania Avenue, just a few blocks from the White House, but the CIA is miles away and across the Potomac River, in Langley, Virginia. The NSA is even farther away, in Fort Meade, Maryland, midway between Washington and Baltimore. The NIH is in Bethesda, Maryland. The PHS is nearby, but the CDC is based in Atlanta, Georgia. The Department of Health and Human Services oversees the NIH, PHS, and CDC, and its offices are just a few blocks from the Capitol in downtown Washington. Long distances also separate the federal government's emergency response agencies. FEMA is in downtown Washington, but its Fire Administration is more than an hour's drive away, in Emmitsburg, Maryland. The Department of Homeland Security is far from the Capitol and the White House.

Of course, technological advances, including secure teleconferences, make it possible for officials of different agencies to share information and counsel. Physical distance, however, contributes to the difficulty of bridging different agency cultures. At HHS, for example, Secretary Tommy Thompson announced a new "One HHS" strategy that was meant to integrate the department's agencies into a single, well-functioning operation. The goal, according to one HHS report, was to "help create 'One-HHS' that looks at our programs from the citizens' perspective and closes the performance gap by providing seamless and integrated services to our constituents."[17] However, officials in some of HHS's far-flung operations, especially in drug approval and public health, had long been accustomed to operating with great independence. They wondered whether Thompson's plan made sense, what its object was, and whether he and his senior staff could understand the technical complexity of their work. In short, they showed all the classic signs of agency officials seeking to protect and increase their autonomy.

Managing technology can further frustrate coordination. There is no more fitting symbol for the technical barriers to securing better coordination than the FBI's Trilogy system. One of the organization's problems was that its information systems continued to run largely on paper instead of electronic systems, and the paper simply did not flow fast enough to the right people to help key officials make critical decisions before September 11. After the attacks, the FBI accelerated development of its computer information system, called Trilogy, but the costs of the project quickly soared. "Unfortunately, Trilogy has become a large disaster," complained Senator Judd Gregg (R-N.H.), chairman of the subcommittee overseeing the bureau's budget. "FBI software and hardware contracts for Trilogy have essentially become gold-plated. The cost is soaring. The schedule is out of control." New systems for conducting criminal background checks and checking fingerprints ran into long delays and cost overruns. In the trial of Oklahoma City bomber

Timothy McVeigh, the agency failed to turn some documents over to his lawyers because they'd been lost. An FBI agent who spied for the Russians, Robert Hanssen, used the agency's own computer system to check whether anyone inside the FBI had discovered that he was passing secrets.[18]

The Trilogy project had three parts: upgrading the desktop computers throughout the agency, upgrading the data networks and servers, and loading investigative programs onto the World Wide Web. For years, antiquated computer systems had crippled the ability of field agents to track information. When the FBI launched Trilogy in 2001, many of its computers were more than eight years old, and replacement parts for some of them were no longer available. Many of the computers did not even allow the use of a mouse to navigate the screen. When agents wanted to search for evidence, they often could do little more than conduct simple word searches of text documents. In the pre–September 11 days, the bureau struggled to manage forty-two different data systems, none of which was adequate. Because the databases were not electronically linked, every time an agent needed to search for information, he or she had to check each system.[19] It was also impossible to connect the different databases. When the FBI tried to upgrade the computers in its field offices, it found that the offices lacked fiberoptic cables to provide network access; after the computers were installed, there was insufficient software to run them. Pressed for funds, the bureau planned to reduce funding for Trilogy, and that infuriated some Democrats. "The FBI continues to operate with a 20th century computer system as terrorists are engaging in 21st century cyber-warfare," said Senator Charles E. Schumer (D-N.Y.).[20] Even after September 11, applicants submitting information for security checks had to find a typewriter to complete the forms and then mail them; online filing was not available.

High personnel turnover in the information technology area also plagued the FBI. Top officials sometimes were not supportive of technology upgrades. Moreover, external pressures, especially from members of Congress, whipsawed the agency among competing priorities. An anonymous source recalled a conversation with former director Louis Freeh. The bureau director had been frustrated and complained that "every time there was a sound bite by a powerful congressman or senator saying, 'We need to devote more attention to car jacking,' for example, someone in the bureau would call a press conference and transfer 400 agents. Although [there were] voices crying in the wild saying we need a much more sophisticated and secure [technology] system, the bureau was always being pulled in different directions."[21]

The FBI's difficulty in managing Trilogy led to the purchase of $7.6 million in equipment that simply disappeared. The GAO questioned another $10.1 million in contractor cost. In the end, the GAO not only raised doubts regarding the FBI's management of the program, but also concluded that "the lack of accountability for Trilogy equipment calls into question FBI's ability to adequately safeguard its existing assets as well as those it might acquire in the future."[22] If it was hard simply to buy and install the equipment, it was even harder to use it to connect the information dots.

Congressional Jurisdictions

Some of the most difficult homeland security coordination problems flowed from congressional decisions. The complicated homeland security mix was the product of organizational design decisions that had accumulated, quite literally, over hundreds of years. As political scientists Kenneth A. Shepsle and Mark S. Bonchek put it, "the bureaucracy is created by Congress and sustained by Congress."[23] Congress establishes agencies and the programs they manage, passes the budgets they spend, oversees their work, and proposes fixes for agencies and programs that work poorly. The president might be the "chief executive," but most agencies interact much more frequently with Congress and especially with the committees and subcommittees that oversee them.

Executive branch structure reflects the complexity of the congressional committee system. Early in the long debate over how to strengthen the nation's homeland security system, analysts counted eighty-eight congressional committees and subcommittees that had jurisdiction over some aspect of homeland security. Any reorganization of homeland security agencies would also require a reorganization of Congress— or strong action by agency administrators to overcome the splintering worsened by Congress's own fragmented structure. Senator Pat Roberts (R-Kan.) pointed to the problem of accommodating "old bulls [on Capitol Hill] who don't want their turf scratched." He continued, "How on earth do you give one person cabinet status and budget authority over the eighty federal agencies that are now involved without involving the Congress?" One Republican aide, in describing the debate over restructuring the nation's homeland security agencies, said, "There's no question this will be one of the most complicated undertakings of legislation in a long time."[24]

In *The Accountable Juggler*, political scientist Beryl A. Radin explores the art of leading a federal agency. She explains that American political institutions, by design, fragment power to prevent concentrated power from developing anywhere. Moreover, "the internal structure of Congress mirrors the larger fragmentation of political power."[25] The nation's founders were sensitive to the risks posed by power concentrated in the hands of a king and determined to guard the new nation against them. Some scholars have wondered since if they overcompensated, creating a system too prone to fragmentation and hence ineffective in tackling tough problems requiring coordinated action.

Indeed, this is one of the central dilemmas of homeland security: at its core, homeland security requires coordination, but the government agencies that must cooperate find themselves pulled in different directions by the fragmented institutions—especially Congress—that oversee them. Because of its sheer size and sprawl, political scientist James L. Sundquist explains, "the bureaucracy appears to those on Capitol Hill to be beyond anyone's control."[26] Members of Congress see their job as making good policy. Their oversight of the bureaucracy requires a tight rein, and within Congress, this leads to irresistible pressure to allow fragmentation. The connect-the-dots arguments made in response to September 11 required just the reverse, setting the stage for an epic battle over control of a hypersensitive issue.

Structured Organizations, Networked Threats

Complicating the federal government's strategy was a bureaucratic form of "asymmetry." The government organized its agencies along traditional lines of hierarchy and authority. Each agency had its own job, and each person within each agency had an assigned task. Bureaucracy requires that people do their jobs and not meddle in the jobs of others, or else risk having things falling through the cracks. Moreover, *government* bureaucracy actually requires agency managers to do *only* their respective jobs. Bureaucracies operate under authority delegated from Congress. As a safeguard, Congress delegates authority narrowly, and federal law prohibits spending government cash for anything other than the purposes for which it has been appropriated. Bureaucracies in general, and government bureaucracies in particular, work within a model that assumes that careful definition of roles and responsibilities is the most effective way of operating.

By contrast, terrorists tend to operate in a distinctly nonbureaucratic fashion. In an analysis by the RAND Corporation of the possibility of technology-based attacks, what distinguishes terrorism "as a form of conflict is the networked organizational structure of its practitioners—with many groups actually being leaderless—and the suppleness in their ability to come together quickly in swarming attacks."[27] Thus, the asymmetry lies not only in differences of power and strategy involving razor-sharp attacks against broad and powerful forces, but also in differences of organization, the attackers being organized primarily in loose networks and the defense structured principally in formal bureaucracies. In fact, the RAND analysts concluded, "the more a terrorist network takes the form of a multi-hub 'spider's web' design, with multiple centers and peripheries, the more redundant and resilient it will be—and the harder to defeat."[28] Moreover, the more terrorists organize through networks, the more important coordination among the defenders becomes.

FIRST STEPS

When Tom Ridge began settling into his White House office in September 2001, he found himself surrounded by problems. The nation remained edgy. Intelligence analysts warned that al-Qaeda might launch more attacks at any moment. Anthrax suddenly became a big threat. Everyone concluded that the key intelligence agencies had to do a much better job of sharing information, but each one quickly circled the wagons to prevent the new Office of Homeland Security—and the other agencies—from encroaching on its power and autonomy. Ridge had perhaps the toughest job in government after the president's. He had a prime piece of West Wing real estate near Bush's Oval Office, but he also faced sweeping challenges with few resources. He had an office but no bureaucracy; a mandate to make the entire country safe but few tools with which to do it.

To further complicate his job, Ridge faced immediate tussles with Congress, some of whose members insisted they wanted to pass a law authorizing his new office and setting out his powers. "If he is not granted a certain amount of authority, he is not going to be very effective," an aide to one Democratic member of Congress said.[29] What members of Congress left unsaid was that if Ridge remained a presidential appointee without congressional confirmation, they would have little control over his operations. If they could pass legislation authorizing the office, setting out its powers, gaining the right to confirm him in office, and controlling the office's budget, they could dramatically shift the balance of power. Many members of Congress saw this as one of the biggest new initiatives in decades, and they wanted to ensure they could control its direction. Bush turned them down, saying through his spokesman that the president didn't need congressional action to do what was required. On October 8, 2001, less than a month after the September 11 attacks, Bush signed an executive order creating Ridge's office.[30]

Ridge stepped into his job as one of a long line of White House "czars" charged with coordinating government policy on important problems. The history of such czars—in every arena, from faith-based social services to energy conservation to drugs—has generally not been happy. They start their jobs with strong presidential support, high-level public attention, and a broad mandate. But they typically find, as Ridge quickly did, that without power over agency budgets and the authority to issue orders to federal employees, they must rely on the job's bully pulpit. Ridge could call attention to homeland security issues, try to get agency officials to work together, and talk to the American people about how to reduce the risk of terrorism. He could not order anyone to do anything. Ridge could encourage the FBI and CIA to share intelligence better, but he could not force them to do so, and he lacked any leverage but the power of persuasion. As one observer pointed out, Bush's executive order establishing the Office of Homeland Security had used the word *coordinate* more than thirty times. It did not use *command* or *control* even once.[31] Members of Congress were convinced Ridge needed legislative authorization to do his job; Bush feared that would lead to congressional meddling. At least at first, Bush won.

Then came a fierce debate about how best to prevent a repeat of the September 11 hijackings. With lives on the line, no one wanted to be blamed for another attack. Everyone agreed on the need for a dramatic change in the screening of passengers and their baggage, and the White House and many members of Congress raced forward with their own airport security plans. The FAA immediately put into place new rules that prohibited carrying a wide variety of potentially dangerous items onto airplanes. Waits in airport screening lines grew from minutes to as much as two hours. When passengers passed through the machines, screeners confiscated anything that might be used to harm flight crews. Just to make sure everyone got the message, the government put out a long list of banned items, from the obvious (hand grenades and black-jacks) to the less obvious (chlorine for pools and turpentine, which could be used to disable flight crews or to start fires).

More difficult was the question of who ought to do the screening. Before September 11, screening was the responsibility of the airlines, with private security companies enforcing federal rules. Everyone agreed that the responsibility could no longer rest with the airlines, and disturbing stories had accumulated about the performance of some of the private companies doing the work. Investigators found that one company, Argenbreit Security, had hired dozens of screeners with criminal records. Low pay—often lower than what fast food workers in the terminals earned—and poor working conditions led to massive turnover, as high as 400 percent per year at St. Louis's Lambert Airport and 375 percent at Atlanta's Hartsfield International Airport. Moreover, in tests, screeners missed twice as many mock weapons as European screeners did.[32] Because the airlines paid for the system, it was part of their operating costs. With the threat of hijacking low and pressures on profits great, airlines had little incentive to spend more money or make the process more difficult for their passengers—until September 11.

A consensus quickly emerged among the president's advisers and members of Congress that the screeners ought to be under federal control. But should the screeners be federal employees or private employees under far stricter regulation?

The last thing the Bush administration wanted, after pledging to shrink the size of government, was to create a new federal bureaucracy. Federal officials counted 429 airports across the nation, and they estimated that they needed a force of more than forty thousand screeners. The administration argued that private companies, under tough federal standards, could do the job, as was the case across Europe. "My approach gives the government the flexibility it needs to assemble a skilled and disciplined screening workforce," Bush said in his October 27, 2001, weekly radio address.[33]

Senators had a different idea. They were convinced that only a full federal takeover could eliminate the problems of the existing private system. Air travel had collapsed, with people afraid to get on planes or discouraged by long lines at security gates, and the Senate was convinced that travelers would never return to the air in large numbers without the strong assurance that would come from full federalization. Senator John McCain (R-Ariz.) put it plainly: "The American people do not have the confidence they need to have to fly on an airplane."[34] A privatized system would not restore confidence, senators concluded, and without fresh confidence in aviation, the economy would be crippled. By a rare unanimous vote of 100 to 0, the Senate approved a fully federalized airport screening system, a plan to deploy air marshals to provide added security aboard planes, and new requirements for the installation of secure cockpit doors.

Members of the House, especially those in the Republican majority, sided with the president. They wanted to restore the confidence of the flying public, but they also fought hard against expanding federal employment. The Senate refused to budge, however, and the Thanksgiving holiday weekend—comprising the busiest flying days of the year—was drawing near. Bush wanted to keep the employees private, but he wanted the bill even more. He signaled that he was willing to compromise, the House agreed, and Congress passed a bill close to the Senate version. It created a new Transportation Security Administration (TSA), within the Department of Transportation, to hire airport screeners and enhance airline security. In a signing ceremony on the Monday before Thanksgiving, November 2001, Bush and congressional leaders went across the river to Reagan National Airport. They all agreed that the new TSA team would make it safe to fly again. Bush pointed to provisions that he likened to practices in the private sector, which would make it easy to remove screeners who performed poorly. Democrats praised the new federal agency. Of course, it would take the new TSA months to get up to speed and to hire new federal employees; the changes would make no difference for the upcoming holiday weekend. But federal officials hoped the bill would prove an important symbol, at a symbolically important travel time, of the nation's resolve to enhance security.

Ultimately, it had two effects. There were no new terrorist attacks, and travelers began returning to the air. The new TSA scarcely solved the problem, however. Determining how best to balance travelers' security with convenience became a perpetual balancing act.

THE RESTRUCTURING STRUGGLE

Despite the passage of the transportation security bill, Democrats in Congress continued to press for a stronger congressional role in homeland security. They didn't like the way President Bush had seized the initiative, and they feared that his efforts would shift power away from Capitol Hill to the White House. They continued to argue for a full-scale department of homeland security. Congressional Democrats also pressed for the creation of an independent panel to investigate the September 11 attacks, what could have been done to prevent them, and what the nation needed to do to increase its security. In presenting the Democrats' case, Senate Majority Leader Tom Daschle (D-S.D.) said that the events demanded "a greater degree of public scrutiny, of public involvement, of public understanding."[35]

Administration officials, including Vice President Cheney, countered that further terrorist attacks were virtually certain and that the nation needed to join with the president to enhance security. His implication was that it was not the time to engage in what he suggested was a side battle over a new department. Now was not the time to divert attention away from preparing for the future to examine what had happened in the past.

The sparring ended abruptly in June 2002 with the explosive testimony of Minneapolis FBI agent Coleen Rowley before the Senate Judiciary

Committee. She complained that top FBI officials had not responded quickly to hints that possible terrorists were training to fly planes. They had refused requests for a search warrant to examine the computer of the man some federal agents suspected of being the "twentieth hijacker," Zacarias Moussaoui. (Many federal investigators later concluded that he was likely not directly involved in the September 11 plot but that he might have been positioned to help conduct a future round of attacks.) As senators listened intently, Rowley detailed her worries about Moussaoui before September 11 and her frustration in working her way through the FBI's layers of authority to obtain approval for the search. She criticized the FBI's culture, which had made it impossible to communicate her concerns to the right officials. "There's a certain pecking order, and it's real strong," Rowley said. In the FBI's way of doing things, agents were not to go over the heads of their immediate supervisors, and working her way up the chain of command proved daunting. Headquarters officials often second-guessed the decisions of field agents. "Seven to nine levels is really ridiculous," Rowley told the senators.[36]

It proved an explosive revelation. It suggested that, if senior FBI officials had better processed the information they had, they might have been able to detect and prevent the attacks. (The 9/11 Commission concluded later that a more aggressive investigation might have helped the FBI uncover the core of the plot. At the least, publicity might have derailed it.)[37] More fundamentally, the testimony illustrated the bigger problems of coordination for homeland security—and it raised large questions about whether the president's plan for Ridge's Office of Homeland Security had gone far enough. Bush sensed that Rowley's testimony would provide support for the Democrats' efforts to create a homeland security department. He decided to steal their thunder—and to ensure that if there was going to be a new department it would be on his terms, not theirs.

In Bush's new plan, twenty-two federal agencies with homeland security responsibilities would be combined into a single new department, with a secretary, structure, and budget subject to congressional approval. Bush told the nation, "As we have learned more about the plans and capabilities of the terrorist network, we have concluded that our government must be reorganized to deal more effectively with the new threats of the twenty-first century." To counter the fears of conservatives and balance his own earlier objections, he explained that the reason for creating the new department was not to increase the size of government, "but to increase its focus and effectiveness."[38] Its budget would start at $37.5 billion and it would have 160,000 employees, more than any other department except Defense and Veterans Affairs.

Agent Coleen Rowley, from the FBI's Minneapolis field office, testifies before the Senate Judiciary Committee on June 6, 2002, about the office's investigation of Zacarias Moussaoui, whom officials charged with conspiring with the September 11 hijackers. (In a thirteen-page memo, Rowley detailed roadblocks headquarters officials had set up to block the investigation of Moussaoui's activities. Later that evening, in a speech proposing the creation of a new department of homeland security, President Bush told the nation that he expected top government officials to treat such inquiries seriously.

Congressional leaders in both houses and in both parties welcomed the plan. It effectively deflated the pressure for a comprehensive investigation of the September 11 attacks, an examination that the Republicans wanted to avoid. It also stopped short of the much broader reorganization that some wanted but that many Republicans opposed, under which the CIA and FBI would both have been swept into the new department.

There was grand irony in the immediate political success of Bush's proposal. While Coleen Rowley's testimony stirred up serious concerns about the effectiveness of the nation's intelligence services and their ability to share information effectively, the proposal for a homeland security department short-circuited questions about the intelligence community without revamping it. To be sure, launching the new department would be sufficiently difficult and complex even without including the FBI and CIA. "What I'm proposing tonight is the most extensive reorganization of the federal government since the 1940's," Bush said in his June speech.[39] Bush's plan avoided the toughest problems while providing a large connect-the-dots symbol.

In many ways, the administration's plan was the most complicated restructuring of the federal government ever proposed. Besides bringing together the aforementioned twenty-two federal agencies and a vast number of employees, it proposed increasing these agencies' focus on homeland security without sacrificing any of their existing missions. The department would include the major federal agencies responsible for border security and emergency response but leave out many others with homeland security responsibilities, notably those responsible for intelligence collection and interpretation (see Table 3.1). Intelligence officials inside the Bush administration argued successfully that with the terrorist threat continuing, this was no time to upset existing expertise. The restructuring therefore concentrated on the government's border security, airline security, infrastructure protection, and emergency response agencies.

In the act of creating the department, Congress resolved the question of which agencies ought to be included with relative speed. The House quickly passed the bill in July 2002, but tensions sharpened in the Senate about the rules for staffing the new department. The Bush administration, backed by key Republican senators, desired greater flexibility in hiring and firing employees and wanted to limit employees' collective bargaining rights. Bush said he needed additional flexibility to act promptly in times of national emergency. Bobby Harnage, then the head of one of the government's largest unions, countered, "We see the administration's use of 'flexibility' as a code word for denial of due process to federal employees." The Senate version, he charged, would make it too easy for the administration to crack down on whistleblowers. The administration's plan "means nothing less than gutting the civil service merit system and busting employee unions," Harnage said.[40] Senate Majority Leader Daschle supported the union's position, but Senator Phil Gramm (R-Tex.) staged a filibuster to block passage of anything but the president's plan. The homeland security bill remained in legislative limbo until after the November 2002 midterm congressional elections.

Those elections, however, produced stunning gains for congressional Republicans, who kept control of the House and won control of the Senate in the new Congress that convened in January 2003. Senate Democrats were stung, and they quickly worked out a compromise on the personnel issues that had held up the bill. The department's senior officials would have great flexibility in pay, promotions, job classification, performance appraisals, discipline, firing, and collective

Table 3.1 Agencies Incorporated into the Department of Homeland Security (2003)

Before September 11	Today
U.S. Customs Service (Treasury)	U.S. Customs and Border Protection—inspection; border and ports of entry responsibilities U.S. Immigration and Customs Enforcement—customs law enforcement responsibilities
Immigration and Naturalization Service (Justice)	U.S. Customs and Border Protection—inspection functions and the U.S. Border Patrol U.S. Immigration and Customs Enforcement—immigration law enforcement: detention and removal, intelligence, and investigations U.S. Citizenship and Immigration Services—adjudications and benefits programs
Federal Protective Service	U.S. Immigration and Customs Enforcement (until 2009; currently resides within the National Protection and Programs Directorate)
Transportation Security Administration (Transportation)	Transportation Security Administration
Federal Law Enforcement Training Center (Treasury)	Federal Law Enforcement Training Center
Animal and Plant Health Inspection Service (part) (Agriculture)	U.S. Customs and Border Protection—agricultural imports and entry inspections
Office for Domestic Preparedness (Justice)	Responsibilities distributed within FEMA
Federal Emergency Management Agency (FEMA)	Federal Emergency Management Agency
Strategic National Stockpile and the National Disaster Medical System (Health and Human Services)	Returned to U.S. Department of Health and Human Services, July 2004

(Continued)

Table 3.1 (Continued)

Nuclear Incident Response Team (Energy)	Responsibilities distributed within FEMA
Domestic Emergency Support Teams (Justice)	Responsibilities distributed within FEMA
National Domestic Preparedness Office (FBI)	Responsibilities distributed within FEMA
CBRN Countermeasures Programs (Energy)	Science and Technology Directorate
Environmental Measurements Laboratory (Energy)	Science and Technology Directorate
National BW Defense Analysis Center (Defense)	Science and Technology Directorate
Plum Island Animal Disease Center (Agriculture)	Science and Technology Directorate
Federal Computer Incident Response Center (General Services Administration)	U.S. Computer Emergency Readiness Team, Office of Cybersecurity and Communications in the National Protection and Programs Directorate
National Communications System (Defense)	Office of Cybersecurity and Communications in the National Protection and Programs Directorate
National Infrastructure Protection Center (FBI)	Dispersed throughout the department, including the Office of Operations Coordination and Office of Infrastructure Protection
Energy Security and Assurance Program (Energy)	Integrated into the Office of Infrastructure Protection
U.S. Coast Guard	U.S. Coast Guard
U.S. Secret Service	U.S. Secret Service

Note: Departments in which agencies were previously located are noted in parentheses.

bargaining. Union officials won some modest protections, but on the whole, the Bush position won. The changes were, in fact, not quite as radical as they seemed. The Internal Revenue Service (IRS) and the FAA's air-traffic control system had been operating for years under similarly flexible rules. But this was a huge federal restructuring involving a giant new department. Union leaders and their Democratic supporters wanted to avoid further erosion of their power. Bush and the Republicans were just as determined to avoid creating a big new group of federal employees represented by Democratic-leaning unions. The Republicans' surprise victories in the 2002 midterm elections quickly resolved both the political and the policy questions. As he signed the bill, Bush praised the new department, which he said would ensure "that our efforts to defend this country are comprehensive and united."[41]

The new department faced daunting tasks, from hiring and training air marshals and integrating the vast new airport screener workforce to developing new strategies for screening checked baggage and securing the nation's ports. Tom Ridge, named as secretary of the new department, not only had to get the department geared up and functional— he had to do it while ensuring that terrorists could not exploit cracks in the system during its startup. He and his management team had to pull together twenty-two different federal agencies, bridge their cultures, and integrate their missions. He had to deal with a Congress whose organization—and oversight—had changed little with the creation of the new department and whose fragmentation could tear the department apart. Ridge and his top advisers moved into a new headquarters on Nebraska Avenue, three miles from the White House and twice as far from Capitol Hill. The new department's constituent agencies and workers remained in their existing locations, with headquarters scattered around Washington, and the majority of its employees—the airport screeners—were dispersed across the country. The logistical challenges alone were huge.

So, too, was the challenge of balancing the new department's relationship with the public. As the symbol of the nation's fresh attention to homeland security, the department needed to be firm and effective— quickly. It needed to do everything humanly possible to prevent a repeat of the September 11 attacks or the anthrax attacks. This would require tough action to screen passengers and luggage at airports and containers arriving aboard ships from abroad, as well as to carefully scrutinize people trying to enter the country. At the same time, the department had to be careful not to make harried travelers even more anxious. The attacks had knocked several airlines into bankruptcy, and the tourist industry around the world had suffered. Citizens worried about threats to civil rights and civil liberties. Somehow, the new department had to determine how best to balance security and service. More of one often meant less of the other. Tighter airport screening could mean longer waits to board airplanes, but efforts to speed up transit through airports could leave vulnerable cracks that terrorists could exploit. The central task of the department's new leaders was to determine, somehow, the best way to balance these competing goals—without drawing political attacks for making the wrong choices.

THE BATTLE OVER BOUNDARIES

At the very least, the new Department of Homeland Security served as a symbol to reassure the American public. Left largely untouched was the biggest problem the September 11 attacks revealed: the great difficulty the nation's intelligence services, especially the CIA and FBI, had in sharing and digesting collected intelligence. Almost two years after the September 11 attacks, one reporter concluded that "even though they both need their relationship to work, they have such different approaches to life that they remain worlds apart. In fact, they speak such different languages that they can barely even communicate." The cultures are hugely different. FBI agents tend to focus on specific things that can lead to identifying suspects and making arrests. The bureau's culture rewards individual achievement, especially in putting criminals behind bars. By contrast, the CIA's employees tend to be more informal and place greater importance on developing relationships. "It's not that [FBI agents and CIA officers] don't like each other, but they're really different people," explained one former CIA analyst. "They have a hard time communicating."[42]

The fundamentally different cultures that made it difficult for the two agencies to connect the dots before September 11 changed little in the first years after the attacks. Changing organizational culture is hard, especially when the risks are great and when preexisting missions (such as catching bank robbers and finding spies) continue to be important. Moreover, the traditional boundaries between CIA and FBI operations multiply the conflicts, with the CIA being responsible for foreign threats and the FBI being charged with defending against domestic ones. The Terrorist Threat Integration Center established by President Bush to be the repository for all information related to terrorism helped bring CIA and FBI employees into the same room, but it also generated new turf battles. In 2004 Congress and the president finally created a new central office to integrate the collection and analysis of intelligence: the Office of the Director of National Intelligence. But the office quickly found that negotiating the turf battles among the intelligence agencies proved just as difficult as uncovering what terrorists were plotting.

Some analysts compared the communication problems of the CIA and FBI to the ones John Gray discussed in his bestseller *Men Are from Mars, Women Are from Venus*.[43] Some insiders despaired that either side would ever be able to push its culture aside to build a strong working partnership with the other. Other experts suggested that it might take a decade or more, during which time the nation would remain vulnerable to attacks. One sixteen-year CIA veteran observed, "I don't think the domestic al Qaeda is worried about [how to coordinate with] the foreign al Qaeda."[44] And some in Washington suggested that bridging the cultures might prove impossible and that integrating intelligence might require the creation of a new agency. They looked to Britain's famous security intelligence agency, MI-5, which has substantially greater powers than either the CIA or the FBI. Created in 1909 to help Great Britain protect its ports from German espionage, MI-5 has long had the responsibility of assessing all threats against the country, regardless of their source. With no history of separating domestic from foreign threats, MI-5 has never suffered from rivalries such as those between the CIA and the FBI. Of course, pushing aside the FBI and CIA to create a new agency would create an epic bureaucratic turf battle, and Washington officials continued to search for other solutions. The one option not on the table was bringing the two agencies into the new Department of Homeland Security, which now had responsibility for connecting all the dots—except for the very ones that proved most troublesome before September 11.

Beyond the intelligence questions, the new Department of Homeland Security struggled to define its mission and determine what "homeland security" meant. Just which problems were within its province, and which were not? Given the substantial—and justified—criticism that a lack of coordination had increased American vulnerability, the instinct of the department's leaders was to be inclusive. If a problem *might* be a homeland security problem, then they would act on it accordingly. However, that instinct sometimes led to "mission creep." For instance, intelligence analysts studied the Internet and concluded that a determined hacker could infiltrate the system, flood it with e-mails, and cripple transmissions. Given the nation's increasing dependence on the Internet for everything from commerce to communication, crashing it could have devastating consequences. Indeed, several attempts in 2003 showed just how serious the damage could be. The Department of Homeland Security therefore took on Internet security as one of its concerns. In short order, however, its concern about Internet-based terrorists spilled over to an initiative designed to help protect children from pornographers, child prostitution rings, and other predators who operated in cyberspace. In announcing "Operation Predator," Secretary Ridge said, "Harming a child in any manner or form is a despicable, despicable thing."[45] Although that statement was unquestionably true, its connection to homeland security stumped many observers.

The new focus on "homeland security" and the difficulties of merging twenty-two separate agencies inside a single department inevitably created tensions between the agencies' traditional missions and the homeland security mission overlaid on top. For FEMA, the strain was especially difficult. Should it concentrate primarily on preparing for and responding to terrorist threats? How much attention should be paid to its more traditional missions, including helping citizens recover from natural disasters? Those tensions spilled over when Katrina struck, as we shall see in the next chapter.

But these two tales—the difficulty of coordinating intelligence and the difficulty of defining the department's boundaries—provide powerful evidence for a fundamental truth in the homeland security debate. Although much of the discussion centered on the department's mission—what needed to be done to protect the nation, and how best to do it—the most important decisions flowed more from political than from mission-based motives. To say that is not to impugn the motives of those involved in the debates. Those discussions were long and difficult, and they produced few clear answers. The lack of any real, black-and-white answers left decision makers trying to see subtle differences in shades of gray. With little else to guide them, they had to sort out questions according to the values they shared, and this made the key decisions political in the most essential sense of the word. Everything about restructuring the nation's homeland defense system revolved around trade-offs: of safety versus service, of protection versus freedom, of presidential leadership versus congressional oversight. Given the high stakes and even higher uncertainty, decision makers had to rely on their best sense of what to do.

The September 11 attacks subjected the national government to a brutal stress test. Congress and the president responded in different ways. Each sought both a symbol to show their determination to prevent a recurrence of the attacks and a response to ensure that, in fact, future attacks were prevented. Both sought a strategy to make the nation's homeland defense far stronger. And officials in both branches struggled to ensure that no matter what the strategy, they would retain a measure of control over what had suddenly become the most important policy issue in Washington.

Bush fell back on a presidential instinct to solve problems by focusing on people and relationships. He wasn't interested in a large restructuring of the nation's homeland security organizations, because he believed that would only enmesh his efforts in ongoing turf wars and frustrate his ability to act. Members of Congress, by contrast, focused on structures, budgets, control, and oversight. Congress passes laws; it doesn't carry them out. For Congress to get traction on the issue, it had to think and act legislatively—and laws meant money, organization, and power.

Events (especially FBI agent Rowley's testimony, which was based on a memo she wrote about the issue) forced Bush to move toward the congressional position, but as he did so, he ensured that he got a bill to his liking. The Democrats held up final action on the home-land security bill in the hope that the November 2002 elections would strengthen their hand. When the elections put both houses of Congress in Republican hands, Democrats beat a hasty retreat and gave Bush most of what he wanted. But they hardly gave up on the homeland security issue. Several key strategists believed that the Democrats could make Bush vulnerable on the issue during the 2004 presidential campaign, especially with respect to coordinating intelligence, but at least in the Homeland Security Department's first years, Bush and the Republicans held the upper hand.

Coordination—connecting the dots—was thus as much a political as an operational issue, one over which the Republicans and Democrats tussled. It provoked constant turf battles among powerful bureaucracies. Dramatically upended by the September 11 attacks, the nation's political system struggled to right itself. At the core of the difficulty, though, one question remained more important than any other: can there be exec-utive branch coordination as long as legislative fragmentation remains? Here, as with everything else the federal government does, the nation's system of separation of powers remained one of the most important touchstones.

At the operational level, the difficulties of getting such a vast array of federal agencies to coordinate carefully created a huge hurdle for ensur-ing and maintaining coordination. Multiple and conflicting missions dis-tracted agency managers. Different cultures made it hard for agency officials to synchronize their operations. And no agency wanted to sur-render its autonomy to others. Put together, these forces magnified the problems with coordination and also increased the difficulty of sustain-ing effective coordination over the long haul. As the painful memories surrounding September 11 began to fade, old instincts reemerged and pulled the agencies back into their familiar patterns. Despite the crea-tion of the new department, there were already signs that pressures for backsliding were building, even as the demands for coordination grew.

4

Federalism Jumble

NEAR DAWN ON AUGUST 29, 2005, as the winds howled and the rain hammered the city, New Orleans residents huddled and hoped. Katrina, forecast to hit the city as a monster Category 5 storm, had weakened to a Category 4 hurricane. More important, it had jogged slightly to the east and spared the city the full force of its winds. Everyone had expected epic damage. "The smell of pine is in the air," one caller to WWL radio told the host—pine trees were snapping in the fierce winds, and the scent of their sap was everywhere.[1] The roof of city hall was leaking, but, as Walter Maestri from Jefferson Parish's emergency operations center reported, "it looks like we've done fairly well." (In Louisiana, counties are known as parishes, and Jefferson Parish is adjacent to New Orleans.) "We have had no reports of serious wind damage, and we don't see any indication of tidal surge problems." However, he added, "It's still really early. The next four to five hours will tell the tale."

Most of the region's residents had heeded local officials' calls to evacuate, but thousands of refugees couldn't get out and huddled in shelters. Others had decided to ride out the storm at home, but they quickly regretted that decision. Water in the streets developed white-caps. A pregnant woman, left alone after a spat with her companion about whether or not to evacuate, had to flag down a police officer to get to the hospital. The Superdome, one of the prime evacuation centers, developed a hole in the roof, and evacuees there were forced to shift to the arena's drier side. One calico cat, named Peekaboo, insisted on standing up to the storm with her face into the wind. "She came in to eat," her owner said, but then despite the storm she "demanded to go outside." The owner lost that battle. "When she gives an order, you listen—and you obey."

Marc Levitan, director of the Louisiana State University Hurricane Center, was initially relieved. The last-minute shift in the storm's direction

When the levees failed near New Orleans's Lower Ninth Ward, flood-waters quickly filled the neighborhood. Within ninety minutes, the water at the Louisiana National Guard's Jackson Barracks rose more than twelve feet, to the level shown by General Hunt Downer. The Guard's rescue boats tied up to the columns as they shuttled the neighborhood's beleaguered residents to the relative safety of the flooded barracks.

and strength promised to spare the city the worst. New Orleans was suffering serious damage, with roofs blown off and curtains from broken downtown skyscrapers waving in the gales. But the city seemed to have escaped the biggest fears of emergency planners.

Major General Bennet Landreneau of the Louisiana National Guard, stationed in Baton Rouge to coordinate the state's response to the storm, called to check with his troops in New Orleans. They had assembled their equipment and gathered at the Jackson Barracks, a historic military post named in honor of Andrew Jackson, who had staged his famous battle for New Orleans from nearby land. General Landreneau asked an airman about the water. The airman replied that there were just a few puddles in the parking lot, but then he hesitated. "Would you hold the line a minute?" he asked the general. "I need to look at something." He quickly returned to the phone and said, "I don't know why, but there's probably a foot of water on Claiborne Street." (Clairborne Street was outside his post.) He looked outside again. "Sir, there's two feet of water on Claiborne Street." Then he stopped himself. "Cars are beginning to float out of the parking lot," he reported. "There's a river of water moving into this area."[2]

That river of water was the first indication that the levees in New Orleans were starting to fail. National Guard commanders knew that, with the water rising so rapidly (fifteen feet in just ninety minutes, one commander later recalled), it could be coming from only one place. Within the hour, the 300 soldiers at Jackson Barracks went from being rescuers to fighting for their own lives. Their power went first, and then the waters flooded the backup generators. Without power, the communications center went down. Mobile communication systems on fifteen high-water trucks were under water. The National Guardsmen trapped at the barracks recognized that within minutes they had gone from dodging a bullet to fighting off the worst-case disaster for New Orleans—a breach of the levees and water filling the bowl. The storm had spared the city on its initial onslaught, but its backwash had punched through the city's flood protection systems.

Within hours, 80 percent of New Orleans was under water, twenty feet deep in some places. Damage was so widespread that it was hard to fully grasp the extent of the destruction, especially with electric power and communications out. Within the first few days, civil disorder began creeping into the waterlogged neighborhoods. Looters grabbed garbage bags and filled them with clothes, shoes, and an endless variety of goods from the abandoned stores. Some cheerily greeted each other in passing on the street while others road around in pickup trucks, honking their horns. Several teens gathered beer and liquor and floated their booty down the flooded street in plastic garbage cans. Others filled a boat with goods stolen from a convenience store. At a Wal-Mart, looters hauled away bicycles, computers, and wide-screen televisions. In amazement, a nearby firefighter watched one of them carry out a basketball goal. The police finally regained control of the store, but in many parts of town there was no order. In several neighborhoods, newly armed vigilantes patrolled in pickup trucks to provide protection.

The state police sent 250 officers to supplement the beleaguered local force. Even that was not nearly enough. At the Children's Hospital, looters tried to break in to steal food and drugs. The 100 patients and staff members trapped inside by the rising waters were terrified, but neither the police nor the National Guard was able to respond. Looters marauded at will, especially after dark. One church custodian compared the scene to the widespread rioting in Los Angeles that followed the 1992 acquittal of four white police officers charged with savagely beating Rodney King, a black motorist who had tried to evade the officers. "I lived in Los Angeles during the Rodney King riots," the church custodian sadly explained. "That was a piece of cake compared to this."

On the streets, the misery continued. Clara Wallace had rescued her brother, who had diabetes and was struggling to recover from a stroke.

Pushing his wheelchair down St. Charles Street in an attempt to find shelter, Wallace pointed to her brother, wearing only a hospital gown, and told a passerby, "Nobody has a bathroom he can use." In fact, she said later, "nobody would even stop to tell us if we were at the right place." Along with about fifty other refugees, she found temporary relief from the baking sun beneath a highway underpass. A worker from the Louisiana Department of Wildlife and Fisheries drove by. He pointed them toward the New Orleans Convention Center, which had become a shelter for a growing number of New Orleanians, some of whom, like Clara Wallace, walked in. Some had been dropped off by patrolling government officials. The convention center had no power or air conditioning. No one had any water or food, and no one knew what was going to happen to them or what they should do next. By the time National Guardsmen arrived with a truck to take Wallace and other elderly refugees off to a better spot, her brother had died in his wheelchair and they had to leave him behind. One bystander, looking at Mr. Wallace's body, shouted to no one in particular, "This is 2005." He went on, "It should not be like this for no catastrophe. This is pathetic."

THE STRUGGLE TO REGAIN THE CITY

For the first time in anyone's memory, it was impossible to tell who (if anyone) was in control of a major American city. Analysts and senior government officials had long debated how to manage "continuity of government," a polite euphemism for ensuring that government leadership remains intact and effective in time of emergency. It had been a recurring theme in planning for the possibility of a nuclear attack following World War II. The worry became real on September 11, when President Bush was circling the nation on Air Force One, Vice President Cheney was in a White House bunker, and Congress itself was the apparent target of the fourth suicide hijacking. But never before in modern times had government failed so completely.

After Katrina hit New Orleans, the "continuity of government" problem became real. The storm savaged the first responders. Police, firefighters, emergency medical technicians, doctors, and nurses all became victims as well as public servants. The police on the streets had little food or water and very limited supplies of gasoline for their cruisers. They had little ammunition and, without laundry facilities, they often had to patrol without the uniforms that lent power to their commands. Many of the city's police officers were also victims of the storm. With their homes under water, they didn't report for work. Some officers simply left town. The city's hospitals were unusable because of storm damage, inaccessible because of the flooding, or both.

If police officers ran into trouble, they couldn't call for backup. The storm had blown down all the radio and cell phone towers, and the generator serving the main police radio transmission site was no longer working. Most officers were out on the streets without any support. The National Guard resorted to a communications technology that troops hadn't used for more than a century—commanders would write messages on scraps of paper and hand them to runners to pass along to other commanders.

To compound the problem, the city's officials were separated and couldn't effectively communicate with each other. September 11 had painfully taught the lesson that major homeland security events could completely disrupt communications and isolate top government officials. Everyone had pledged to make sure that such disruption never occurred again. But during the first major event following September 11, the communications system collapsed again, this time with catastrophic consequences. "Continuity of government" had broken down. The city still had a mayor, Ray Nagin, but looters controlled the streets.

Huddling at the Hyatt

Mayor Nagin huddled with a handful of city leaders in the Hyatt Hotel, between the French Quarter and the banks of the Mississippi River.[3] Compared with much of the city, which was under water, the hotel was dry. It was better stocked with food and water than the city's emergency command post, and Nagin and his senior managers thought they would be better off there. They settled into several fourth-floor conference rooms to ride out the storm.

At the height of Katrina's rampage, the hurricane spun off a tornado that tore off one side of the hotel. "You could hear the windows popping out like gunfire," Greg Meffert, the city's chief technology officer, reported later. The storm knocked out the power and, with it, the air conditioning. But the officials who had hunkered down at the Hyatt thought they would soon be able to move back to their offices. When the levees failed, they were soon marooned and had no communication with the outside world. When several hundred gang members converged on the hotel to seize its food and water, some of the officials disguised themselves by ripping their shirts to copy the gang's insignia. The city's leaders then retreated to the twenty-seventh floor of the hotel.

Communications was their biggest problem, and Scott Domke, a staff member of the city's information technology office, remembered that he had set up an Internet telephone account with Vonage. He found a working Internet jack in the conference room and rigged his laptop to connect with the jack. For the first time in two days, the mayor could make a telephone call to the outside world, but a single telephone line was not enough to take back the city. So shortly before dawn on Wednesday morning, August 31, Meffert, several aides, and the city's chief of police, Eddie Compass, clambered aboard a military Humvee and made their way through the flooded streets to an Office Depot to stock up on more computer and office equipment, from routers to fax machines. While they were rooting through the store for printer cartridges, the looters returned, only to confront Chief Compass. He was an imposing figure with a stern glare. The looters quickly decided not to give the chief a chance to make his day and ran for the door.

Meffert knew he needed a powerful computer to act as a server for e-mail. They found one hooked up in the store's back room. Chief Compass found one of the store's workers and asked, "Do you really need this?" The employee replied, "Yes, we do." But the chief decided that the city needed the computer more, bent the rack holding the equipment, and ripped it out. It was soon on its way back to the Hyatt, where it became the hub for the city's jury-rigged communications system.

The cordless phones they took with them up to the twenty-seventh floor worked, but they had a range of only 300 feet. To connect with the server and the Vonage account downstairs, users had to hang over the railing into the building's atrium. "This was when the last parts of the government were about to come undone," Meffert recalled later. "It felt like the Alamo—we were surrounded and had only short bursts of communication."

All the city's advance planning had fallen short. The commercial systems had failed, and the city's satellite phones, designed to communicate through systems in earth orbit, had run out of power on the ground. City officials later said that local budget cuts and slashed federal aid had made it impossible for them to spend more to get ready. Critics countered that the city had a long reputation of poor management and low investment in technology.

By the end of the week, thousands of Sprint walkie-talkie phones had arrived. A former Army Ranger from the Unisys Corporation led a team of experts to help the city build a wireless network for emergency communications at the Hyatt and city hall. He also brought along bottles of Wild Turkey whiskey.

Gauging the Federal Response

As conditions deteriorated in New Orleans, Americans were horrified at the scenes they were watching on television. How, they asked, could the nation prove so poorly prepared for a storm that had been forecast days in advance, especially when the implications of a major strike on New Orleans had been on the top list of worries for years? Even worse, where was the federal government? The city government of New Orleans was completely overwhelmed and teetered on being knocked completely out of commission. The state government didn't have the resources to respond to a catastrophe on such a scale. The armed forces had combat meals in their warehouses and large numbers of helicopters, but nothing had arrived. The Federal Emergency Management Agency (FEMA) hadn't brought in the other federal agencies with capacity for transportation, health care, and other forms of emergency response. "Where is the government?" was the constant refrain. Meanwhile, broadcast news reporters were beaming live pictures of the disaster. Why, Americans asked, could the reporters get there when the government could not?

On the day before the storm hit, FEMA Director Michael Brown briefed President Bush on a conference call. "My gut tells me—I told you guys my gut was that this [inaudible] is a bad one and a big one." Katrina, he said, could be "a catastrophe within a catastrophe."[4] Dr. Max Mayfield, director of the National Hurricane Center, eerily forecast the implications of the storm's winds blowing water across Lake Pontchartrain against the levees. Everyone knew that a big disaster was on the way, and the president issued declarations of emergency, but the White House was late in recognizing the full impact of the storm—and in responding. The levees broke on Monday, but not until a day later did the president and his staff understand what had happened in New Orleans. The president spent most of the time at his Texas ranch while critics complained he seemed disconnected from the tragedy. As the Senate Committee on Homeland Security and Governmental Affairs bluntly concluded later, "the White House failed to grasp the gravity of the situation as it unfolded."[5]

As the damage reports mounted, the president cut his Texas vacation two days short to fly over the devastated area. From Air Force One, on the third day of the disaster, he surveyed the damage from high above, but that only added to the dismay of many Gulf Coast residents. Not only was the federal government late in recognizing the scale of the problem and in mounting a response, but when the president did visit, he did so from a sanitized altitude.

Compounding the rising criticism was FEMA's sluggish response. Governor Kathleen Blanco said later, "I asked for help, whatever help you can give me." Mayor Nagin was more salty. On his Internet telephone line, he told President Bush that "we had an incredible crisis here" and that his flying over in Air Force One didn't do it justice. The next day, he went on a local radio station to complain about the tepid federal response. "I don't want to see anybody do any more goddamn press conferences," he complained. "Put a moratorium on press conferences. Don't tell me 40,000 people are coming here. They're not here!" Michael Chertoff, the former federal judge who had succeeded Tom Ridge as secretary of Homeland Security, was in the middle of his first major disaster. He told the public, "We are extremely pleased with the response of every element of the federal government." But on the radio, Mayor Nagin countered, "It's too doggone late. Now get off your asses and let's do something! And let's fix the biggest goddamn crisis in the history of this country!"[6]

Stranded evacuees at the Superdome and convention center pleaded for water, food, and help. Live television broadcasts chronicled the misery. Behind the scenes, FEMA Director Michael Brown was criticizing Governor Blanco and Mayor Nagin for not doing their jobs. They shot back complaints that FEMA's help was nowhere to be found. "We haven't eaten in, like, five days," one woman shouted into a network camera. Brian Williams of NBC News asked Brown, "Where is the aid? It's the question people keep asking us on camera." He replied, "Brian, it's an absolutely fair question, and I got to tell you from the bottom of my heart how sad I feel for those people. The federal government just learned about those people today."

That was the repeated federal response, from both the White House and FEMA: the federal government had just learned about the depth of the problem, and help was on the way. Brown repeated the same statement to two other reporters. Later, he admitted to a reporter from the PBS *Frontline* program that he had misspoken—that, in fact, he had known about the full seriousness of the issue a full day earlier. Brown explained later, "I understand why people can—can now look at that tape and say, 'Brown's saying he just learned about that? He really must be an idiot.' I simply misspoke. I knew about it 24 hours before, and I should have said, 'We just learned about it 24 hours ago, Brian.'" The *Frontline* reporter countered, "I just don't understand how you would misspeak three times about that situation." Brown snapped back, "Well, I'll tell you what we'll do. Next time there's a really big disaster, we'll put you in charge of it, we'll not give you any sleep, and we'll put you on this side of the chair, this side of the camera, and we'll pepper you with questions for a couple hours at a time and then see how tired you are."[7]

Criticism about FEMA from residents, state and local officials, and even reporters grew sharper. On Friday, September 2, the White House concluded that it needed to get the president back in front of the issue. He flew to Alabama, whose coast had taken a direct hit from the storm, to view the damage firsthand. He promised residents, "If it's not going exactly right, we're going to make it go exactly right. If there's problems, we're going to address the problems. And that's what I've come down to assure people of." Then, in a statement that came back endlessly to haunt him, he turned to Brown and said, "Brownie, you're doing a heck of a job"[8]—at a time when it was clear to everyone that FEMA was not doing a heck of a job.

Critics pointed to Brown's relative inexperience in disaster management. Before coming to FEMA as counsel, general counsel, and eventually as director, he had served for nine years as president of the International Arabian Horse Association. That relationship ended badly amid acrimonious lawsuits over his enforcement of the association's rules. Brown defended himself by pointing to the 164 presidentially declared emergencies on which he had worked. But the *New Orleans Times-Picayune*, on its way to a Pulitzer Prize, published an open letter to President Bush on the Internet edition that came out even though it couldn't publish paper copies. "We're angry, Mr. President," the paper said. Brown had told reporters that food was coming to the convention center, and that "they've gotten at least one, if not two meals, every single day." The paper countered, "Lies don't get more bald-faced than that, Mr. President. Yet, when you met with Mr. Brown Friday morning, you told him, 'You're doing a heck of a job.' That's unbelievable." Most of those huddled at the convention center had traveled to it on foot. If they could walk there, it seemed that rescue vehicles should have been able to get there, too. "Every official at the Federal Emergency Management Agency should be fired, Director Michael Brown especially," the paper scolded the president.[9]

The government investigations of FEMA's response produced a remarkably uniform and grim collection of criticisms. The Senate Homeland Security Committee's report concluded, "FEMA was unprepared for a catastrophic event of the scale of Katrina."[10] The report from the House of Representatives was stinging: "Our system of federalism wisely relies on those closest to the people to meet immediate needs. But faith in federalism alone cannot sanctify a dysfunctional system in which DHS [the Department of Homeland Security] and FEMA simply wait for requests for aid that state and local officials may be unable or unwilling to convey. In this instance, blinding lack of situational awareness and disjointed decision making needlessly compounded and prolonged Katrina's horror."[11] The White House's own report concluded that the storm quickly outstripped FEMA's capacity. "Hurricane Katrina was a deadly reminder that we can and must do better," the report said.[12]

FEMA had been slow and clumsy in responding to the city's communications and health issues, even though the federal government had the

Following a news conference at the New Orleans airport on September 2, 2005, President Bush shook hands with Mayor Ray Nagin. In the background stood FEMA Director Michael Brown, who became the symbol of the federal government's poor performance. A week later, the president replaced Brown with Coast Guard Admiral Thad Allen as the federal government's commander on the scene.

capacity to move stockpiles of food in military warehouses with military helicopters and the Department of Transportation had offered help in managing the logistics. There was a National Response Plan to bring other agencies on board, but FEMA had neither tested it thoroughly nor determined how best to incorporate the contributions of other federal departments. Coast Guard Admiral Thad Allen, sent by President Bush to restart the vast recovery when the first efforts failed, explained it like this. The National Response Plan, he said, "doesn't contemplate" an event on the scale of Katrina. "When it goes off the scale," he continued, "you need a separate plan for how to deal with something that massive. In this case, there were some things that were unique to this event that can only be handled by an almost different approach to what you're doing."[13] FEMA's failure was not only one of response. If the failure to prevent the September 11 attacks was a "failure of imagination," as the 9/11 Commission reported, Katrina represented the "failure of initiative" that the House Select Committee discovered.[14]

Local officials complained for months that they couldn't get speedy answers from FEMA. Officials in other federal agencies claimed that their offers of help had gone unanswered. FEMA officials quietly said that too many decisions had to go too far up into the bureaucracy to get answers, and outside observers suggested that top-level decisions were sluggish because "everything got over-lawyered"—carefully scrutinized to check the legal authority for actions and to document them in case of future problems.[15] Responsible management, of course, is essential. In FEMA's case, however, that led to a slow and poorly coordinated response.

As FEMA officials struggled, Gulf residents suffered. The Senate report concluded, "Despite knowledge that Katrina was a looming 'nightmare scenario,' DHS and Secretary Chertoff failed to adequately prepare the federal government for what became one of the most destructive natural disasters in the nation's history. As Katrina approached the Gulf Coast, those in the top ranks of DHS failed to understand the potential scope of the pending catastrophe and FEMA's limited capacity to address an event of this magnitude."[16]

FEMA's problems didn't end as New Orleans and the rest of the Gulf slowly came back to life. Federal investigators found massive waste, fraud, and abuse in the emergency recovery effort. To help victims recover, FEMA had distributed emergency checks and debit cards. Officials tried to make the process easy. The Government Accountability Office (GAO) found it had been too easy. Individuals could apply over the phone, and FEMA didn't check their identities. Some individuals used fabricated identities to receive multiple $2,000 checks. Some applied for aid for vacant lots or properties that did not exist. Prisoners behind bars received checks. Of the eleven thousand people who received debit cards, five thousand received duplicate payments. FEMA inadvertently paid for five season tickets to New Orleans Saints football games, a vacation in Hawaii, weapons, champagne, "Girls Gone Wild" videos, a divorce lawyer, and a sex change operation. FEMA claimed that it was simply trying to minimize red tape and to get help to victims as quickly as possible following the storm. The GAO countered that the mistakes totaled as much as $1.4 billion, one of every six dollars spent in relief. Control over the money, the GAO concluded, had been "weak or nonexistent."[17]

State and Local Response

In the hard days after Katrina struck, some government workers showed uncommon bravery and initiative by (temporarily) seizing private boats to rescue trapped citizens. Helicopter rescuers put in long, long hours to pluck people from rooftops. As on September 11, emergency workers made the extraordinary routine.

But state and local governments proved just as sluggish as FEMA. There had been decades of warnings about the risks of a hurricane strike on New Orleans in particular. In 2001, FEMA itself had identified a hurricane in New Orleans as one of the three biggest threats the nation faced. The year before, an exercise labeled "Hurricane Pam" had tested the ability of state and local officials to respond to such a storm, and the results were grim. The emergency preparedness offices were understaffed, and officials knew they didn't have the ability to evacuate the citizens from the danger area. "In short, when it received warnings of Katrina's approach, the state had reason to know that its emergency response systems were likely to fail, however diligently they were implemented," the Senate Committee report concluded. "And fail they did."[18]

At the state level, the National Guard was the main instrument of response. Each state has its own militia, equipped and trained by the federal government but under the command of the governor except when needed for national defense. Most members of the National Guard serve part time, one weekend a month and two weeks a year. They are a "national" guard because the federal government has the right to call them up as needed to supplement the regular Army and Air Force, but most of the time they remain under state control.

This had long been standard policy—until the war in Iraq strained the regular armed forces and the Pentagon called up many National Guard units for deployment, in some cases for repeated tours of six months or more. As the storm neared the Gulf Coast, the governors mobilized the National Guard; six thousand troops were on duty as Katrina struck. But the Iraqi war limited the governors' ability to send in reinforcements. Louisiana had sent three thousand National Guard troops to Baghdad, and 40 percent of Mississippi's Guard units were either in Iraq or on their way. The strain of fighting the war had also made it hard for the states to recruit members of the Guard. "We're just losing too many out the back door," said Norman Arnold, a spokesperson for the Alabama National Guard.[19]

Once the Guard's equipment arrived in Iraq to support the troops, it often remained there when the troops rotated home. New troops needed the equipment, and much of it had already been altered for Iraqi conditions, such as Humvees fitted with armor. The Pentagon was slow in replacing the equipment in the states, since first priority went to the troops on the front lines. The troops called up to fight Katrina, therefore, were not only undermanned but also underequipped. They were short on helicopters, heavy trucks, and earth-moving machinery. Some Guard units had to borrow helicopters fitted with slings to deliver supplies to isolated refugees. The shortage of choppers with hoists limited their ability to rescue people.

Before the storm, city officials had planned to use the Superdome as an evacuation center for special-needs citizens, but they had no list of the people likely to need the shelter. Mayor Nagin put out an evacuation order on Sunday. More than one million people from the area got out, but tens of thousands remained. Some were tourists who had no way to leave. Others had physical handicaps and medical conditions that made it impossible for them to travel. Many lower-income people had no cars. The last airline flights filled up quickly and there were no rail options in place. Even for those who did get out of town, shelters within a short drive of New Orleans had only limited accommodations, so any evacuation meant a long trip. To make things worse, the storm was approaching at the end of the month. Many residents on public assistance had run out of money. Many who lived paycheck to paycheck were running short.

Some critics later showed little sympathy for those marooned in the city because they had passed up the chance to leave. The critics overlooked the fact that many people were not able to get out. Some couldn't afford to leave or had no place to go. Some stayed to be with their pets or to keep an eye on their property. And some were stubborn and insisted that, since they had ridden out previous storms, they were not about to leave in the face of this one.

For many people without other options, the Superdome became the shelter of last resort. It was a cavernous facility that had hosted basketball's Final Four and football's Super Bowl, as well as the New Orleans Saints, the city's long-suffering professional football team (until, in 2010, it finally won the Super Bowl). It quickly opened its doors to ten thousand people. Officials had pre-positioned nine hundred thousand military "meals ready to eat" at the dome, but no one had thought about portable toilets. It didn't take long for the sanitary facilities at the Superdome to become overwhelmed.

In the storm's initial assault, windows blew out and some roofs came off. The power went out everywhere. Some famous landmarks took heavy hits. The storm ruined much of Brennan's, a noted French Quarter restaurant. Jimmy Brennan, one of the restaurant's partners, defended his thirty-thousand-bottle wine cellar with his chef and a couple of guns. When they were finally able to taste the wine a few weeks later, they discovered their efforts had been for nothing. Mold and heat, which had risen in the cellar to 130 degrees, had ruined every bottle. Another New Orleans restaurateur, Emeril Lagasse, nationally known because of his television show and line of Cajun products, suffered similar losses. At one of his restaurants, looters tried to pry open the door but couldn't get in. They did manage to open it just enough to let in hot air, which ruined the wine in his cellar.

The breach of the levees caused the worst damage, however. As the storm moved inland, its counterclockwise winds pushed water across the lake, up the navigation and drainage canals, severely straining the walls and eventually breaking through in several places. New Orleans is a bowl with much of its land below sea level, and after the levees failed it didn't take long for more than three-fourths of the city to fill with water. At that point, Katrina moved from a huge storm to a worst-case disaster.

Bodies floated down city streets. Thousands of refugees at the Superdome and convention center clamored for help. Supplies of essentials ran low and then disappeared. City officials lost control. And all of it was broadcast live on national—indeed, international—television. Viewers everywhere were horrified at third-world scenes. And no one could miss the faces, which were mostly African-American. Katrina's floodwaters had wiped out the mostly black Lower Ninth Ward as well as predominantly white upper-income neighborhoods on the opposite side of the city. The refugees trapped at the evacuation centers, and most of the bodies in the sad photos of people suffering and dying, were black. It was an unimaginable tragedy, but it was also an inescapable portrait of America's continuing struggle to deal with issues of race and class. Gun sales soared, not only in the affected areas but also in the surrounding states, which harbored many of the evacuees. It was impossible to miss the racial overtones that made Katrina not only a natural disaster but a social one as well.

One of the most poignant symbols came with the desperate effort of two hundred people to find a way out of New Orleans. Blocked by water on one side, they tried to cross the Crescent City Connection, one of the few roadways that still offered an escape. It was a motley group. Some were residents of New Orleans (known locally as the Crescent City), and many of the residents were black. Some were tourists from other countries who had become trapped in the city. All were desperate. The bridge led to Gretna, a suburb across the Mississippi River. And local police there had decided to close the bridge to all traffic, including victims trying to walk to safety. "If we had opened the bridge," the city's police chief told reporters, "our city would have looked like New Orleans does now: looted, burned, and pillaged." As the group neared the bridge, according to the accounts of several of its members, Gretna deputies formed a line to block their path and fired in the air. Several officers said later that the situation was dangerous and that they were trying to protect themselves. Members of the group suspected that Gretna officials were determined to block blacks from entering their town.[20] The motivations remained muddy, but the facts were not. Local officials confirmed that shots were fired, one of the most notable examples in recent American history of conflict at the political boundary between neighboring communities.

At New Orleans's Danziger Bridge, an even bigger tragedy unfolded. A team of officers jumped onto a Budget rental truck to respond to a report of problems on the city's east side. When they got there, they opened fire on members of a family who were looking for food. They killed a 17-year-old family friend, James Brisette, and seriously wounded four others. Then they chased down Lance Madison and his brother Ronald, a 40-year-old with mental disabilities, as the two tried to escape to the other side of the bridge. One officer shot Ronald in the back and another stomped on him. The police arrested Lance and accused him of opening fire, but a grand jury later exonerated him. Seven years later, a federal judge sentenced five officers involved in the event to prison—not for the shooting (which would have been a state charge) but for civil rights violations and lying to the investigative team (the charges federal prosecutors could pursue). The federal government acted when the local government did not.

Collapse of the Levees

In the investigation that followed, the focus quickly fell on the levees: why had they failed to protect the city? In advance of the storm, officials had told citizens that the levees were designed to defend the city against a Category 3 hurricane (one whose winds ranged between 111 and 130 miles per hour). Federal, state, and local officials had long before anticipated the possibility of such a storm, so they had built a massive system of levees 125 miles long to protect the area. A levee is a large interlocking network of walls designed to hold back water. It is typically a tall, wide structure made of stone or earth and frequently has a core of metal to provide extra support. The walls protecting New Orleans are part of a larger system of floodgates, pumps, and drainage canals designed to prevent flooding and make navigation easier in the busy Mississippi River port.

As Katrina neared the coast as a fearsome Category 5 storm and took aim at New Orleans, the situation seemed grim. But when the storm veered east at the last minute and weakened to a Category 3 at the areas of peak force, New Orleans seemed to have gotten lucky. Given the wind patterns around hurricanes, the strongest winds were to the north and east of the eye wall—on the side of the storm farthest from New Orleans. The maximum winds that hit the city were certainly severe, but the levees failed with a storm that fell below their top design strength.

Of course, even Category 3 hurricanes, by any measure, are frightening events. In Katrina's case, the storm's fiercest attack on New Orleans came from the rear, a surge of water that barreled across Lake Pontchartrain. The levees failed at multiple points—at a canal used by boats on the way to the Gulf of Mexico and at several drainage canals normally used to empty water out of the city. At one breach, the force of the water pressed the top of the levee backward, allowing water to flow down into the front of the levee and separate the floodwall from the foundation. A large section of the levee collapsed and water spilled with frightening force into the city.

The levee system was a collaborative effort of the U.S. Army Corps of Engineers, the Louisiana Department of Transportation, and five local levee boards responsible for the region's flood control system. The Corps had designed and built the system. The state oversaw the levee districts, which were responsible for raising revenue and assisting in maintenance. The districts had enormous tax raising capacity, and they spent a great deal of the money on activities other than flood protection (e.g., licensing a casino, operating marinas, leasing space to a karate club and to a beautician school), which distracted them from their core mission of protecting the city.[21] In the lively and sometimes boisterous world of Louisiana politics, they were hotbeds of patronage.

There were thus three main players in charge of the levee system. However, there was little coordination among them. The Senate Committee report found that no state agency "made sure that the state's levee districts were integrated into the state's emergency-planning process, much less genuinely prepared for an emergency."[22] The Corps of Engineers believed that the system would protect the city against a Category 3 strike, but some of the system was under construction or repair and other parts had sunk into the soft soil over time. Some parts couldn't protect the city against even a basic hurricane, let alone a Category 3 storm. The local levee boards hadn't properly maintained the system, including rebuilding sunken parts of the levees, and inspections were sporadic at best. Complaints by neighbors that the levees were leaking went unanswered. There was no clear agreement on who was responsible for fixing what.

Once the levees broke, officials couldn't begin to pump out the city until they had at least temporarily plugged the holes. Confusion reigned over who was responsible for what pieces of the effort. As Colonel Richard P. Wagenaar, commander of the Army Corps of Engineers office in New Orleans, explained later,

> Who was doing it, who was in charge, you know, and what parish was what and who could build what road and what trucks could be used and what equipment could be used, you know. . . . I mean, the issue was, is the . . . [West Jefferson] Levee District had like five trucks, dump trucks and an excavator. And here we bring in a contractor

that's ready to go that's got 20 trucks. . . . I mean, we're bringing federal contractors—we're bringing the federal government to bear on the problem. And they [the West Jefferson Levee District] were like, "Well, you can't do that, that's our road." They were working on building this road back there. "Well, you can't"—you know, "We're building the road, you can't do that." . . . I mean, all—pretty much a turf war almost. . . . And it just got to the point where, you know, we were mobilizing contractors . . . and they wouldn't let us operate on the bridge [the Hammond Highway Bridge]. Mike Stack [with the Louisiana Department of Transportation] and—you know, Giuseppe [with the West Jefferson Levee District] blocked some of our equipment from moving with his vehicles.[23]

It took three days of haggling to decide who was in charge of the repairs. That meant three more days in which the city was under water, and three more days before officials could begin to dry it out. Quite simply, there was no plan for dealing with levee collapse. Was the ineffective response due to a federal, state, or local failure? The only possible answer is: all of the above.

The military, together with state and local officials, finally began a frantic effort to plug up the levees. Helicopters dropped enormous sandbags the size of small cars into the breaches and at last managed to keep the water from flowing in. But as the pumping started to take effect, another storm, Hurricane Rita, took aim at the Gulf Coast west of New Orleans. Its strong winds and heavy rains breached the temporary sandbags and the city filled with water yet again. This time, the effect was more psychological than physical. The flooded neighborhoods were deserted and the damage was already done, but New Orleanians wondered how much more they could take. And government officials, at all levels, knew they had a serious problem on their hands: making the temporary repairs at least semipermanent before the next hurricane season began and devising a better flood control strategy that wouldn't continually subject the city to the same risks.

LEARNING FOR THE FUTURE

The legacy of Katrina's furious assault on the Gulf Coast, and especially on New Orleans, is one of profound intergovernmental failures. None of the key players performed well. Despite long-standing warnings about the risks of major storms and the lessons from the Hurricane Pam exercise, not one of the key officials was ready. Communications broke down almost completely. Help was slow to arrive from state and federal agencies, and FEMA's performance, in everyone's estimation, was unacceptably poor.

Why, if everyone knew that the day of a major hurricane would one day dawn for New Orleans, was the government—at all levels—not better prepared? And why, given all the post–September 11 promises, did so many problems recur, beginning with the difficulty in establishing communications?

Fixing the Problem?

Some analysts decided that the problem was the sheer scale of the storm. It was impossible, they concluded, for any government to prevent it from occurring, and because it caused enormous damage, it was understandable that it would take the government some time to respond. There was surely some truth in this argument, but no one found it acceptable. Everyone believed that government could—and should—do better.

Some analysts pointed to the historical problems of government management and corruption that had afflicted Louisiana and New Orleans governments. There were quiet conversations in Washington about the risk of sending billions of dollars of aid into the storied nooks and arcane crannies of Louisiana politics. There was no question, in the judgment of all the federal investigations that followed the storms, that both the city and state governments should have been more prepared and that their response should have been far better. In particular, careful observers pointed to the continuity-of-government problem in New Orleans, where it took days for top officials to simply find a telephone. But the repetition of so many problems that had plagued local governments on September 11 suggested that the issues were far larger than the quaint traditions of Cajun politics.

Some analysts suggested that these problems argued for a stronger role for the military. If state and local governments became overwhelmed, and if the military had heavy equipment, supplies, and personnel, then perhaps the military ought to be called in sooner. In particular, some critics pointed to the fact that New Orleans officials had been disabled and that Louisiana state officials had difficulty in formulating the request for additional federal help. Perhaps, President Bush suggested, the military ought to assume command more quickly in such circumstances. The nation's governors quickly shot down that plan. Although they saw the need for an important federal role, they rejected the idea of federal control. A month after the storm hit, *USA Today* published a survey of state governors, to which thirty-eight had responded. Only two supported the president's plan. Mississippi Governor Haley Barbour, a

Republican who had once headed the party and whose state took a direct hit from Katrina, said the states might need some federal help. "But we don't need them coming and running things," said the governor's spokesman. Michigan Governor Jennifer Granholm, a Democrat, was blunter. "Whether a governor is a Republican or Democrat, I would expect the response would be, 'Hell no,'" she said.[24]

Some analysts suggested that FEMA's problems demonstrated that the decision to move the agency into the Department of Homeland Security after the 2001 terrorist attacks had been a terrible mistake. FEMA, in fact, had gone through a long series of reorganizations throughout the course of its history. (A 2006 Congressional Research Service study of the structure of federal emergency management includes a chart of the function's structural evolution that stretches over five pages.[25]) But the organization's problems went far deeper. Even though FEMA was an independent agency in 1992, it didn't perform well when Hurricane Andrew struck southern Florida. It did far better in dealing with a string of disasters later in the 1990s, including major hurricanes and a California earthquake, but that was mostly due to the agency's leadership, especially from its director, James Lee Witt.

When Congress mandated a "no-notice" exercise in 2000 to test the nation's ability to respond to terrorism, FEMA demonstrated serious problems that foretold its Katrina failures in 2005.[26] This exercise, christened TOPOFF 2000 (for "top officials"), simulated bioterrorism attacks in Denver, Colorado, and Portsmouth, New Hampshire. Even though FEMA was then an independent agency, problems surfaced in TOPOFF 2000: identifying who was in charge of producing results; ensuring adequate communication; clarifying uncertainty over decisions; and creating effective coordination among federal, state, and local officials. Many of these issues returned in the wake of Katrina. The problems found in TOPOFF 2000 were all fundamentally based in process, not structure. That is, their roots did not lie in FEMA's structure; changing the agency's structure would not, in itself, have solved them.

Rethinking Emergency Response

The answers lay fundamentally in shaping the homeland security mission—and then building the capacity to get things done. FEMA's basic responsibility is to respond to natural hazards, such as hurricanes and earthquakes. Effective response involves a wide range of functions, including evacuations, medical support, provision of basic food and water, and communications.[27]

However, FEMA's mission also includes functions specific to terrorism response. For example, FEMA is responsible for ensuring the provision of not only basic medical care but also the specialized medical care that would be required following attacks with biological agents or nuclear materials. Firefighters and police officers responding to the first stages of a major event, for example, not only need to rescue people who are trapped but also need to assess whether the cause of the disaster was an accident, like a gas main or chlorine tank explosion, or a terrorist attack, which might pose additional risks.

The frontline realities of this mission define the federal strategy. All homeland security events, whether caused by terrorists or natural disasters or public health issues, begin as *local* events. Response to the September 11 terrorist attacks began as firefighters in southern Manhattan rolled to the scene of a very large fire, perhaps, they were told, caused by an airplane accident. Response to Katrina began when Louisiana National Guard troops in New Orleans noticed that the water was rising very, very quickly outside their Jackson Barracks. They concluded that could happen only if the levees had failed. The medical response to the monkeypox outbreak in 2003 began the same way the 2001 anthrax attacks had: patients arrived at physicians' offices with unusual symptoms.

On the front lines, where the first critical decisions must be made, there is no neat line between terrorist and nonterrorist events. Only after New York City firefighters, police officers, and emergency medical technicians had already begun to respond to the first World Trade Center fire did everyone realize—as the second plane hit—that it was a terrorist attack. When Washington-area physicians treated the postal workers exposed to anthrax, they didn't know for some time that they were dealing with a terrorist attack. Frontline first responders must be prepared to respond to all such events. Moreover, we have only one set of local first responders—not completely separate teams for terrorist and nonterrorist events.

For decades, local first responders have been trained on an all-hazard system: a flexible response system built to deal with a wide range of possible problems, from chlorine tank explosions to large building fires and floods to earthquakes. Because of events since the September 11 attacks, first responders now know that they could also encounter highly lethal substances like anthrax or radioactive materials. This means they must take additional care in assessing and responding to suspicious scenes. It doesn't mean they can send out completely different fire, police, and emergency medical service teams for different disasters, although they may supplement their basic response teams with specialized units for new-generation terrorist threats. In short, they have developed new operational strategies based on the traditional all-hazard system—plus new capabilities for responding to terrorist events. The Senate Committee on Homeland Security and Governmental Affairs calls this an "all-hazard-plus" system (see Figure 4.1).

Response works best when tightly linked to preparedness. It's hard for responders to plan a response without closely coordinating their work with the officials analyzing the threats. It's even harder to develop critical close partnerships among all participants when artificial lines separate preparedness and response. The job of first responders becomes vastly more complicated if they need to establish separate relationships with officials charged with preparedness and those charged with response. Trying to switch teams in the middle of a major event—or starting from scratch to build new teams in the middle of an event—is even harder. Indeed, part of what complicated and delayed the response to Katrina was the great difficulty of putting together new partnerships, from scratch and on the run.

Pulling FEMA out of DHS would create wasteful duplication of efforts. The new, spun-off FEMA would still have to work closely with the homeland security elements that remained inside DHS, or it would

Figure 4.1. Common Emergency Management Elements

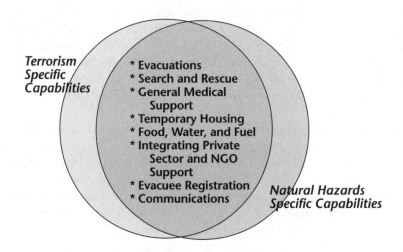

Source: Senate Committee on Homeland Security and Governmental Affairs, *A Nation Still Unprepared,* 109th Cong., 2nd sess. (2006), "Recommendations," 5, http://hsgac.senate.gov/_files/Katrina/FullReport.pdf.

separate DHS emergency planning from the major agency responsible for carrying out the response. Either way, costs would be greater and response would be worse. For the same reason, preparedness and response belong in the same agency. To do otherwise would either require duplication of efforts or risk creating fundamental fissures between those functions at precisely the moment they most need to be joined.

Finally, the steps taken to reduce the consequences of natural disasters can also help reduce losses from terrorism. Efforts to shore up foundations against earthquakes can also help make them bomb resistant. Individuals who stock up on water, canned food, and batteries are better prepared to deal with major events, whatever their cause. It makes great sense to build remediation into the strategy—and to avoid creating artificial barriers between terrorist and nonterrorist events.

In many ways, we face a fundamental choice. We can continue to try to force problems to fit poorly designed organizations, or we can try to build organizations nimble enough to respond to a wide variety of problems. If we attempt to make our problems fit our organizations, the problems will always win. We will face more Katrina-like failures. Our hope lies in building nimble organizations capable of flexible response. We need organizations that can rise to the challenges of the problems we face.

The Future of Federalism

The challenge, to which we will return in the last chapter of the book, is how to construct these organizations within the nation's marvelously complex system of federalism. Too often the system's boundaries have become barriers, such as when police lined up along the line between communities and fired over the heads of refugees to keep them out. In many less dramatic ways, that event is a metaphor for the conflicts that frequently accompany efforts at administrative coordination and political collaboration.

As Peter Eisinger explains, we deal constantly with the "loose arrangements of a highly decentralized federal partnership." Our challenge is to devise strategies to address the "deficiencies of imperfect federalism."[28] The bad news is that these issues, and the conflicts that accompany them, are hardwired into the constitutional structure of American government. They are deeply rooted and long lasting. Still, the problem is not impossible to solve.

Coast Guard Admiral Thad Allen and his wife were among the many Americans who, transfixed, watched the Gulf tragedy unfold on television during that long Labor Day weekend.[29] At the time, they were vacationing on Maryland's Eastern Shore. At one point Allen turned to his wife and said, "The president ought to send someone down there to straighten that out." An hour later the phone rang. It was President Bush, and he asked Allen to go immediately to New Orleans. As a long-time Coast Guard officer (Allen had helped the National Guard manage the response to the 1989 oil spill from the *Exxon Valdez* in Alaska and had led its efforts to evacuate trapped office workers from lower Manhattan on September 11), he had proven experience. A no-nonsense commander with a long "gets results" reputation, he was an obvious choice for the president.

When he arrived in New Orleans, a small helicopter carrier had tied up at the dock. It was one of the few places in the city with reliable communications, electric power, a dry place to sleep, air conditioning, and hot food. Allen brought in the parish's emergency services commander and asked him what he needed. The response was simple. "Hope," he said. Allen choked back his emotions and set to work supplying just that. He became the coordinator-in-chief of the government's recovery operations, and things began to happen. He didn't manage by command— even though, with his military position, his presidential charge, and his bulldog-like demeanor, he could have done just that. Rather, he worked hard to establish partnerships among the players: to define the mission that had to be accomplished, to identify the contributions of each organization to that mission, and to motivate everyone to contribute their part. That approach quickly began to pay off; it was how the things that got done, in fact, got done. Allen later called this a focus on "unity of effort" instead of "unity of command."[30] Results, not control, mattered most. He built the partnerships on the results the region needed, and results were what he got. His experience and skill proved so valuable that, when the Deepwater Horizon oil drilling rig exploded in the Gulf in April 2010, a different president picked up the phone and yet again dialed Allen to ask him to lead the government's response to the disaster.

The Political Costs of Managing Risk

PUBLIC POLICY, WHETHER IT INVOLVES DEFENDING AGAINST TERRORISM, responding to a natural disaster, or dealing with a financial crisis, usually raises tough problems. Government officials can anticipate and plan for every challenge they can imagine but struggle when the time comes to act—and they can fail to imagine the possibilities they will face. A system that works 99.9 percent of the time can still allow one terrorism attempt or unforeseen disaster in a thousand to sneak through the defenses, with devastating costs in terms of both human lives and property damage. Before the 2008 economic collapse, no one fully anticipated the way major financial crises would ripple through the system and bring the economy to the edge of collapse. New Yorkers pride themselves on being able to recover from anything, but Hurricane Sandy's assault in the fall of 2012 staggered the city for weeks.

Citizens expect total protection. Elected officials have a strong incentive to exaggerate their successes. And because no system can be completely foolproof, there is always political tension. The problem of grappling with "unknown unknowns" is enormous, since threats can come from anywhere and government's preparedness has to be everywhere. The best that policy planners can realistically do is anticipate likely problems, prepare a flexible response to things that might happen, minimize the costs if the worst happens, and maximize the government's response. These are extremely difficult steps, however. No official wants to suggest publicly that full protection is impossible, that anything less is acceptable, or that even the smallest amount of risk is tolerable. At the same time, no public official could long survive the furor that would come from imposing the costs and restrictions required to bring the risk as low as theoretically possible. Moreover, the likelihood that terrorist attacks will be a reality for generations—and the certainty that natural disasters will continue to afflict human societies—make the tough dilemmas inescapable. Inevitable, too, are economic crises, as the world's financial systems become more intricately interwoven and one problem anywhere can quickly become a problem for everyone everywhere. Climate scientists are warning that global temperature changes are making storms more severe, more often. These issues not only sharpen the old trade-offs, but they also create difficult new puzzles of how to provide protection without intruding unnecessarily into individual liberty and the role of free markets.

Policymakers must constantly face this dilemma. In writing rules on a host of issues, they must balance risks to the public's health and safety with the costs of compliance. How much research should a pharmaceutical company be required to perform before the government allows a new drug onto the market? How safe is safe enough? How much should a company be required to invest in reducing air pollution? If that pollution threatens to kill or injure people, how much investment is an appropriate trade-off for the lives that are saved? Every year, the news media capture stories of people made sick or killed by food poisoning from bacteria. How much should government spend inspecting stockyards, farms, transportation systems, restaurants, and grocery stores to save those lives? What is the risk of mad cow disease—and how far should the government go in trying to prevent its spread? Accidents at railroad crossings kill hundreds of people annually and cause approximately a billion dollars in damage every year.[1] These accidents could be completely prevented by building an overpass at every crossing, but such a remedy would be extremely expensive. What new savings instruments or loan programs should the government allow—and what might happen if they fail?

Puzzles like these ripple through the system, dominating the debates over terrorism and natural disasters and financial policy—issues that not only carry the potential for catastrophic damage, both physical and economic, but also create images that seize the public's mind and dominate the media. This adds an important emotional layer to the public debate and makes it even more difficult to choose an appropriate balance between risk and cost.

More protection usually incurs higher costs. Some of the costs are monetary, through investment in sophisticated new technology. Others might involve less individual liberty, as we shall see in the next chapter. Moreover, it is very easy for citizens to see only the costs and none of the benefits that come from government policies to address low-probability, high-cost events. For example, no passenger arriving for a long international flight wants to come extra early for luggage screening and answer a battery of questions before being allowed to board. No one wants to stagger off one of those flights and suffer long delays before retrieving their luggage, answer questions about goods being brought into the country, go through passport control, or face a long list of inquiries regarding immigration. During the 1990s, the federal government invested a great deal of energy in reducing those costs. Following the September 11 terrorist attacks, the government ramped up all of its inspections. Citizens proved remarkably tolerant of these costs, but as the immediacy of the attacks faded, so did the public's patience. And no one wants to be told what to do with their money.

A blockade of the borders and hand searches of everyone and what they are carrying might dramatically reduce the odds that terrorists could carry dangerous materials into the country. But given the long, open border with Canada and the miles of unpatrolled shoreline, even that wouldn't be enough. It's possible to greatly reduce the vulnerability of homes to hurricane storm surges by installing stormproof shutters, sturdier roofs better connected with the rest of the structure, stronger walls—and elevating everything above the highest tide of the largest storm imagined. Although that would prove enormously expensive, some homeowners have done just that, including in the areas ravaged by Katrina on the Gulf Coast. Others have decided that the gain isn't worth the investment—either because they're betting their homes can withstand the surge or because they believe such a storm is unlikely to occur. The government could insist on tough regulations for American banks, but a way to make a financial bet is always open somewhere in the world, and money knows no national boundary. The real questions are far more difficult: how much—in money, time, and energy—do citizens want to spend to protect themselves? And how much constraint on their liberty are they willing to accept?

BALANCING RISKS

How can a system guard itself against events—natural or manmade—that are rare, unpredictable, and, when they do occur, very costly? For many analysts, the answer has long been *redundancy:* calculated overlaps to reduce the odds that any part in the system might fail. For example, the space program uses redundant computer systems to protect against system crashes. There are multiple checks on every component. Ground crews and the flight crew cross-check their work. Engineers have built redundancy into airliners. They conduct tests to ensure that two-engine planes can safely take off and land on just one engine, in case one fails at a critical time. They blast bird carcasses into engine cowlings and across the pilots' windshields to make sure the plane can endure such an impact. The landing gear has multiple tires and the electronic systems have backups. Redundancy has been designed into each of these systems to minimize risks and maximize safety.

Experts have long accepted, even celebrated, such redundancy. In a famous 1969 article, political scientist Martin Landau argued that redundancy and overlap provide greater security and improved results. In fact, he concluded, such redundancy could actually be efficient because duplication reduces the odds of catastrophic losses.[2] Multiple programs, duplicative organizations, and overlap among them all provide a robust defense—if one agency misses a problem, the odds of catching it improve if another agency's jurisdiction overlaps. Some "waste," by Landau's argument, is not really waste at all but an insurance policy against disaster.

Critics, in contrast, have long complained about the redundancy approach, which celebrates the advantages of duplication but doesn't provide a clear guide for just where duplication ought to be implemented, how much is enough, how much is too much, and how to tell the difference. Taken to its logical extreme, redundancy could prove little more than a justification for massive inefficiency. This is especially true for homeland security, where threats are by definition uncertain and unpredictable and where, therefore, massive redundancy could theoretically be emotionally comforting but economically inefficient. Redundancy as a basic operating procedure could provide an excuse for sloppy planning and the waste of scarce human and monetary resources—including higher taxes.

Of course, resources are always limited. No one ever has enough time or money. No one likes paying taxes. But no one wants to suffer the consequences of a terrorist attack or catastrophic storm loss either. Everyone would like protection, but no one really wants to pay for it. These cross-pressures limit the extent to which redundancy can plug gaps in the system. Moreover, redundancies could actually open the door to well-planned attacks: terrorists could avoid areas where the government has created rigorous defense and seek areas where defense is much thinner. This is precisely what the terrorists did on the morning of September 11. Government investigators now believe that a system designed to prevent gun-toting terrorists from hijacking planes and holding passengers hostage allowed terrorists using legal blades to kill the crews and crash the planes. This is the core of asymmetric attack: avoid the areas with redundant strengths, identify areas of weakness, and then exploit them.

Homeland security is fundamentally different from most government programs because there is zero tolerance for mistakes. After all, if the sanitation department misses garbage collection on a street or a teacher doesn't provide high-quality reading instruction, the consequences can be serious but are rarely catastrophic. And although no one wants to see errors in disbursing Social Security checks or processing building permits, mistakes in those programs are rarely fatal. There are a few policy areas, however, where errors are never acceptable. Navy pilots landing on aircraft carriers, for instance, have to get it just right. Over- or under-shooting the deck can be catastrophic, and there is no side-to-side margin. The same is true for the operation of nuclear power plants, where tiny problems have proved to be disastrous. In high-risk programs with zero tolerance for error, the system must work all the time.

In extensive writings about "high-reliability organizations," political scientist Todd LaPorte and his colleagues have crafted a theoretical approach to solving this problem. Their theory provides a foundation for understanding homeland security problems. In a 2002 article about the management of zero error tolerance, George Frederickson and LaPorte contend that such complex systems can suffer two kinds of errors: false positives and false negatives. "False positives" are investments in efforts to prevent terrorism when there is no terrorist risk. In such cases, government may spend money and focus energies on solving problems that turn out not to be problems and thus get nothing in return. In contrast, some errors are "false negatives," cases in which managers fail to detect risks until catastrophes occur. Resources are saved, but everyone suffers from the mistake.[3] This is what happened when terrorists exploited loopholes in the system on September 11.

Ideally, of course, we minimize both kinds of errors: resources wasted on situations that are not problems and damage from problems that the system fails to detect. False negatives—problems that sneak through—have the potential for catastrophe, so public officials worry most about eliminating them. At the core of all this, however, is a tough trade-off. Investing more in the system to reduce false negatives can impose big costs and inconveniences for little gain. For example, following the unsuccessful 2001 attempt to sabotage American Airlines Flight 63 with a shoe bomb, airport travelers found themselves subjected to far more extensive searches. Travelers got used to removing their shoes for x-ray inspection. Some shoe manufacturers put their design teams to work substituting "security-friendly" plastic supports for metal ones. But the whole process confused many older travelers, and fliers complained that searches were inconsistent from airport to airport and sometimes within the same airport. Experienced fliers often chose shoes they knew wouldn't set off the alarms, only to be told to take off their shoes anyway. One executive complained that the screening rules were "often capricious." As a result, it was "difficult to predict when [it was] going to be an easy process." Another frequent-flier complained that he occasionally came upon a gate agent who seemed to suggest, "You'll do what I say or you're not going anywhere." On one flight, he was pulled over for a random screening and groaned, "Oh, man." The agent brusquely told him, "Don't raise your voice. I can keep you from getting on that airplane."[4]

If someone managed to get through security without a full screening, or if someone tripped the alarm at an emergency exit, security officials would pull everyone back into the lobby and force them to undergo screening and x-rays of their carry-on baggage again. Pilots sometimes taxied from the runway back to the gate if a passenger made a poorly timed joke about security, and travelers wearing protest buttons found themselves escorted off planes. Passengers often complained about the inconvenience, but neither security guards nor pilots were in the mood to tolerate even a joke about the new risks they faced. In analytic terms, the balance in the system had been recalibrated to prevent more false negatives—allowing people to fly who might later turn out to be a threat—even if that meant far more false positives—subjecting people who were not threats to much greater inconvenience. In 2012, one flier going through the security line in the Portland airport retaliated by taking off all his clothes. The police arrested him for disorderly conduct.

In the first years after the September 11 attacks, the new federal Transportation Security Administration (TSA), charged with safeguarding air travel, constantly checked the system's standards. Its officials increased screening for shoes but eased up on files attached to nail clippers. They ratcheted up examination of laptop computers and, for a brief time, asked travelers with fold-up umbrellas to open them (despite the old wives' tale that opening umbrellas indoors is bad luck). Following the 2006 threat to use liquid explosives to blow up transatlantic flights, TSA officials required travelers to put toiletries into clear plastic bags. In general, however, TSA was cognizant of the need to balance the rigor of security checks with their effect on the flying public. With the airlines bleeding red on their balance sheets, the TSA wanted to do everything possible to avoid discouraging travel. But everyone knew that nothing could discourage travelers more than another attack, and the TSA worked to identify the most important threats and to focus security screening on them.

The fundamental question became how to find the right balance between allowing false positives and false negatives. At some point, more investment to prevent one kind of error will not prevent the other kind. For example, at some hard-to-define point, a greater investment in passenger screening and luggage searches will not improve airline safety—and it might push potential terrorists to use other techniques instead. Moreover, if policymakers invest more money, energy, expertise, and time in preventing one kind of error, and if they prove successful in preventing attacks, they might conclude that they have invested too much or imposed too much inconvenience. If citizens conclude that they are being overprotected and overly inconvenienced, they are likely to press for an easing of restrictions. Money is always tight, and money spent on protection could always be spent on other things, from teachers' salaries to prescription medicines. How can policymakers know how much is enough? Or too much? Even with minimal investment, the country might simply be lucky. Al-Qaeda has been famously patient, willing to wait many years for just the right moment to launch attacks, or to shift its strategy to try to exploit different gaps in the security

The discovery by British authorities that hijackers were plotting to blow up transatlantic jetliners with liquid explosives led homeland security officials to raise the terror warning to red, the highest level. Passengers, like the ones here at Washington's Dulles International Airport, had to surrender all containers of liquids and gels before boarding their flights.

system. The only way to test how much is enough is to tempt fate by lowering one's guard. Frederickson and LaPorte conclude that "no system is entirely efficient"; therefore, there will always be errors.[5]

This dilemma points to three inescapable tensions in the homeland security system. First, there is the problem of *collecting enough information to make reasoned judgments*. How can policymakers calibrate the system and balance the risks they face? They can use experience and intelligence estimates to frame educated conclusions. The best way to do this is to make a decision, test it to see how well it works, modify it if necessary, and repeat the process. Indeed, many complex, high-risk systems, such as aircraft carriers, provide many opportunities for testing new tactics and gathering feedback. Everything known about the process of launching and trapping high-speed jets on a relatively tiny surface bobbing on the waves has grown from decades of naval experience.

The fewer opportunities there are to test the system, the harder it is for those who manage it to have confidence that they have set just the right balance. This was part of the challenge of running the space shuttle program, which involved only a few launches, each of which carried a high risk. As the investigation into the 2003 disintegration of the shuttle *Columbia* revealed, it had been easy for shuttle managers to talk themselves into the conclusion that their systems were safe, because small mishaps—such as the foam that flew off the external fuel tank and struck the shuttle on launch—had not previously caused major damage. Their confidence proved tragically misplaced. When a large piece of foam flew off the tank and damaged the *Columbia*'s wing, a very rare false-negative error proved fatal.[6] Homeland security events can be even rarer. Skillful terrorists constantly seek new cracks in the system. Financial problems occur regularly, but true crises capable of bringing the global economy to its knees are, fortunately, very uncommon. Severe storms don't happen often, but they roar in often enough, somewhere, that emergency planners need to be ready. And that's the point: big problems that occur rarely pose special problems for policymakers.

The second problem is the *risk of backsliding*. As we saw in previous chapters, powerful forces deeply rooted in the political system can pull against efforts to strengthen homeland security. LaPorte argues that, to minimize homeland security risks, we will likely be forced to accept more costly false-positive errors than we might like in order to reduce the false-negative errors that we cannot accept. We will likely have to accept higher costs and more inconvenience than might be necessary so as to reduce the risk of terrorist attacks as much as possible.

That means that policymakers are likely to be plagued constantly by complaints about overspending, inconvenience, and excessive intrusion into civil rights and civil liberties. As more time goes by without an attack, pressures to reduce false positives are likely to grow, demands to reduce investment in homeland security and shift spending to other areas will increase, and cries to eliminate inconvenience and lessen the invasion of civil rights and civil liberties will ring out louder. Such backsliding might seem sensible in resetting the balance, but it could increase the risk of terrorist attacks and damage from the other policy problems we've been exploring.

The third issue is the problem of *calibrating risk*. The way people perceive risk is often not in proportion to the objective facts. As political scientists David Ropeik and George Gray found, individuals tend to fear new risks more than existing ones, risks that attract big headlines more than quiet ones, and risks that are controlled by others more than ones they choose.[7] The highly public September 11 attacks, with people watching on live television as one of the planes hit the World Trade Center, terrified many away from flying altogether. As researchers Paul Slovic and Elike U. Weber observed, "differences in risk perception lie at the heart of disagreements about the best course of action between technical experts and members of the general public."[8] Indeed, dangers are real, but risks are inherently subjective. Social forces can amplify the sense of danger that individuals feel.

Risk analyst Baruch Fischhoff argues that "managing risk is a human enterprise." It depends on how individuals perceive risk and on how public officials communicate about risk. Nevertheless, Fischhoff has found, risk management suffers from a profound "lack of behavioral realism." Public officials often operate on shared lore or on anecdotal experience. Citizens tend to exaggerate some short-term risks and ignore longer-term threats. This, in turn, tends to mislead citizens into relying on faulty plans and to blind public officials to better options that might not flow easily from their experience.[9]

Researchers warn that when nerves are on edge, as they were in the days after September 11, public officials may overreact. So not only is it impossible to know what level of protection is best, but raw nerves can drive the system to hyperinvestment in protections that may not, in the long run, really make the country safer. The false-positive costs may rise quickly. This also can encourage backsliding if further attacks do not occur. The homeland security system could thus find itself lurching between extremes of overreacting and underreacting. Both can make citizens more vulnerable, impose more costs, and further limit personal freedom.

To address these three concerns, the Pentagon explored an experimental new method to predict what risks were most likely. Its Defense Advanced Research Projects Agency signed a contract with the Policy Analysis Market, an online service, to create a market to allow Middle East experts to bet on likely political and economic events in the region. The Policy Analysis Market would enroll one hundred experts, give each a hypothetical account of $100, and allow them to buy and sell online futures contracts on scenarios such as the overthrow of one of the region's leaders or the assassination of a major political figure. This was to be a mechanism to collect the judgments of many experts, do it in real time, and allow the assessments to change over time with new events and new analyses. Its value, experts believed, lay in improving the ability of analysts to predict what was likely to happen next. Similar online markets allowed betting on everything from the outcome of the Super Bowl to the winners of reality television show jackpots. Researchers at the University of Iowa had run a presidential futures market for years: anyone could log in, create an account, and bet on who would win the next election.[10]

But the plan died an almost instant death when news stories labeled it state-sponsored "gambling on terrorism," a notion that quickly proved unpalatable to Americans struggling to recover from the deaths of thousands of their fellow citizens. "This is just wrong," said Senator Tom Daschle (D-S.D.). Senator Byron Dorgan (D-N.D.) called the plan "unbelievably stupid." Senator Ron Wyden (D-Ore.) observed, "Trading on corn futures is real different than trading on terrorism and atrocity futures. One is morally fine and represents free enterprise, and the other one is morally over the line."[11] Defense Department analysts believed otherwise. They continued to think that rapidly collecting the best judgment of experts in the field would enhance their assessments of likely threats, but following such a political storm they dared not make their argument publicly.

Analysts have struggled, through both political pressures and great uncertainty, to estimate which problems the nation is likely to face and how best to solve them. Ultimately, the question of how to balance the risks and costs of the homeland security system is one that elected officials must answer. The analysis implicitly warns that people might have to accept higher costs than seem warranted to secure the level of protection desired. This will come as little surprise to homeland security experts, but it raises stark warnings for policymakers and citizens alike about the difficulty of balancing risks and costs and of keeping that balance over the long haul, over a vast range of policy puzzles.

USING THE MARKET TO MANAGE RISK

One strategy for managing risk is to allow market forces to work. Public officials struggle to frame policy, especially because of two things: the imbalance between the expectations of citizens and the ability of public officials to respond, and the difficulty of matching short-term decisions about risks that are relatively unlikely with long-term policy on the investments required to meet them.

Policy analysts have long debated the comparative advantages of market versus governmental forces.[12] Through supply-and-demand forces, markets provide incentives for individuals to do things and choices about how to get them done. Insurance companies have created such markets for dealing with the costs of property damage from hazards. They have typically steered clear of terrorism insurance because such events are so unpredictable and expensive. However, insurance companies do offer homeowners and business operators insurance to deal with a wide range of other risks, including fires, thefts, earthquakes, winds, and floods, and reinsurance companies provide backup to insurers in case of catastrophic claims. Residents living in hurricane-prone areas can insure themselves against the damage such storms can bring. Moreover, mortgage lenders typically require homeowners to buy flood insurance for property located in flood plains, either along inland rivers and streams or near the coast. The same insurance is an option for most other homeowners as well.

Research shows, however, that most homeowners do not buy insurance against such hazards even when it is available to them. About 80 percent of homeowners living in areas that require flood insurance purchase it. (Some homeowners don't because they don't want to pay the extra cost and because the enforcement provisions for this requirement are weak.) In areas where flood insurance is not required, about the same share of homeowners do *not* buy it, because they see their chances of exposure as relatively low. In sum, only about half of homeowners living in areas that have a 1-percent chance of suffering flooding damage in any given year—the one-hundred-year flood plain—buy insurance.[13] In New Orleans, a majority of those living in areas officially defined as being in the flood plain had flood insurance. The city's tragedy is that much of the area that ended up under water was not defined as flood prone—and many of these residents had not purchased flood insurance.

The cost of insurance is important, and many people don't want to pay the extra money. But so too is the perception of risk. The odds of a flood high atop a mountain are, of course, infinitesimal. For a

Many Gulf area residents had no insurance to cover their losses from Hurricane Katrina. Others, like the owner of this home, fought with their insurance companies over the size of their payments. Many insurance companies invoked clauses in the policies to pay only for wind damage, although most of the damage was caused by flooding.

very long time, however, individuals have settled near water and, as people have become more affluent, many have enjoyed vacationing along rivers, lakes, and oceans. How high is their risk? Individuals often take an "It can't happen to me" approach. In reality, flooding is a far more prevalent risk than many people believe. More people are killed in hurricane storm surges than by the winds and, as Katrina showed, storm waters can impose a staggering cost.

Experts tend to assess flooding risk by looking at past floods (although information is limited by the quality of records from the distant past), the kind of weather events that prompted them (how large a storm occurred, over what period of time), and how the land has changed over time (since replacing farmland with strip malls vastly increases the amount of water that accumulates and the speed at which it runs off, potentially creating more floods). They assess the odds that a flood of a certain intensity will occur in any given year. A "one-hundred-year flood," for example, refers to the largest flood in the last century, prompting the calculation that there is a 1-percent chance that a similar flood will occur within the coming year. Megastorm Sandy, which hit New York and New Jersey in 2012, was a "thousand-year storm," with the highest storm surge recorded in the city's history.[14]

However, individuals are not very good at incorporating such information into their thinking. Homeowners living in a one-hundred-year flood plain often conclude that they are unlikely ever to see such a flood. If their time horizons are short, they might conclude that there is only a tiny chance that they are likely to see a big flood in the coming year and, therefore, do nothing to reduce their risks. In fact, they have better than a one-in-five chance of seeing such a catastrophe in the course of a typical thirty-year mortgage. Those who grasp this concept may therefore decide to reinforce their homes—and buy flood insurance. The difficulty of communicating and understanding risk, however, often leads people not to take relatively easy steps that could greatly help in the long run. Then, when large disasters occur, they may find that ten feet of water has destroyed their homes and everything in them—and have no insurance to rebuild their houses or replace their possessions.[15]

Even when individuals want to purchase insurance, there is the tough question of trying to determine just how many people should buy flood coverage. Oceanfront property in Florida is at high risk and insurers are reluctant to write policies there. Mountaintop properties are a low risk, and there is little reason to buy flood insurance there. In between lies a vast gray area. If a property lies in the one-hundred-year flood plain, are the risks sufficiently high to warrant buying insurance? What about a five-hundred-year flood plain? A thousand-year plain? The longer the time horizon, the more properties that become swept in and the harder the area is to define, since we obviously don't have good weather records stretching back over several centuries. No one wants to spend money unnecessarily, but experts can't offer clear guidance on where to draw the line. That quickly became one of the most important issues in rebuilding New Orleans: just where should the flood plain lines be drawn?

Caught with major damage and no insurance, many individuals turn to the federal government for help. This instinct is understandable—where else can they turn? And government's response is reasonable, for Americans are a generous people; they hate to see their fellow citizens in trouble, and their elected officials understand the political gains that result from helping large numbers of people in desperate need. Whenever the federal government arrives with emergency rebuilding aid, however, it weakens the case for individuals to buy private insurance. Why should they pay in advance if federal help arrives when needed? Of course, private insurance often provides more relief than federal aid, and it provides a check without the uncertainty of whether Congress will act. Nevertheless, many individuals and companies have drifted into a policy of avoiding the purchase of individual insurance and counting on the government to come to the rescue.

This implicit policy has created enormous budgetary problems for the federal government, to the point that it has developed its own label for some of the costliest beneficiaries of the National Flood Insurance Program (NFIP): "repetitive loss properties." In fact, the Government Accountability Office (GAO) found in 2004 that such properties "represent[ed] a significant portion of annual flood insurance program claims." The NFIP insures 4.4 million properties. But even though repetitive loss properties represent just 1 percent of those properties, they account for 38 percent of all claims—or about $4.6 billion paid out between 1978 and 2004.[16]

These forces have combined to create a difficult dilemma. Many individuals do not accurately perceive the risks they face and thus do not purchase private insurance. When trouble comes, they look to the government for help, and elected officials often find it impossible to say no. Individuals rebuild, often bigger and better in the same spot, again fail to buy insurance, and when trouble recurs the federal government bails them out yet another time. The result is a drain on the federal budget, poor incentives for individuals, and a growing tendency to relive the same problems over and over.

Even insurance is no guarantee of payment, however. Insurance companies advertise that they will be there when disasters occur, but they naturally don't want to write more checks than they have to. Following Katrina, many residents complained that they had insurance for hurricanes but that their insurance companies argued that their damage was caused by floods. Individuals whose roofs blew off sometimes had an easier time getting their check than those whose homes had been destroyed by the storm surge, since some policies covered damage where the primary cause was wind but not water. Other individuals found themselves battling with their insurance companies over the amount of payment they received. One homeowner in New Orleans returned to find that the force of the water had pushed his refrigerator into the kitchen wall. Mud covered everything and the home was a wreck. He had $1.2 million in coverage on a 3,000-square-foot home. His insurance company offered him $10,000. "I want people to drive by my home and decide for themselves: Could I repair this for ten thousand dollars?" he plaintively asked a reporter.[17]

Markets can provide a useful way of generating incentives to minimize risk and speed recovery. Sometimes insurance companies will ask homeowners to make repairs that reduce the risk of damage in storms, which helps homeowners and reduces the companies' costs. But the insurance market for terrorism and natural disasters functions poorly. It is full of what economists would call market imperfections, and those imperfections inevitably bring government back in. Reforms could help, but public officials cannot escape a central role in the most basic functions of signaling risks and responding to disasters.

Of course, the economic crisis that began in 2008 starkly shows the limits of markets in managing risks. Major financial firms thought they had done just that in creating financial instruments whose risks demanded higher premiums and in providing safe investments for savers who wanted little risk. In addition, private rating firms like Moody's, Fitch, and Standard & Poor's examined financial products and told investors just how risky those investments were. Layered on top of the system was a complex web of federal regulators charged with keeping the system safe and stable. Despite the multiple levels of defense, the safeguards failed. It became clear that financial firms did not fully understand the investments they were selling, that investors did not know what they were buying, that the rating firms misjudged the risks, and that government regulators missed the emerging threats to the system. These were market imperfections taken to frightening heights, and worried investors wondered whom they could trust to protect their money.

WARNING SIGNALS

As homeland security officials planned their strategy following the September 11 attacks, they confronted a tough question. Because the intelligence agencies couldn't connect the dots in advance of the attacks, the terrorists gained complete surprise. But what if analysts had detected the possibility of an attack in advance? How would the government have notified state and local officials and citizens?

In the case of Katrina, officials had clear warnings days in advance about how big the storm would be and where it was heading. Everyone knew that the consequences could be enormous. Mayor Nagin issued an evacuation warning the day before the storm hit, but critics later suggested he had waited until it was too late. Some observers suggested that, having been harshly criticized for ordering an evacuation for an earlier storm that proved a lamb instead of a lion, he was reluctant to act too quickly. Of course, the longer he waited, the less chance citizens had to flee. Moreover, Mayor Nagin realized that an evacuation order could impose enormous financial costs on the city's economy, especially on the tourist industry on which it so heavily depended.

When Hurricane Rita headed toward Houston a few weeks later, city officials ordered the city completely evacuated. Most citizens complied, but they turned the evacuation routes into long parking lots, and a bus carrying senior citizens from a nursing home burst into flames, killing twenty-five seniors being driven to safety. Evacuations are never easy and certainly not risk free. How should the government best manage and communicate risk?

In the weeks after the September 11 attacks, warnings were almost nonstop. Federal officials cautioned that more assaults on planes might occur. They struggled to understand the possibility of more anthrax attacks. Intelligence officials detected "chatter" among suspected terrorists that could be a harbinger of other attacks. Following September 11, no federal official wanted the responsibility of knowing—or even suspecting—information about possible attacks without sharing it. State and local officials, however, complained that they were already at heightened alert. They were trying hard to protect possible targets, but such targets were everywhere: buildings, roads, bridges, tunnels, airports, and power plants, among many others. Vague warnings about the possibility that bad people might at some point do bad things told them nothing about what to do. Some analysts suggested that the constant warnings only increased anxiety without increasing protection, adding that some all-news television channels only aggravated the problem by putting the terror alert level on a constant crawl at the bottom of the screen—a signal that the terror threat could change at any moment.

To provide better guidance, Homeland Security Director Tom Ridge, in March 2002, announced a new alert system. The federal government would notify citizens about the level of risk of terrorist attack using five color designations, ranging from green for low risk to red for severe risk. Each level represented a different degree of threat, and each called for different levels of response from citizens and public officials. Ridge started the system with a yellow alert, which indicated an "elevated" level of threat and was supposed to prompt increased surveillance around critical areas and a heightened state of readiness.

In general, Ridge received high marks for his work in bringing the twenty-two disparate agencies together into a new department and for strengthening the nation's homeland security system. The difficulty of communicating with citizens, however, generated an endless supply of jokes. Writing in the *St. Petersburg Times*, Jan Glidewell said, "It still doesn't tell you what kind of attack is expected or where it is expected, and it doesn't say what you should do while you are on alert. Basically, it seems, your job is to stand or sit in one place, elevate your blood pressure, secrete excess stomach acid and, well, fret, until the color changes and tells you to be more or less agitated."[18] Jay Leno quipped, "This thing is so confusing. Yesterday the alert went from blue to pink; now half the country thinks we're pregnant."[19] The jokes were predictable—perhaps even a healthy sign that a skittish nation was beginning to regain its footing. Behind the humor, though, was the inescapable lesson about how hard it is to communicate clearly about risk.

In February 2003, just two weeks into his job as secretary of the new cabinet-level department, Ridge changed the terror warning from yellow to orange because of intelligence that suggested al-Qaeda might be preparing for another attack. Intelligence officials worried in particular that terrorists might be plotting biological or chemical attacks, and Ridge suggested that citizens buy plastic sheeting and duct tape to prepare a "safe room." Shoppers, especially in New York and Washington, swamped home supply stores and cleared all the tape and sheeting from the shelves. Some experts doubted that the plastic-and-duct-tape combination would provide much security. Such safe rooms would work only if people put up the protection in advance of an attack, but chemical and biological attacks typically can be detected only after they occur. Moreover, most such chemical and biological agents are harmful only in small areas and sometimes only on contact with the skin. It would make little sense for everyone to lock themselves in on the off chance that an attack might occur. If an attack did occur, its effects would arise before anyone could put up the plastic and apply the tape.

Ridge found himself roasted at the annual Gridiron Dinner, at which top journalists and politicians trade off-the-record spoofs. To the tune of the wartime standard "Over There," a journalist playing Ridge (and wrapped in duct tape and plastic sheeting) sang, "We're sealed, we're shipshape/The axis of evil lives in fear/Over here, over here."[20] The wife of Bush's budget director, Mitchell E. Daniels Jr., said that the message for the upcoming Valentine's Day holiday should be, "Say it with duct tape." Daniels obliged and asked the florist to send his wife a special bouquet with the stems wrapped in the tape. "I think they got into it," Daniels said of the florist.[21]

Despite the jokes, Ridge's advice was sound. As anyone who has ever attempted a repair knows, duct tape is useful for an infinite variety of problems. (It even helped the Apollo 13 astronauts in 1970 piece together an air-treatment system for their spacecraft, seriously damaged by an explosion on their way to the moon, and get them safely back to earth.) Plastic sheets can provide temporary repairs from storm damage or supply provisional shelter if necessary. Together with a battery-operated radio, a flashlight, extra batteries, and a supply of water and food, duct tape and plastic sheeting are useful supplies that citizens everywhere can use in a wide variety of emergencies, from terrorist attacks to tornadoes and from power outages in thunderstorms to winter blizzards. In New Orleans, thousands of citizens learned painfully that they needed to be able to cope on their own until government could rescue them. But the commonsense nature of the recommendations became lost in the fuzzy nature of the threat. In the meantime, the announcement fueled endless jokes by stand-up comedians.

Beyond the jokes, many critics worried that the duct tape episode showed real problems in the nation's homeland security strategy. A columnist for London's *Guardian* wrote that it had taught him "that the country's rulers haven't the faintest idea what they are doing."[22] Former Democratic presidential candidate Gary Hart put the point more sharply: "Because the government has done so little against terrorism at home, it sounded as if they were saying, 'You're on your own.'" Homeland security expert Ivo H. Daalder added, "Homeland security is a difficult job, but they've been at it for 17 months, and they're certainly not getting any better at it. . . . They want to be absolutely sure that if anything happens they can say they've warned us about it. But by covering their backsides, they're making terrorism into something more awful."[23] The "You're on your own" comment, however, proved eerily prescient. It was precisely the reaction of many Gulf Coast residents after Katrina struck. As the government mobilized at an excruciatingly slow pace, many citizens in fact found themselves on their own and without many supplies. Ridge's message was that citizens had to take a measure of responsibility for their own protection. It was a lesson that many citizens didn't want to hear.

Ridge and his staff faced a tough—perhaps impossible—challenge. No one wanted casualties to occur because the public didn't have access to all the information available. However, because terrorists are secretive and unpredictable, the best that the Department of Homeland Security (DHS) could typically do was to share a sense that risks had increased, that something might happen somewhere. Department officials could never say that a particular thing would happen at a particular place at a particular time. Indeed, if the department had such specific information it surely would work with law enforcement officials to arrest the perpetrators. The nature of the risk was always vague. Sometimes intelligence officials detected more specific threats, such as a plot to attack New York's Brooklyn Bridge, but the intelligence supporting the threat was often not solid enough to broadcast the specifics publicly. Often the best that government officials could do was to suggest that people—and local officials—needed to be even more careful than usual. But vague warnings, some suggested, only increased fear without increasing security.

The chief of the Portland, Maine, police department said simply that he relied on CNN. On one occasion when the threat level was raised, the official notification came eight hours after he saw it on the news channel. When warnings occurred, responding to them was expensive for local officials, who sometimes resisted. Philadelphia Mayor John F. Street, for example, refused to close a street near Independence Hall following a DHS warning. Moreover, the Congressional Research Service found, the DHS system was one of eight separate warning systems about potential catastrophes—severe weather, contamination from chemical and biological weapons stockpiles, and others—which were not integrated.[24]

The United Kingdom, which has long struggled with terrorist attacks by the Irish Republican Army, uses a different system. Home Secretary David Blunkett, whose department is in charge of the United Kingdom's homeland security, explained it this way:

> We have internally seven different layers of threat level. We announce the heightened threat level only when we believe that the public themselves are at risk, or when we have to take obvious action, as we did six weeks ago [in early 2003] to ensure that there wasn't a threat to Heathrow Airport. In other words, we're pronouncing publicly at a moment when we believe either that we should engage the public in their own surveillance, or at a moment when the threat level has heightened to a position where either in heightened policing or in terms of using military hardware, as we did six weeks ago, it would be obvious to the public that we're taking action.[25]

British policy tips the balance between public access and secrecy of sources toward secrecy. The Web site of the British Home Office tells citizens, "We are committed to giving you as much information as we can about terrorism." But, it adds, "we also have a responsibility to protect people working in the intelligence and security fields," and the government wants to avoid giving out "information that could compromise their safety."[26]

British officials thought that the American color-coded system was too vague. As the Home Office explained, "We do not believe it is beneficial to the UK to have one single national system to indicate the current general level of threat. Rather than one blanket system, we operate specific systems in various public sectors and key industries, like aviation and the utilities. This reflects the fact that when alert states need to be raised in one sector, the threat assessment for other sectors could stay the same. Our concern is always to minimise the damage to the economy and our prosperity caused by alarms of this nature."[27]

The British, with a long history of terrorist attacks, had been working to enhance their own warning system. One strategy focused on communicating better with citizens in times of emergency, an issue that became even more important after September 11. The New York terrorist attacks had not only destroyed the two World Trade Center towers, but they had also taken out a major telephone switching center, many cellular phone towers, and the transmitters of most New York television stations, which were atop one of the towers. In Manchester, Leeds, and Liverpool, British officials had already installed a pager warning system. After September 11, the British Home Office further evaluated using new technologies, including pagers, instant messaging, e-mail, and digital services, to transmit warnings. When the September 11 attacks overwhelmed cell phone service in Washington but left BlackBerry wireless e-mail service relatively unaffected, congressional leaders issued each member of Congress a BlackBerry to transmit emergency evacuation messages and keep in touch with one another in case of another attack. Efforts to make the cell phone system more robust failed following the 2011 East Coast earthquake, a relatively modest temblor that sent everyone to their phones—which clogged the system so badly that emergency calls couldn't get through. Hurricane Sandy collapsed the system, and cell phone companies sent a stream of messages saying they were working as hard as they could to get their systems back online as soon as possible.

Of course, other problems also proved capable of seriously disrupting communications. The massive August 2003 blackout that darkened vast portions of the Midwest and Northeast in the United States as well as parts of Canada swamped and then cut off cell phone service in some cities, New York in particular. Without electric power, citizens couldn't turn on their televisions to receive timely updates. Many relied on battery-operated radios and word of mouth to learn—to their relief—that the blackout was just a blackout, not a terrorist attack. Everyone determined to avoid such communication gaps in the future, but communications failures were the first step in the breakdown of government in the Gulf when Katrina hit.

Public officials needed to determine how best to educate citizens about the new risks they faced without "crying wolf" or aggravating an already scary situation. They needed to couple warnings with specific responses or risk losing credibility. They needed to get the word out, quickly and effectively, to the frontline first responders who would have to deal with any attack that occurred, along with specific advice about what to do when and where. They needed to develop better ways of communicating with each other. And they needed to develop the technical means of communicating advice in ways that would get through during an emergency that disrupted communication systems.

In 2011, Homeland Security Secretary Janet Napolitano ended the confusion over the infamous color-coded alert system by announcing the department would scrap it. It was none too soon, argued Representative Bernie Thompson (D-Miss.). "The old color coded system taught Americans to be scared, not prepared," he said. "Each and every time the threat level was raised, very rarely did the public know the reason, how to proceed, and or how long to be on alert." CNN reported that the general alert level had been raised from yellow (elevated) to orange (high) five times. On three other occasions, the alert went to orange for specific industries.[28] Then, for long periods, the alert level did not change, which suggested to Americans that they always need to be frightened—and to security analysts that the system was too clumsy to convey changes in the threat level. "This new system is built on a clear and simple premise," Secretary Janet Napolitano said. "When a credible threat develops that could impact the public, we will tell you and provide whatever information we can so that you know how to keep yourselves, your families and your communities safe."[29] The new system aimed to send alerts only to law enforcement officials or parts of the private sector in some cases, and in other cases to the general public. It characterized threats as "imminent" or "credible," and contained "sunset" provisions so they would not continue indefinitely.

The TSA also deployed new full-body scanners that used less radiation to produce clearer images of passengers. When many fliers complained they amounted to virtual strip-searches, TSA replaced the machines in 2013. Some passengers found themselves singled out for trace detection, where TSA employees swabbed luggage and inserted the samples into machines programmed to test for explosives. New scanning systems came on line to screen carry-on luggage, while behind-the-scenes scanners x-rayed checked luggage. Meanwhile, the TSA invested heavily in behavioral analysis to identify characteristics of individuals who might be planning terror attacks. Every new threat, real or suspected, generated another round of technological response to bridge the gap between warnings and trust.

TRUST

Despite the warnings, jokes, and debates about technology, these issues fundamentally boil down to politics and values. The greatest difficulties of coordinating such issues are not the managerial ones. Post–September 11 public opinion polls showed that many Americans wanted government to play a stronger role in protecting them from future attacks.[30] Following the financial collapse, Americans agreed on the need for tougher financial regulations, although support dropped from 76 percent in 2009 to 62 percent in 2010.[31] The kind of government role that citizens wanted, however, varied significantly. In a poll taken a year after the attacks, Americans favored creation of a national identification card by a two-to-one majority. Support for the monitoring of cell phone calls, however, had dropped from 54 percent to 32 percent.[32] Following the financial collapse, Americans agreed on the need for tougher financial regulations, although support dropped from 76 percent in 2009 to 62 percent in 2010.[33] Citizens wanted safety, but they were unsure about what that meant or what price they ought to pay. In New York, New Orleans, and the rest of the Gulf, the pledge was to rebuild bigger and better.

Two fundamental problems characterize these policy issues. One is the level of safety that public officials can responsibly guarantee. Citizens, not surprisingly, expect full protection from all risks, and rapid response if problems occur. They look to their government to provide it. Sluggish response courts strong attacks against public officials. The revelation that FBI field agents in Minneapolis and Phoenix had identified suspicious individuals receiving flight training in advance of September 11 led to widespread criticism of the intelligence agencies and, ultimately, to the creation of the Department of Homeland Security. Bush's praise of FEMA director Brown—"You're doing a heck of a job, Brownie"— became a national joke. Government officials plan and train, budget and design, coordinate and test, but they can never cover all contingencies. They can never fully *guarantee* protection to citizens—they can only guarantee their best efforts. In the Gulf, no one tried to do poorly; one of the great tragedies is that the problems cascaded despite the fact that everyone was trying to do his or her best. Still, an argument that officials did their very best could prove a thin reed on which to rest the defense of their work.

The other problem is that security cannot be pursued in isolation. Rather, it is the product of continual trade-offs between protection from risks and limits on freedom. Just how far are citizens willing to go to secure protection? Which freedoms are they willing to sacrifice, and to what degree? Are they willing to accept the implicit risk that comes when citizens rise up to defend their freedoms? Will they accept government restrictions on where they can build and on how they must strengthen their homes to resist storms? Are their tolerances of risks and of limits on freedom likely to change as memories of September 11 and Katrina recede into the past?

The civil rights battles in the last half of the twentieth century focused the debate over how much discretion state and local governments ought to have at the expense of nationally guaranteed rights. Homeland security produces the same tension between national power and local discretion but does so in a context that, in an instant, could prove fatally unforgiving. National defense is mainly a function of the national government, although the National Guard, managed by the states, plays a role. Homeland security is inevitably an intergovernmental function, pushing questions of values onto the agendas of officials at all levels.

Homeland security, in all of its facets, is thus far more than a technical issue. It is more than a national security issue or a puzzle of federalism. It is, at its core, a problem of governance. And it is one that demands strong and effective political leadership to make the necessary decisions and to shape the necessary trade-offs.

Public officials and citizens rarely discuss these big political trade-offs explicitly. Amid tough and sometimes insoluble problems, it is easier to build consensus and cobble together coalitions if some of the toughest issues are kept vague and the most difficult trade-offs are pushed to the background. This helps make politics work. Making everything explicit can make the trade-offs—who wins and especially who loses—all too painfully clear. Politics runs on the subtext; new battles are the product of past victories and losses. Any deficit from one battle can potentially be made up in the next. Terrorism, however, has made that game much harder to play. The enormous losses of September 11 were vivid and painful, and the implications of further attacks were made clear. Katrina demonstrated that natural disasters can impose costs and consequences just as great. A political system traditionally built on keeping such trade-offs below the surface suddenly has found itself grappling with them in the open.

This is a key challenge that can be solved only through political leadership. The job of leaders is to define reality for others.[34] They help resolve ambiguity. They motivate employees and they are the faces an organization presents to the world. They build and maintain administrative capacity. Most important, they fill the gaps that other processes and strategies leave. They are responsible for effective operation across government's complex boundaries and problems. In homeland security, that means defining what level of risk is acceptable and deciding how to set the balance between freedom and security that any level of risk entails.

Leaders must shoulder the burden of making, and accepting accountability for, decisions that have profound implications, stretching to the very safety and survival of citizens. That is a huge responsibility with equally huge political implications. It requires public officials to feel their way gently toward defining acceptable levels of risk, and citizens to find appropriate ways of holding officials accountable for securing them. It requires leaders to make critical decisions about the balance of risk and protection, something they didn't have much experience with before September 11. As Richard A. Clarke, former White House counterterrorism coordinator, said, "Democracies don't prepare well for things that have never happened before."[35] It was true for the September 11 terrorist attacks, and it is just as true for natural disasters.

At the core of these difficult challenges for democracy is the role of citizens. For all the jokes about duct tape and plastic sheets, or about who is doing "a heck of a job," the issue revolved around the responsibility that citizens have in homeland security. How much information should citizens receive? What should they do with it? Which risks are acceptable—and what price should be paid for reducing them? How much protection is possible—and reasonable—in the risky and uncertain world of terrorism and natural disasters and financial crises? To what degree should citizens hold public officials accountable for these decisions? Few issues of democracy and political leadership have been so difficult. Faced with such tough puzzles, it has been tempting for leaders and citizens alike to try to duck the trade-offs and slide back to the more comfortable—if far more risky—world they knew before September 11.

6

Balancing Liberty with Protection

OF ALL THE SURPRISES IN THE AFTERMATH of the September 11 terrorist attacks, one of the biggest was the discovery that the four teams of hijackers had been living undetected in the United States for months. Two had settled in San Diego in January 2000. Several had spent time in the United States in the early 1990s, taking language instruction and, later, flight lessons. The "muscle" hijackers, whose job it was to overcome the pilots and control the passengers, began arriving in April 2001. Early in the year, the four pilot hijackers traveled across the country in dry runs and, for reasons investigators could never determine, spent layovers in Las Vegas.[1]

All the hijackers had entered the country with what appeared to be valid passports. By the day of the attacks, the visas of two of them had expired, and a third hijacker had failed to register for classes and thus violated the terms of his student visa. But federal authorities did not discover any of this until after the attacks. Just as important, sixteen of the hijackers were in the country legally. All managed to live comfortable lives, blending into the fabric of American society.

Americans have always treasured their ability to go where they want when they want. They have long valued the freedom to choose their jobs and chart their careers, to live their lives without government scrutiny, and to associate with people of their own choosing. So important are these values, in fact, that many states refused to ratify the U.S. Constitution until, in 1789, Congress proposed a bill of rights. But at the same time, Americans have always expected their government to protect them from threats. That the country was attacked by people who had so easily integrated themselves into the nation's daily life raised a dilemma: how much should government intrude into the lives of citizens in its quest to provide protection?

That question raised a second point. Americans have always accepted any expansion of government power grudgingly. When government has expanded, people have tended to trust state and local governments, to which they are closer, more than the federal government. But to the degree that homeland security strengthens government power, it tends to strengthen the power of the federal government. Therefore, it not only shifts the balance from individual freedom to government control, but it also shifts the balance from state and local authority to federal power. In the long run, the most lasting and important effects of the September 11 attacks could prove to be these changes in individual liberty and governance.

The 2008 economic collapse raised precisely the same questions. Initial efforts to halt the collapse, through massive government intervention in the financial markets, vastly expanded federal power. To help the economy recover, the federal government became the owner of banks and auto companies. And to shore up the system against further assaults, both Congress and the White House proposed tough new regulations. These strategies combined to shift the balance from individual freedom to governmental control. The federal government also became the cornerstone of a global effort to forestall the collapse, thus greatly increasing governmental power over the private sector. In all these cases, efforts first to respond to and then to prevent policy crises significantly shifted the balance of power within government and between government and citizens. That spotlighted the challenge of balancing liberty with protection.

ASSAULT ON AN OPEN SOCIETY

The discovery that the September 11 attackers had so easily entered the country and managed to plot the attacks without detection (except by a handful of suspicious FBI agents, whose memos had not gained attention at headquarters) stunned federal officials. A congressional investigation, released in 2003, offered a scathing assessment. "At home, the counterterrorism effort suffered from the lack of an effective domestic intelligence capability. The FBI was unable to identify and monitor effectively the extent of activity by al Qaeda and other international terrorist groups operating in the United States." Coupled with the CIA's difficulty in tracking foreign threats, "these problems greatly exacerbated the nation's vulnerability to an increasingly dangerous and immediate international terrorist threat inside the United States."[2] Sixteen of the nineteen hijackers had come from Saudi Arabia, and an American who had worked for the Saudi foreign ministry said, "The visa operation is a joke over there." Nationals from other countries handled the initial processing of the applications, which made it easy for even questionable individuals to slip through the process. "The State Department does not do a quality control check," the former employee charged. As a result, *Boston Globe* reporters concluded, the United States, "with its borders so porous and its recordkeeping so unreliable[,] . . . has little ability to keep all criminals—or terrorists—out of the country and has no system to track them once they're in."[3]

According to the *Washington Post*, the whole star-crossed system produced "a portrait of terrorists who took advantage of America's open society as they planned their murderous assault on the Pentagon and the World Trade Center."[4] The story was dismaying: a student visa process exploited by one terrorist; easy issuance of new passports to foreign travelers; a lack of careful screening at American immigration facilities; failure to create effective watch lists and match them to individuals trying to enter the country; and weak information systems to track foreign travelers once they entered the country. Americans and their officials wondered if the nation's tradition of openness and minimal intrusion of government had allowed the hijackers an advantage that they had exploited to horrendous result.

Americans were rocked not only by the enormity of the attacks but also by the fact that the terrorists had walked among them for months or years. The warning of intelligence analysts that more al-Qaeda operatives might be waiting in "sleeper cells" to stage more attacks kept anxiety high and led Americans to look over their shoulders, especially at individuals with Arabic names or differences in color. Then there were new threats. Investigators found evidence that some of the September 11 hijackers had studied crop dusters. Was al-Qaeda planning to distribute anthrax or some other biotoxin from the air? Was another round of airline hijackings in the offing? Would the terrorists dream up a new strategy for attack?

In short, how could the nation protect itself without becoming a police state? The *Boston Globe* said that the terrorists had "exploited one of the most enduring tenets of American freedom: its open society."[5] A week after the attacks, columnist Martin Wolf sharply summarized the budding dilemma in London's *Financial Times*: "The biggest long-term challenge to any open society vulnerable to assaults on so vast a scale is striking the balance between safety and freedom. The attack of 9/11 took advantage of the ease of movement and low security levels of air transport inside the U.S." He concluded, "We must balance the needs of security with the demands of freedom."[6] Even the staunchest advocates of civil liberties knew that the horror of the September 11 attacks and the fact that the terrorists had exploited American freedom in an effort to weaken the nation would inevitably mean some sacrifice of civil rights and civil liberties to provide greater security.

It would also mean a vast investment in new technology. Intelligence analysts discovered that the terrorists were using satellite phones and coded e-mail. By contrast, American officials charged with guarding the borders and ferreting out terrorist cells often had to sift through reams of paper without good computer support and deal with government data-bases that didn't connect. Senator Edward M. Kennedy (D-Mass.), long an advocate of an open immigration policy, nonetheless recognized that things had to change. "We're dealing with horse-and-buggy technology," he said. "We're dealing with handwritten notes. It's a shocking indict-ment."[7] U.S. intelligence would have to enter the twenty-first century to deal with the twenty-first century terrorism threat.

These issues were central to what President Bush called the "global war on terror." Although he received fierce criticism for the strategy, including using the label as justification for the war in Iraq, he faced tough issues. Especially after September 11, no president would ever want a major attack to occur on his or her watch. Compounding the problem for the president is an important part of the job that almost no American ever sees: the "President's Daily Brief," a digest of foreign policy issues and intelligence findings. The brief contains an endless list of things the president must worry about on behalf of American citizens, from possible threats from domestically based terrorist organizations to the dangers posed by operatives abroad. After teams of suicide terrorists hit the Madrid train system in 2004 and the British underground in 2005, and after an American Customs agent in 1999 caught terrorists trying to sneak explosives into the country in the trunk of a car, and after Canadian agents in 2006 broke up a ring planning explosions throughout Toronto, it was clear that the risks were more than hypothetical. Compound these terror worries with the very real threats from public health crises and natural disasters and the long economic crisis that continued after the 2008 collapse, and it's easy to see why presidents so often seem to age in office. Their daily reading would put deep creases on anyone's face.

After the September 11 attacks, the nation found itself in the midst of a struggle that, in the assessment of many experts, was likely to stretch on for generations. The president carries responsibility for ensuring the safety and welfare of the nation's citizens. But in defending the nation against clandestine operatives who can burrow into American society and then appear suddenly with terrifying effect, just how far can—and should—the president go? No one wants the nation to suffer terrorist attacks. Yet no one wants to sacrifice individual liberties, and it's impossible to defend the country against certain kinds of threats without some sacrifice of liberty. Just where should that balance be set? And who has the right and responsibility to set it?

THE PATRIOT ACT

For the Justice Department officials shaping the new policy, the issue also had a sharp personal side. Barbara Olson, a CNN commentator and the wife of Solicitor General Ted Olson, had been aboard hijacked American Airlines Flight 77. As she and her fellow passengers tried to figure out what to do, Olson twice called her husband at his Justice Department desk. Soon it didn't matter—Flight 77 crashed into the Pentagon, killing everyone on board and many in the building, and the smoke was visible from the Justice Department's door. The officials working on the new policy had known Barbara Olson well. Her story gave them an extra measure of determination. Terrorism had taken on a personal face.

For the first days after the attacks, Attorney General John Ashcroft was at a secure location away from Washington along with other senior administration officials. Worried that more terror cells might be plotting follow-up attacks, Ashcroft huddled with advisers to put together tough new programs to break up any cells and protect the country from future attacks. One of Ashcroft's aides later remembered that his charge was clear: "all that is necessary for law enforcement, within the bounds of the Constitution, to discharge the obligation to fight this war against terror."[8] Not only did department officials feel the need to act, but the heat of press scrutiny created an inescapable need to be *seen* to be acting as well.

This imperative created a flurry of proposals on the floor of Congress. Some members proposed an aggressive new authority that would allow the federal government to intercept e-mail and telephone calls. Plans surfaced to allow the government to increase the monitoring of foreign agents and to infiltrate religious services, even if there was no prior evidence of criminal activity. Investigators, in fact, had complained that the existing law made it easier to infiltrate the Mafia than al-Qaeda cells. Civil libertarians, for their part, worried that Congress would rush to enact sweeping new legislation without stopping to consider what impact it might have on civil rights and civil liberties. Security experts struggled to find a way to balance concerns for liberty with the need for stronger homeland defense.

Under heavy pressure from the Bush administration, Congress agreed on new legislation to make it easier to track the origin and destination of telephone calls and to increase the authority of government to track e-mail. They agreed on broader wiretapping authority and new measures to track the flow of money to terrorist groups. The administration, however, wanted to go much further. Ashcroft, for example, wanted the authority to indefinitely detain noncitizens who might be planning acts of terrorism. He wanted greater flexibility in sharing grand jury and eavesdropping data throughout the federal government and in tapping into e-mail chats. And he wanted the new authority to be made permanent, so that the federal government could create new and aggressive long-term strategies to go after potential terrorists. Just a week after the attacks, Ashcroft announced at a press conference that he expected the administration's proposal to be ready very shortly—and that he wanted Congress to act on it within a few days. "We need these tools to fight the terrorism threat which exists in the United States," Ashcroft said.[9]

Most members of Congress agreed that the nation needed tougher penalties for terrorists and that the federal government needed broader investigative powers. But Senator Patrick J. Leahy (D-Vt.), chair of the Judiciary Committee, warned that "the biggest mistake we could make" was to conclude that the terrorist threat was so great "that we don't need the Constitution."[10] He added, "The first thing we have to realize is this is not either/or—this is not the Constitution versus capturing the terrorists. We can have both."[11] The American Civil Liberties Union (ACLU) echoed Leahy's concern in a set of ten principles endorsed by scores of civil rights and civil liberties groups. "We need to consider proposals calmly and deliberately with a determination not to erode the liberties and freedoms that are at the core of the American way of life," the ACLU said on September 20.[12]

Fundamental issues were at stake. Citizens expect the right of privacy in their homes and workplaces, but government intelligence analysts believed that they needed broader powers to wiretap phones and track e-mail. They sought new powers to search the homes and belongings of individuals suspected to have terrorist links without informing the individuals in advance. The rationale behind all this was that the government suspected that terrorists worked in secret cells. Conducting a search of one cell member's home might alert the others that the government was on to them and frustrate the government's ability to arrest all the cell's members.

Civil libertarians worried that in its zeal to capture and interrogate potential terrorists, the government might violate the long-standing principle of habeas corpus. Literally translated as "You have the body," this principle traces its lineage back to 1215 and the Magna Carta. A writ of habeas corpus, issued by a court, requires the government to bring a prisoner to court to show that it has reasonable cause for holding the person; otherwise, the prisoner must be released. But federal officials said they believed some potential terrorists should be held as "enemy combatants," which would allow them to be imprisoned indefinitely, without trial, to permit prolonged investigation and questioning. Civil libertarians worried that these steps would open the door to broad abuses of government power.

Congress did not come close to meeting Ashcroft's deadline, but it did complete its work in near-record time, just six weeks after the September 11 attacks. The legislation's authors formally labeled it the "Uniting and Strengthening America by Providing Appropriate Tools Required to Intercept and Obstruct Terrorism Act," or the "USA PATRIOT Act" for short, surely one of the most clever and symbolically powerful Washington acronyms of all time. Given the pain of the terror attacks, who could be against an act supporting patriotism and fighting terrorists? The bill won House approval on October 24, and the Senate agreed the next day by a vote of 98 to 1, with Senator Russ Feingold (D-Wis.) casting the only "nay" vote. President Bush signed the bill promptly on October 26. "Today, we take an essential step in defeating terrorism, while protecting the constitutional rights of all Americans," Bush said that morning. "With my signature, this law will give intelligence and law enforcement officials important new tools to fight a present danger."[13]

The Patriot Act gave the federal government broad new powers to investigate and detain potential terrorists:[14]

- *To facilitate the tracking and gathering of information with new technologies.* The law allowed federal officials greater authority to use a kind of "secret caller ID," which can identify the source and destination of calls made to and from a particular telephone. Existing laws allowed such "trap and trace" orders for phone calls. The new law permitted them for other electronic communications, including e-mail.
- *To permit "roving surveillance," or allow observation not limited to a particular place or instrument.* In the past, court orders had allowed surveillance only on telephones or places identified in advance. Since terrorists may change locations often, discard their cell phones after a single use, frequently switch the SIM cards in their cell phones, and repeatedly create and change free e-mail accounts, court orders were often a step behind. The new law permitted investigators to obtain authority to track targets as they moved or switched phones and e-mails. It also allowed investigators to obtain a court order to examine any "tangible item" rather than just business records. For example, investigators could probe voicemail messages and library records showing who borrowed which books.

- *To increase federal authority for investigating money laundering.*
  The new law required financial institutions to keep more complete
  records of the financial activities of suspicious individuals and to
  allow federal investigators broader access to them. In the aftermath
  of September 11, federal officials had discovered that hundreds of
  thousands of dollars had flowed through the financial system to
  terrorist cells undetected, and they wanted stronger authority to
  trace this flow of money.
- *To strengthen the authority of border agents to prevent possible ter-*
  rorists from entering the United States. The new law gave authorities greater power to detain and deport suspicious individuals and
  those suspected of supporting them. To signal that these provisions
  were not aimed at punishing foreigners, the law also provided
  humanitarian assistance for foreign victims of the September 11
  attacks.
- *To define a broader array of activities—terrorist attacks on mass*
  transportation facilities, biological attacks, harboring of terrorists,
  money laundering to support terrorism, and fraudulent solicitation
  of money to support terrorism—as federal crimes. Federal officials
  were concerned that the ingenuity of terrorists had grown faster
  than criminal law, and they were intent on creating a broader net
  to snare terrorists.
- *To allow so-called sneak-and-peek searches, in which investiga-*
  tors can enter homes and facilities and conduct searches without
  informing those searched until a later time. Whereas previous law
  specified that individuals who were searched had to be informed
  before the search began, federal officials said that giving even a
  few minutes' notice might disrupt their investigations and tip off
  members of a terrorist cell. Sneak-and-peek searches, they said,
  would permit more effective investigations.
- *To expand the government's authority to prosecute computer*
  hackers. Government officials increasingly worried that terrorists,
  or even ordinary hackers, would exploit vulnerabilities in the
  Internet to flood the system with e-mails or damage computer
  records. With the growing dependence of the world economy
  on electronic commerce and communication, officials wanted to
  increase the system's protection against cyberterror attacks and to
  provide stronger remedies to those hurt by hackers. Such attacks
  had not occurred on a broad scale at that point, but security analysts warned that the system was vulnerable and that they could
  occur in the future. Over the next few years, hackers proved
  them right.

Within an hour of Bush's signing the act, Ashcroft put ninety-four federal attorneys and fifty-six FBI field offices to work implementing its provisions. In September 2003, he hailed the Patriot Act as one of the Justice Department's best tools to "connect the dots" in fighting terrorist activity.[15] But almost immediately, critics began worrying about just how the government would use the act's new powers. Administration officials maintained that the governmental powers granted by the Patriot Act were ones that only terrorists needed to fear. The line, often repeated, was that the government needed the same power to investigate potential terrorists that it had long used to stop organized crime. Civil rights experts acknowledged the need for new government powers but worried that there were few checks on the new powers and that the government would push them too far. The government could conduct searches without informing those searched. It could hold prisoners without informing them of the charges or bringing them to trial. And the issue was not only *what* the government could do, but also the uncertainty about how the new powers would be used and what protections citizens would have to ensure that government officials didn't abuse those powers.

BROADENING THE WAR

In his September 20, 2001, address to a joint session of Congress, President Bush condemned the Taliban government in Afghanistan for sheltering al-Qaeda terrorists. He bluntly demanded, "Deliver to United States authorities all the leaders of al-Qaeda who hide in your land." Bush continued, "These demands are not open to negotiation or discussion. The Taliban must act, and act immediately. They will hand over the terrorists, or they will share in their fate."[16] A few weeks later, Bush made good on his threat, launching a major military campaign in Afghanistan, and in less than a week, the United States and its allies swept the Taliban forces from most of the northern part of the country.

The October 2001 military campaign quickly brought into the spotlight the issue of the rights that should be accorded suspected terrorists. As U.S. forces captured territory in Afghanistan, they also captured members of al-Qaeda along with other suspected enemy combatants and Taliban soldiers. How should the United States treat non-Americans that officials suspected were terrorists? What about armed fighters allied with governments, such as the Taliban, that had sheltered terrorists? What rights should those captured be granted, and how, if at all, should those rights differ from those guaranteed Americans? In particular, should they be treated as prisoners of war, and given the rights provided under the Geneva Conventions? President Bush had promised that the war on terrorism would be a new kind of war. This new kind of war also raised tough new issues about how to treat those involved in it.

These big questions generated a steady stream of other issues. What about security? Captured terrorists had to be held so that they couldn't escape or be freed by their colleagues. The United States had to protect them so that deaths or suicides wouldn't create new martyrs, whose legacy would help recruit new terrorists. U.S. officials also wanted to minimize the chance of hostage taking, with the terrorists' colleagues trying to bargain for their release. Who would have authority to try the terrorists, and where would such trials take place? How could the United States pursue trials without undermining the intelligence value of captured al-Qaeda members? Indeed, did those involved in terrorism deserve trials? If so, how long could they be held before the trials occurred? What punishments could be meted out? Given the widespread opposition to the death penalty in many parts of the world, especially among European allies of the United States, would executing suspected terrorists be considered?

The United States decided to place captured individuals under tight guard at the American naval base at Guantanamo Bay, Cuba. The base, the nation's oldest beyond its shores and the only one in a communist country, dates from a 1903 lease to establish a coaling station for naval vessels. For the military's purposes, it was a great choice: far from the Middle East and South Asia, surrounded by water and communist Cuba, it was easy to control and difficult to penetrate. It was on American-controlled soil but outside the United States, so officials could assert that different rights and liberties applied to prisoners held there. In January 2002, the government established a bare-bones installation, "Camp X-Ray," to house the first of the captured fighters and suspected terrorists. International criticism immediately erupted. When the first prisoners were flown to Guantanamo from Afghanistan, they were blindfolded and kept in heavy restraints and earmuffs. Their beards had been shaved—an action considered by many to be a sacrilegious insult to the prisoners' Islamic faith. The pictures, which were taken by soldiers and found their way into the press, outraged human rights activists, especially in Europe. Other photographs showed prisoners kneeling shackled in front of wire cages with corrugated metal roofs, which served as temporary cells. Critics charged that the prisoners were being held unlawfully, without a right to trial and other rights customary under international law, and that they were being treated inhumanely, deprived of adequate shelter and the practice of their religion.

At first, senior American officials maintained that the Guantanamo prisoners were not prisoners of war but "unlawful combatants," armed fighters who were not covered by the Geneva Conventions. According to the Geneva Conventions, prisoners of war have certain guaranteed rights and need only give interrogators their name, rank, and serial number. Even though many foreign government officials and human rights advocates acknowledged that the prisoners were not clearly entitled to prisoner-of-war status because they didn't wear uniforms, fight for a regular army, or respect the rules of war, images in the media suggested to many critics that those guarantees were not being met. Human Rights Watch, a monitoring group, charged that the United States had implicitly acknowledged that the conditions were inadequate when officials stated that more permanent facilities would soon be constructed. Indeed, the military began construction of "Camp Delta" shortly thereafter. The facility opened in 2003 and was equipped to house more than eight hundred detainees.

As their detention stretched on, however, new problems surfaced. In the first fourteen months, at least fourteen prisoners attempted suicide. In 2006, three prisoners succeeded in what appeared to have been a suicide pact, shortly after other prisoners had faked a suicide in a failed effort to ambush their captors. Outside experts said that the prisoners faced enormous stress, in part because of their isolation (they were kept apart from each other except for two 15-minute exercise periods each day) and uncertainty (they were far from home and didn't know when—or if—their detention would end). Prisoners who cooperated, both by observing the rules and providing useful information, could win transfer to better, barracks-style quarters, where they were less isolated. That option, however, scarcely satisfied the critics. Human Rights Watch charged, "Rather than relying on international law as an essential tool in the fight against terrorism, the Bush Administration increasingly treated it as an encumbrance. An increasingly powerful faction within the Bush Administration pursued a radical vision of the United States as above international law."[17] Administration officials rejected the charge, saying that the detainees were being treated humanely, and they reminded critics that the nation had a responsibility to learn as much as possible from the prisoners to reduce the threat of future attacks.

Most difficult were the matters of how long the prisoners would be held and what kind of court would deal with them. Critics both in the United States and abroad argued that the administration could not simply hold the prisoners indefinitely without charging them with a crime or trying them. Over the first two years the number of prisoners grew, and only a handful were released. American officials decided that any trials would not be held in American courts but in military tribunals, which would have the power to impose the death penalty on those found guilty of capital offenses. The detainees included citizens not only of Middle Eastern and South Asian countries but also of European nations such as the United Kingdom, which prohibited capital punishment. The prospect of U.S. action that violated the laws and policies of other nations severely strained international relations. Tensions with other nations and with human rights groups grew when the government disclosed that the military was holding children among the Guantanamo detainees.

The constraints that foreign and domestic concern about human rights imposed on its actions led the government to keep the highest-ranking terrorist officials in high-security sites in Afghanistan or to surreptitiously ship them to foreign intelligence services with a reputation for more aggressive interrogation practices. In Afghanistan, for example, metal shipping containers behind three layers of concertina wire held top al-Qaeda and Taliban officials. Detainees who refused to cooperate could find themselves kept blindfolded and standing or kneeling for hours. Some top-level captives were subjected to "waterboarding," in which they were tied to a board and submerged almost to the point of drowning. In addition, their captors might deprive them of sleep with constant bright lights—called the "stress and duress" technique. Those who cooperated, by contrast, received creature comforts.

Interrogators used other techniques to keep captives off balance. For example, they might use disguises and decor to make detainees think they were in another country noted for brutal treatment. They might have female intelligence officers conduct the questioning, which often proved shocking to prisoners from the male-dominated Muslim culture. The CIA did not always conduct such interrogations; sometimes CIA officials relied on foreign agents under the CIA's direction. All these techniques pressed the boundaries of acceptability, and as one official who supervised the process frankly said, "If you don't violate someone's human rights some of the time, you probably aren't doing your job."[18]

Sometimes the United States relied on what it termed "operational flexibility" to transfer especially difficult and important prisoners to third-party countries, especially Jordan, Egypt, and Morocco. According to one American official involved in this process—known as "extraordinary renditions"—the United States handed over such prisoners along with a list of questions it wanted answered. The understanding was, "We don't kick the [expletive] out of them. We send them to other countries so *they* can kick the [expletive] out of them." Others involved in these activities noted that some countries had used so-called truth serums, such as sodium pentothal, in the questioning. The official American position was, "We're not aware of any torture or even physical abuse."[19]

American military police closely guarded suspected terrorists at Camp X-Ray, within the Navy's Guantanamo base in Cuba. The Bush administration struggled for years over the kind of treatment the detainees ought to be provided, as well as whether—and how—they ought to be brought to trial.

The start of the Iraqi war changed the debate fundamentally. American troops captured large numbers of prisoners. Tales of prisoner abuse, especially at Abu Ghraib prison, just west of Baghdad, began surfacing. Photographs emerged, some showing prisoners with their arms outstretched and hooked to what appeared to be electric cables, others of snarling dogs cornering terrified prisoners, and still others of naked prisoners arranged in human pyramids. Hundreds of other pictures began flowing out, all showing Iraqi prisoners being subjected to a vast array of humiliations, including simulated sex acts. In the *New Yorker*, Seymour M. Hersh's scathing account concluded, "As the photographs from Abu Ghraib make clear, these detentions have had enormous consequences: for the imprisoned civilian Iraqis, many of whom had nothing to do with the growing insurgency; for the integrity of the Army; and for the United States' reputation in the world."[20]

Guantanamo and Abu Ghraib were different prisons for different purposes, for captives from vastly different conflicts. The specter of prisoner abuse, however, spilled from one into the other. No one wanted to risk another terrorist attack by missing important information. However, the cascading tales of prisoner abuse, supported by the horrendous images, transformed the issue. Focusing solely on security was not enough. Policymakers faced a powerful surge of concern, both within the United States and around the world, for balancing protection with liberty.

THE FIERCE DEBATE

In the months after the passage of the Patriot Act, worries about the ramifications of post–September 11 policies on civil rights and civil liberties steadily grew. At first, many Americans were simply in no mood to worry about the possible mistreatment abroad of those allied with the September 11 terrorists. Domestic criticism, especially of the Patriot Act, was broad and sharp. The legislatures of Alaska and Hawaii passed resolutions condemning it. So did the councils of more than 160 local governments, including Baltimore, Denver, Detroit, Minneapolis, Oakland, San Francisco, and Seattle. Representative Don Young (R-Ala.), said, "I think the Patriot Act was not really thought out." He added, "I'm very concerned that, in our desire for security and our enthusiasm for pursuing supposed terrorists, sometimes we might be on the verge of giving up the freedoms which we're trying to protect."[21] Attorney General Ashcroft met the critics head on by going on an eighteen-city speaking tour in August 2003 to sell the act and its accomplishments. It was an unusual tactic for a senior official to employ regarding a program that had been in operation for almost two years.

Critics on both the right and the left complained that Congress had rushed to judgment and had vastly expanded executive power. They charged that, under heavy pressure to act, Congress had given too little attention to the measure's effects on civil rights and civil liberties. At the conservative Cato Institute, Robert A. Levy said that "Congress's rush job" had produced a bill that was "unconstitutionally vague" and dangerous. In fact, he charged, the bill had gutted "much of the Fourth Amendment [the protection against unreasonable searches and seizures] in far less time than Congress typically expends on routine bills that raise no constitutional concerns." The Patriot Act, Levy said, did not provide sufficient judicial oversight to prevent possible abuses. He contended that the law was too broad and that it aggressively threatened the rights of individual citizens under the guise of protecting against terrorism. He worried that the law did not provide sufficient opportunity to revisit the broad questions to see how well it was working. "Any attempt by government to chip away at constitutionally guaranteed rights must be subjected to the most painstaking scrutiny to determine whether less invasive means could accomplish the same ends. The USA PATRIOT anti-terrorism bill does not survive that demanding test. In a free society, we deserve better," he concluded.[22]

From the left came equally harsh criticism. "In its rush to pass the Patriot Act just six weeks after the September 11 attacks, Congress overlooked one of our most fundamental rights—the right to express our political beliefs, especially those that are controversial," said senior attorney Nancy Chang of the Center for Constitutional Rights, which filed suit to block the act. Chang added, "Now it is up to the judiciary to correct Congress's excesses."[23] The ACLU filed its own suit against the Patriot Act, claiming that the provision allowing broader searches of "tangible things" was unconstitutional. Even librarians found themselves in the battle. They feared that the extensive powers the act gave the government to probe "tangible things" would enable federal investigators to examine the reading habits of their patrons without their knowledge or consent. These actions, the American Library Association (ALA) warned in a 2003 resolution, could "threaten civil rights and liberties guaranteed under the United States Constitution and Bill of Rights."[24] That drew a retaliatory charge from Ashcroft, in the midst of his multicity campaign, that the ALA was fueling a "baseless hysteria."[25]

The charges and countercharges finally led the Justice Department to release a count of how many times the "tangible thing" provision had been used in the act's first two years: zero. Department officials argued that this was evidence that the critics didn't need to worry. The critics countered that if the provision hadn't been used at all, it couldn't have been important in the antiterror war. Representative John Conyers Jr. (D-Mich.) said that "if this authority was not needed to investigate September 11," he wondered if "it should stay on the books any longer."[26]

Other worries about the act led Representative C. L. Otter (R-Ida.) to champion an amendment to eliminate funding for the Justice Department's sneak-and-peek searches. Otter stunned the administration by winning House passage of the amendment by an overwhelming vote of 309 to 118. The Justice Department counterattacked by labeling it the "Terrorist Tip-Off Amendment" and said that if terrorists and their colleagues had advance warning of searches they could quickly break up their cells and reassemble their work at another location to stay a step ahead of the government.[27] Ashcroft, however, clearly took notice of the amendment, and its surprising passage helped spur his national tour.

An internal Justice Department investigation in 2003 revealed dozens of cases in which department employees had been accused of serious civil rights and civil liberties violations, and this didn't help Ashcroft's defense of the act. The Office of Inspector General found thirty-four credible reports of violations, including charges that Arab and Muslim immigrants in federal detention centers had been beaten. A federal prison doctor received a reprimand for telling an inmate during a physical exam, "If I was in charge, I would execute every one of you" because of "the crimes you all did." In another case, investigators said they were still exploring the allegation that a corrections officer had ordered a Muslim inmate to take off his shirt "so the officer could use it to shine his shoes."[28] Critics on both sides of the partisan fence pointed to the report as evidence that the government was overstepping its bounds, using the

Patriot Act as license for a broad range of activities that stretched—or broke—the bounds of civil rights and civil liberties.

Public opinion polls produced a cloudy picture of the political situation. Ashcroft trumpeted a July 2003 poll by FOX News/Opinion Dynamics in which 91 percent of respondents believed that the act had not affected their civil rights or those of a family member.[29] However, a 2003 poll on the second anniversary of the September 11 attacks showed that 34 percent of those responding were "very concerned" and another 32 percent were "somewhat concerned" that new measures to fight terrorism could restrict individual freedom.[30] The problem with the polls, as a 2004 USA Today/CNN/Gallup survey revealed, was that most citizens supported the general idea of the Patriot Act, but most respondents didn't know what was in it and some supported ideas that fell under the president's war powers. For example, most Americans supported the idea of military tribunals for suspected terrorists, as well as indefinite imprisonment of those captured in Afghanistan. In fact, however, President Bush had asserted the right to such action under his constitutional powers—the Patriot Act did not authorize them. Still, 71 percent of those surveyed disapproved of the act's provision that allowed agents to search citizens' homes and to delay telling them. Respondents were unhappy as well with the act's provisions that allowed searches of library records and detailed financial searches. Much of what citizens supported was not in the act; some of what was in the act they opposed. Citizens liked the idea of being tough on terrorism, but there was wide disagreement on what that meant.[31] A similar poll a year later revealed that 59 percent of those responding favored broad investigative authority for the FBI. But two-thirds opposed provisions that the Senate Intelligence Committee was in the process of approving, which would allow the FBI to obtain records without first getting judicial approval. When the Patriot Act expired at the end of 2005, 80 percent of Republicans favored an extension. But the number dropped to 54 percent of independents and just 43 percent of Democrats.[32]

The act worried many observers. Critics worried about how broadly the law might be applied—how many innocent nonterrorists might find their property searched without knowing about it. Some people remarked that although the act supposedly didn't allow someone's records to be searched simply because he or she had written an article criticizing the Patriot Act, they wondered if the act's language would be interpreted differently if the author was from an Arab country.[33] The lack of public scrutiny raised questions of accountability for searches. How often they were undertaken, and for what reasons, would simply be unknown.

Ashcroft countered that the Patriot Act merely allowed terrorist investigators to use techniques that federal officials had been using for years against organized crime figures. He argued that the act had proved invaluable in helping federal, state, and local officials to connect the dots. The attorney general pointed to the indictment of Sami al-Arian, charged with having financial ties to the Palestinian Islamic Jihad, a terrorist organization responsible for murdering more than one hundred people. The group's victims included Alisa Flatow, who died in a bus bombing in Gaza. Her father said, "When you know the resources of your government are committed to right the wrongs committed against your daughter, that instills you with a sense of awe. As a father you can't ask for anything more."[34]

Ashcroft's Web site regarding the act said that it had "assisted us in obtaining the indictment by enabling the full sharing of information and advice about the case among prosecutors and investigators."[35] The Justice Department pointed to the breakup of terrorist cells in Buffalo; Detroit; Portland, Oregon; and Seattle. Half of al-Qaeda's senior leaders had been captured or killed, and "more than 3,000 operatives ha[d] been incapacitated." Justice officials said that as of late 2003, 143 individuals had been convicted or had pleaded guilty. That list included shoe bomber Richard Reid, who had tried to bring down the American Airlines jet from Paris; John Walker Lindh, the "American Taliban" captured by American troops in Afghanistan; six members of the Buffalo cell, who had been convicted and decided to cooperate with investigators; two members of the Detroit cell; and Iyman Faris, who had pleaded guilty in a plot to blow up the Brooklyn Bridge. "We have expanded freedom over the past two years while protecting civil liberties and protecting people here and around the world from further terrorist attacks," the department claimed.[36]

President Bush, in fact, used the second anniversary of the terrorist attacks to ask for even greater federal powers in a new version of the Patriot Act. The 2001 law, he said, gave investigators important new ammunition in the war against terrorism, but it didn't go far enough. He asked Congress to "untie the hands of our law enforcement officials" by giving them stronger power to investigate and detain terrorism suspects. "Under current federal law, there are unreasonable obstacles to investigating and prosecuting terrorism, obstacles that don't exist when law enforcement officials are going after embezzlers and drug traffickers," he told an audience at the FBI Academy. "For the sake of the American people, Congress should change the law and give law enforcement officials the same tools . . . to fight terror that they have to fight other crime."[37] In particular, Bush asked that federal law enforcement agencies be permitted to issue "administrative subpoenas," which would allow officials to investigate individuals without obtaining advance approval from a judge or a grand jury. In addition, he proposed laws expanding the federal death penalty to more crimes and making it more difficult for suspected terrorists to be released on bail. "If we can use these subpoenas to catch crooked doctors," Bush said, "the Congress should allow law enforcement officials to use them in catching terrorists."[38]

"It's clear the administration, now on the defensive, is trying to use offense as a defensive strategy," charged the executive director of the ACLU, Anthony Romero.[39]

Representative Conyers, the senior Democrat on the House Judiciary Committee, objected to Bush's approach. "Removing judges from providing any check or balance on John Ashcroft's subpoenas does not make us safer, it only makes us less free. Of course terrorists should not be released on bail, but this administration has a shameful record of deeming law-abiding citizens as terrorists and taking away their rights," he said.[40] Many Republicans likewise were concerned about the new proposals. But with the president forcefully making the case, and with his speech coming on the anniversary of the attacks, they felt they had little choice but to remain quiet.

The tough debate on both sides was not enough to stop President Bush's campaign for reauthorization of the act in 2006, when its provisions were due to expire. Despite the strong concerns of the public and considerable debate on Capitol Hill, opponents couldn't resist President Bush's strong push for renewal and the powerful symbol of patriotism wrapped around the act. The renewal included provisions to make it easier to tap phones and obtain personal records, including bank transactions and library borrowing. Moreover, most of the original act's powers, which Congress had created temporarily in 2001, were made permanent. Time limits remained on the power of the FBI to make "roving wiretaps" of suspects who had several e-mail accounts and telephone lines and on the power of the government to obtain business records with the approval of a special court. House Judiciary Committee Chairman F. James Sensenbrenner Jr. (R-Wis.) told his colleagues that the act had been a strong tool against terrorism. But in the Senate, several Republicans blocked passage of the reauthorization until the administration agreed to additional safeguards. "There's no question that the politics of terror is something new to this country," explained one of the senators, Larry E. Craig (R-Ida.).[41]

In the end, though, President Bush got most of what he wanted: a renewal of the act, conversion of most temporary provisions into permanent powers, and expansion of the federal government's powers in several areas. On signing the bill, the president said, "The Patriot Act has served America well, yet we cannot let the fact that America has not been attacked since September the 11th lull us into the illusion that the terrorist threat has disappeared. We still face dangerous enemies. The terrorists haven't lost the will or the ability to kill innocent folks. Our military, law enforcement, homeland security and intelligence professionals are working day and night to protect us from this threat. We're safer for their efforts, and we'll continue to give them the tools to get the job done."[42]

The Patriot Act was a highly unusual piece of federal legislation. Rarely had any public policy issue united critics from both conservative and liberal ends of the political spectrum. On the right, condemnation came from those who had long worried that a strong government might hinder the exercise of individual freedom. On the left, opponents were concerned that innocent individuals would be swept up in the administration's zeal to fight terrorists. Critics from both sides quietly suggested that the administration was using the war against terrorism to promote new governmental powers that Congress had rejected in years past. No one argued for being soft on terrorists and no one wanted to risk another big attack, but many of those involved in the debate felt that some kind of line had to be drawn in the shifting sand of homeland security legislation.

The battle over the balance mushroomed during the 2011 debate over reauthorizing the Patriot Act. Civil libertarians fought hard to repeal the parts they most disagreed with. Senator Mark Udall (D-Col.) said the voters in his state "would be alarmed if they knew" what the Justice Department was doing with the data collected under the act. Intelligence analysts insisted that the act provided invaluable tools. In the end, Congress voted to extend the act, and President Obama signed it moments before it would have expired. "I think it is an important tool for us to continue dealing with an ongoing terrorist threat," he told reporters.[43]

BALANCING SECURITY AND RIGHTS

While the debate raged, there was widespread disagreement on just where to draw the line between the stronger powers the government said it needed and the protections of civil rights and civil liberties that had, for many decades, been fundamental to American democracy. Having stood atop the pile of debris that once had been the World Trade Center, inhaling the pungent smoke and surrounded by determined rescue workers, President Bush had developed an unshakable commitment to making the country as safe as possible. But civil libertarians, conservatives and liberals alike, worried that the post–September 11 changes could transform American society. The Patriot Act, they feared, could have as lasting an impact on the country as the American Revolution. This time, however, the legacy would be one of enduring restrictions on liberty, the opposite of the legacy of freedom established by the nation's founders. Both sides knew that the struggle was titanic. Rarely does a nation face such fundamental choices about its future.

As the nation grew into the new age of terrorism, the landscape often quickly shifted. New problems continued to appear, which forced the administration to rethink its strategy of protection. In 2003, just before the second anniversary of the September 11 attacks, a homesick man, Charles McKinley, managed to have himself shipped by air freight—inside a crate—from New York to Dallas. McKinley billed the $550 cost to the warehouse where he worked, put in a request for a pickup to the air freight company, and addressed the crate to his parents in Texas. Before landing in Dallas, the plane made stops in Niagara Falls, New York, and Fort Wayne, Indiana. No one noticed anything unusual until the deliveryman wheeled the crate to his parents' front door and saw a pair of eyes peering at him from outside. McKinley took a big risk, since some air freight travels in the unheated, unpressurized areas of planes, where subzero temperatures and the lack of oxygen would prove fatal. McKinley ended up in jail on unrelated traffic and bad-check charges, since federal officials couldn't find any law under which to prosecute him for his adventure—even though, according to district attorney Bill Hill, "he violated the law of stupidity if nothing else."[44]

Every new occurrence like this one raised a basic question: Was the homeland security system full of holes, requiring tighter rules and more careful government scrutiny? Or was the incident in question a rediscovery that people sometimes do stupid things without significantly endangering anyone else? The fundamental problem was how to separate genuine threats from ordinary occurrences—and to define the powers that the government ought to have in probing the clues.

Homeland security continued to generate new puzzles, which often put old questions in a new light. Consider these cases:

- *Screening grandmothers and babies.* Many of the airline security system's critics complained that security officials were needlessly delaying and scaring older travelers and small babies, who were unlikely to pose a terrorist risk. Was it really necessary to force grandmothers to take off their shoes or to x-ray babies' toys? Federal officials countered by pointing to a teddy bear seized at Orlando International Airport, in which screeners discovered a loaded .22-caliber Derringer. The Ohio family to whom the bear belonged, returning home after a Florida vacation, was stunned. On questioning, family members told investigators that someone had given the bear to one of the children two days earlier at an Orlando hotel. The person who had passed along the bear was never found, but the pistol was traced to a theft from a Barstow, California, home in 1996. During another incident, screeners picked up a man who had slid a knife down the back of a six-year-old child's shirt. Another man, age sixty-seven, had concealed a nine-inch knife inside a hollowed-out prosthetic leg. Transportation Security Administration (TSA) spokesman Robert Johnson pointedly said, "We are criticized a lot for screening grannies and babies: 'Why are they checking this? My two-year-old isn't a terrorist.' This underscores the need to screen everyone and everything." Johnson concluded, "We can't allow terrorists any opportunity."[45]

The case wasn't an isolated one. In May 2012, airport screeners at Rhode Island's T. F. Green Airport uncovered a clever plot. Their machines found a disassembled .40-caliber pistol and a loaded magazine hidden in carry-on luggage. In just a few seconds once on board, the gun could have been put back together—if it weren't that the often-maligned airport screeners found it. More surprising was where they found the parts—inside three separate stuffed animals, including a smiling Mickey Mouse, carried by a four-year-old child traveling with his dad. Officials carefully investigated the incident and concluded that neither the child nor the father was involved in a plot. Instead, they said, they suspected a domestic dispute.[46] In 2012, the TSA did loosen its screening of older Americans, allowing them to keep on their shoes and light jackets and to skip pat-downs.

- *Fake IDs converted to real driver's licenses.* Investigators from the Government Accountability Office (GAO) set out to assess the

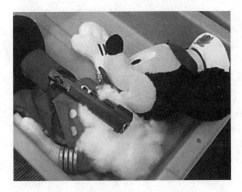

U.S. Transportation Security Administration screeners made a surprising discovery in May 2012 at the Warwick, Rhode Island, airport. While x-raying the carry-on bag of a father and his four-year-old son, they found a disassembled .40 caliber pistol and ammunition—hidden inside a stuffed teddy bear, a bunny rabbit, and a Mickey Mouse toy. Investigators discovered that the hidden gun was the result of a domestic dispute.

security of the nation's system for providing driver's licenses. The licenses, after all, are close to a national identity card, the standard identification accepted at airport security checkpoints as well as for driving cars. GAO investigators used regular desktop computers and inexpensive, off-the-shelf software to create fictitious identification documents, such as driver's licenses, birth certificates, and Social Security cards, and attempted to exchange them for real driver's licenses. At all eight motor vehicle departments where they tried—in Arizona, California, the District of Columbia, Maryland, Michigan, New York, South Carolina, and Virginia—they succeeded. If the GAO can do this, said Senator Charles Grassley (R-Iowa), "obviously terrorists can do it."[47] GAO investigators also obtained valid Social Security numbers for two fictitious infants and used counterfeit documents to enter the United States from Barbados, Canada, Jamaica, and Mexico.[48]

- *Lax security at the back door.* Airplane travelers got used to long lines and heavy screening with increased airport security. Organizations representing flight attendants, however, complained that security was lax for airport workers, some of whom turned out to be illegal aliens. At many airports, employees only had to show an ID to enter, and they received no screening. Cars and trucks rarely received inspection. Nearly a thousand construction workers at the Dallas/Fort Worth airport entered the facility daily without any screening. Although airport officials said they had established tight controls, the International Association of Flight Attendants reported that only San Francisco and Denver had met federal standards for perimeter security.[49]

- *Preferred traveler lines.* Eager to make life easier for busy frequent-fliers, the TSA created a special new "preferred traveler" program, in which fliers could register with the government and submit additional personal information. In exchange for the information and an annual fee, they got fast-track screening priority at the airport. At some airports, members of the airlines' top-level frequent-flier programs and first- and business-class passengers got special treatment through shorter security screening lines. For a fee, other travelers enrolled in the Global Entry program, which allowed them to skip long passport lines and quickly scan their passports at special readers. These programs continued to fuel the simmering debate. Should some fliers get shorter lines because they pay more for tickets or fly more than others? To what degree should airport screening impose equal costs (especially in regard to delay) on everyone?

- *Asleep at the switch*. Flight attendants readying a plane in Pittsburgh for an early morning departure were understandably surprised to discover Louis Esquivel already aboard, sitting asleep in the seventh row. Esquivel told the stunned attendants that he wanted to go to St. Louis. He had managed to get aboard the plane in the middle of the night by ducking behind a ticket counter, crawling along a baggage conveyor belt, prying open a door, getting into a van whose keys were sitting in its ashtray, driving it to the gate, and boarding the unlocked plane. Asked about the breakdown, the head of security for the TSA said, "It raised tremendous alarms for me, and obviously, I'm pretty upset about it."[50] In July 2012, a murder suspect stole a commuter jet in Utah. As he taxied the plane, he clipped the wings of another aircraft and then shot himself. Even with additional security, planes on the tarmac are not always secure.

- *Divulging personal information*. JetBlue Airways was highly embarrassed to confess that it had given personal information about more than one million of its passengers to a private company that was working under a contract with the Pentagon to try to develop a screening system to identify travelers who posed a high risk. Divulging the information had violated the company's own policies for safeguarding the privacy of its customers, and JetBlue's chief executive acknowledged that "this was a mistake on our part" and that "many of our customers feel betrayed by it."[51] The company scrambled to try to repair the damage to its reputation. Several months later, however, Northwest Airlines revealed that it, too, had violated its privacy policy by sharing data on millions of passengers with the federal government. The airlines struggled with how best to balance the search for security with the imperative for privacy.

- *Divulging telephone calling records*. In early 2006, *USA Today* reported that AT&T, Verizon, and BellSouth had secretly been turning over the long-distance telephone records for millions of Americans to the National Security Agency (NSA), apparently without a court order. A western company, Qwest, had refused the NSA's request. Such "data mining" has become increasingly important to intelligence operations. Massive high-speed computers can review vast stockpiles of records looking for patterns or clues about suspicious activity. President Bush defended the actions as an important part of the war on terror. But Representative Jan Schakowsky (D-Ill.) countered, "We've entered a time where consumers' rights and privacy are for sale, and as it turns out, the government may be the best customer."[52]

- *Ownership of the nation's ports.* Dubai Ports World, one of the globe's largest owners and managers of maritime ports, made a deal in early 2006 to purchase the port operations in six American harbors (Baltimore, Miami, Newark, New Orleans, New York, and Philadelphia). A special Treasury Department committee had reviewed the plan and approved it. But when word of the sale of American ports to the company, based in the United Arab Emirates, became public, criticism was scathing. Even some of President Bush's closest allies attacked the deal. After hearing for years that one of the nation's greatest points of vulnerability was the lack of security around its ports, many members of Congress were incredulous that an Arab company would be allowed to purchase the management companies at the ports. Representative Mark Foley (R-Fla.) said, "The potential threat to our country is not imagined, it is real."[53] In reality, most experts concluded that management of the ports by the Dubai company would not compromise homeland security. The company was one of the most experienced in the world. Most of the operations wouldn't change at all—just the ownership structure. And perhaps most important, if any problems developed and the company's financial interests were affected, it was the company itself that would stand to lose the most. But Arab ownership was a symbol in the public mind that the Bush administration could not separate from the complex operating details of the arrangement. The administration and the company both agreed to delay the sale and construct another arrangement that wouldn't produce the same political backlash.

Wherever Americans and their public officials turned, they encountered new issues they had never seen before—and old issues with strange and unfamiliar faces. The issues that became viewed as "homeland security" continued to multiply. None could be viewed in isolation. Whenever the possibility arose that some new twist of behavior could endanger public safety or the nation's security, its importance rose like a rocket, its interconnections with other homeland security issues made those issues harder to manage, and the balance of security and individual liberty became far harder to achieve. Every such issue thus fractured into many pieces, and it became more difficult than ever to put the pieces together.

Compounding the puzzle was the fact that the effort to put the pieces together—to connect the dots—inevitably implied a stronger executive branch and, especially, a stronger president. In the months after September 11, the flow of power down Pennsylvania Avenue from the

Capitol to the White House was almost palpable. President Bush reinforced that flow with his powerful rhetoric about the "global war on terror" and the war in Iraq, justified for years on the grounds that it was just one campaign in this war. Every step in that war on terror, however, also raised questions about balancing the rights of individuals with the power of the government and the power of the president with the other elements of American government.

Complex forces began resisting President Bush's assertion of executive prerogatives. The U.S. Supreme Court ruled that both the Geneva Conventions and American law applied to the prisoners being held at Guantanamo. The Court found that military tribunals set up to try detainees lacked authority to do so. Congress pushed back against the president's claim of broad powers to wiretap citizens and engage in data mining. The American Bar Association (ABA) issued a special task force report that condemned as unconstitutional the Bush administration's practice of issuing "signing statements" as the president signed legislation, which the White House had claimed gave the president the right to revise, interpret, or disregard parts of laws if necessary to protect national security.[54] "If left unchecked," said ABA President Michael Greco, "the president's practice does grave harm to the separation of powers doctrine, and the system of checks and balances that have sustained our democracy for more than two centuries."[55] Republican congressional leaders insisted that the president would have to back away from secret interrogation facilities and put suspected terrorists on trial, and in late 2006, President Bush reluctantly agreed. As criticism mounted, the balance of power among elements of the government shifted back away from the president, although the presidency unquestionably remained far stronger than it had been before September 11.

That increase in presidential power raised tough questions about civil liberties. "When dangers increase, liberties shrink. That has been our history, especially in wartime," explains analyst Stuart Taylor Jr. The nation must surely recalibrate the balance between liberty and security, Taylor argues, but in determining how best to do so, "we are also stuck in habits of mind that have not yet fully processed how dangerous our world has become or how ill-prepared our legal regime is to meet the new dangers."[56] This predicament is especially devilish because the only way to know how low to set the security bar is to take a chance— and risk the devastating consequences that can occur from miscalculation. After September 11, executive branch officials didn't want to defend themselves ever again against charges that they had failed to protect the nation. Everyone recognized that the steps they were taking endangered civil liberties, but Bush administration officials were willing to exchange that risk for an approach they hoped would lead to greater national security.

In his 2008 presidential campaign, Barack Obama pledged to close Guantanamo. Right after his inauguration, he took the first step by signing three executive orders: one banning torture, one creating an interagency review group on detention polices, and one pledging to shut down the Cuban facility within a year. The move was very popular, and both President Bush and Republican presidential candidate John McCain had also expressed hopes of closing the prison. But doing so proved enormously complicated. Raucous opposition arose to bringing any of the Guantanamo prisoners to the United States, and no one wanted to release terrorists. Starting trials proved extraordinarily difficult, because sorting out the role of military commissions versus regular criminal trials was incredibly tough. By the end of 2012, however, Guantanamo was still open and the president had signed a new law that allowed indefinite military detention without trial.[57]

How could officials know whether they had gone too far? The outcome that mattered was the absence of a terrorist attack. The absence of an attack might mean that the administration had calibrated its strategy just right—or that the terrorists had changed tactics, were planning something different, or were patiently biding their time. Restrictions on civil rights and civil liberties might prove crucial in preventing an attack—or they might prove irrelevant. It's impossible to know where best to set the balance; the appearance of safety is no guarantee that the government didn't go too far, and attack isn't necessarily a sign that the government didn't go far enough.

Fresh events continue to play out that dilemma. In September 2012, the FBI arrested an 18-year-old on charges he was planning to detonate a car bomb. For nearly a year, the suspect had been sending e-mails calling for violent jihad, FBI officials reported. An undercover FBI agent connected with the suspect and obtained from him a list of 29 possible targets, ranging from tourist attractions and malls to bars and military recruiting centers. The 18-year-old chose a downtown bar as his target and drove there with the undercover agent in a car containing what the agent told him was an explosive device. The suspect led them both in a prayer that the bomb would kill many people. He then walked to an alley nearby and pressed the detonator—which didn't work because the agent had supplied him with a nonfunctional device. He was quickly arrested.[58]

But a nationwide network of state/local intelligence-sharing offices, called "fusion centers," had produced waste and violations of civil liberties, a bipartisan Senate Homeland Security and Governmental Affairs subcommittee report charged in 2012. The investigation found that federal funds had been used to buy dozens of flat-screen televisions. One local government spent $45,000 on an SUV equipped with lights, flashers, a siren, a public address system, a computer mount, a reinforced bumper, and an external cup holder, and then turned it over to an official who used it mainly for commuting. In sum, the report concluded, the centers produced "'intelligence' of uneven quality—oftentimes shoddy, rarely timely, sometimes endangering citizens' civil liberties and Privacy Act protections, occasionally taken from already-published public sources, and more often than not unrelated to terrorism."[59]

In the years since 2011, the country has struggled to find the balance between protecting public health and safety and protecting civil liberties. There have been remarkable advances, especially in infiltrating terrorist cells and preventing attacks. There have also been disturbing questions about the cost of these advances for civil liberties—questions raised not only by critics of new homeland security politics but also by top officials in the government. On the one hand, the debate is scarcely surprising. With the September 11 attacks, we have entered into a new world with few guideposts. With other crises, including fierce storms and financial meltdowns, we have struggled to redefine just how much power government ought to exercise; how to share it among our federal, state, and local governments; and how to protect the individual freedoms we've cherished for so long. These questions go back to the founding of the nation, but twenty-first century events have brought them under a harsh spotlight. American politics has always been about setting a balance: between executive, legislative, and judicial powers; between the powers of the national, state, and local governments; and between the rights of individuals and the control of the government. In homeland security, the issues are sharper and the stakes are higher because the issue is so new, emotions are so raw, and consequences can be so enormous. And although natural disasters don't typically pose issues of national security so acutely, they often raise many of the same concerns about the balance of governmental power and the balance between individual rights (e.g., to build in flood plains) and governmental action (to help shape the incentives to which citizens respond and to keep citizens out of harm's way). Citizens want financial security as well, and expect to be protected from the decisions of financiers whose misbehavior could undermine the value of homes and savings.

To make the problems even more troublesome, citizens, quite rightly, expect their public officials to provide for their protection and safety, to deliver quick and effective response when problems occur, and to guarantee freedom and liberty in their daily lives. These have always been the great issues of American politics. Homeland security, in all its variations, has brought these problems to center stage.

Goldfish Bowls

OUR PUZZLES AT THE BEGINNING OF THE BOOK WERE THESE: Why doesn't government work as well as it should? And why, once we suffer through mega-problems and tell ourselves we'll make sure they never happen again, do big problems so often seem to recur? Despite the warning of al-Qaeda's threat to the United States that came with the 1993 World Trade Center bombing, we found ourselves vulnerable on September 11, 2001. Despite detailed exercises that demonstrated the risks to New Orleans from a major hurricane, storms twice flooded the city in 2005. And despite the "can't happen again" warnings from the 2008 financial collapse, JPMorgan Chase found its balance sheet drained of billions of dollars because a rogue trader made bad bets no one really understood. It's not surprising that policy lightning occurs. That's an inevitable consequence of "unknown unknowns." But once the unknowns are known, we nevertheless often fall into the same problems again and again.

For fans of the old legend that goldfish have a memory of just three seconds, it might all make sense. As the story goes, goldfish constantly repeat the same patterns in their lives, while remembering none of it. That might be a blessing when swimming in circles in a small bowl where the view never changes. Maybe this is like American public policy, where big problems frequently happen and we vow to make sure they don't recur, but we don't remember them long enough to follow through.

However, it turns out that the legend isn't true. Goldfish are actually much smarter, as a 15-year-old student from Australia discovered. He put a red Lego in a goldfish tank and each day fed the fish right next to it. "At first they were a bit scared of it, a bit wary," he explained, "but by the end of the three weeks, they were actually almost coming before I put the food in." He then removed the red Lego and replaced it a week later. "They remembered perfectly well," he found, and they actually arrived even faster for their food.[1] Goldfish, he discovered, could learn through conditioning. Constant repetition reinforced new instincts. Scientists who have long studied fish were not surprised. And on the Discovery Channel's *MythBusters* show, investigators trained goldfish to navigate an underwater maze, finding their way from starting line to tasty food. With repetition, they learned to negotiate their path faster, but not surprisingly there was a limit to their performance.[2] How long is their memory? Much longer than three seconds, but their memory depends on having the right incentives, and there's a limit to how long they can remember anything.

In public institutions, as in goldfish bowls, memories and incentives become seared into memory. The horrifying images of September 11 and Katrina will be remembered just as the film of the December 1941 attack on Pearl Harbor continues to reverberate through history. The Great Recession that began in 2008 resonates with the Great Depression. But too often, when the immediate memory fades, so does the impetus for reform. In each of these cases, government confronted problems whose consequences demanded immediate action, where action demanded new governmental strategies, where the strategies irresistibly increased governmental power, and where a stronger government posed huge new challenges for constitutional democracy in the United States. Yet, too often, government struggled to rise to these challenges.

TOO BIG TO FAIL

Consider the 2008 economic meltdown, which raised very tough questions about the nation's—and the world's—financial markets. The crisis threatened huge institutions at the very foundation of the American economy. Are there some banks that are simply too big and too important to be allowed to fail? Are there institutions so central that their collapse would create a tsunami so large that they'd gravely injure other parts of the economy? And, if so, what should the government do about this?

In the middle of the crisis, policymakers, especially in the Fed (the Federal Reserve) and the Treasury, constantly faced these tough decisions. They saved one large investment bank, Bear Stearns in March 2008, but six months later they allowed the venerable Lehman Brothers to go broke. In part, this was because the Fed *could* save Bear Stearns, even though its financial support allowed JPMorgan Chase to acquire the company at a very deep discount. By the time Lehman began to crumble, the economy was in deep distress and Fed officials concluded that there was little they could do to save the firm—and that, even if they did make a stopgap loan, they might never be repaid. While Bear

Stearns survived (though not under that name, with JPMorgan Chase swallowing it up), Lehman failed.

Banks began failing because borrowers couldn't repay the real estate loans they had taken out and because the underlying capital of many institutions evaporated as arcane instruments like credit default swaps, subprime mortgages, collateralized debt obligations, and other financial tools quickly lost their value. The list of failed banks grew and grew, to more than 460 banks from the beginning of 2008 through mid-2012.[3] Most depositors didn't lose any money—the federal government's Federal Deposit Insurance Corporation (FDIC) insured deposits up to $250,000 per account owner in each bank, and in 2011 and 2012 the FDIC guaranteed all deposits, regardless of amount, to reassure customers.

Most of these failed banks, however, were relatively small community banks. In the case of some of the larger banks, the federal government stepped in. In January 2009, for example, the FDIC, Fed, and Treasury joined in a late-night rescue of Bank of America with a $138 billion rescue plan. This generated an intense policy debate. Were some banks,

in fact, so big that their failure was unthinkable? Or did a true free-market economy mean that banks and their investors needed to let competition sort out the winners and losers? The core question was this: Where should the government use its tremendous might? Which problems were public problems—and which public problems demanded governmental intervention? Saving all banks would ruin the free market. Saving just the small banks would risk having the collapse of big banks capsize the economy. Saving the larger banks would mean that large concentrations of wealth and power were rewarded while small community banks had to fend for themselves. Nobel laureate Paul Krugman made the case against allowing the big banks to collapse: "Breaking up big financial institutions wouldn't prevent future crises, nor would it eliminate the need for bailouts when those crises happen. The next bailout wouldn't be concentrated on a few big companies—but it would be a bailout all the same. I don't have any love for financial giants, but I just don't believe that breaking them up solves the key problem." The solution, he argued, lay in tougher bank regulation.[4]

Former Fed chairman Alan Greenspan took exactly the opposite view. "If they're too big to fail, they're too big," he said. Once, Greenspan argued, no bank had been too big to fail. But then the feds stepped in to bail out Fannie Mae, Freddie Mac, Bear Stearns, and AIG. That, in turn, created a series of problems. The big federal regulators lost their credibility, "because when push came to shove, they didn't stand up." Greenspan felt that creating a too-big-to-fail mentality could create "a moribund group of obsolescent institutions which will be a big drain on the savings of the society." He concluded, "Failure is an integral part, a necessary part of a market system," and that without a real market test the economy as a whole could be weakened.[5] Even Sanford I. Weill, the former head of Citibank and widely recognized for having created the mega–financial institution that became too big to fail, changed his mind in mid-2012: "What we should probably do is go and split up investment banking from banking, have banks be deposit takers, have banks make commercial loans and real estate loans, have banks do something that's not going to risk the taxpayer dollars, that's not too big to fail."[6]

The *Wall Street Journal* reported that in 2010 and 2011, Bank of America had considered breaking up its operations into smaller pieces but had rejected the idea because it might expose the company to legal and financial problems and could weaken its brand. In 2012, however, famous bank executive Edward Crutchfield, who had made so many deals in the 1990s while leading First Union Corporation that he became known as "Fast Eddie," concluded that putting "gargantuan, completely unrelated businesses under one roof is probably not a good idea."[7]

This framed a debate of fundamental philosophical importance—just what should be government's relationship with the private sector?—and a puzzle of profound practicality—how could the government shore up a badly wounded economy? In the middle of the meltdown, the second question trumped the first. The Fed and the Treasury, with the help of the FDIC, engaged in frantic midnight meetings and ad hoc deals to prevent the financial system from collapsing. Indeed, the system was much closer to the edge than many Americans realized. Although what happened was bad enough, the very worst did not occur, and citizens could readily be forgiven for breathing a huge sigh of relief and trying to cobble the pieces of their lives and jobs back together. But three years after the banking crisis began, the regulations to bring major financial reforms to life had still not been put into effect. Although the refrain in the midst of the crisis was, "Make sure this doesn't happen again," precious little changed in its aftermath. Many parts of the American political system seemed to have the memory of goldfish: longer than three seconds, for sure, but persistent only when new stimuli reinforced old memories, and hyper-vulnerable to new stresses that pushed away old ones.

LEARNING FROM STRESS TESTS

For physicians who administer stress tests, of course, such tales are nothing new. When a patient struggles with the test, physicians have stock suggestions: Eat better. Lose weight. Exercise more. Get more sleep. Cut down on alcohol consumption and stop smoking. The response, of course, is standard as well: "Of course, Doctor. I've learned my lesson. This test changes everything. I'll do things differently in the future."

Of course, the odds of successful weight loss are small; the odds of keeping weight off are smaller yet. Barely used exercise machines clutter the eBay Web site, and in some families the gift of a dust rag follows the gift of a treadmill the year before. The parade of new diet books on and off the best seller list is testimony to how hard it is to truly change anything. A fundamental concern of most cardiologists is that patients, even when thoroughly shaken by their stress test results, often fail to follow sound advice.

As more people are crowded into smaller spaces and as the global economy becomes ever more interconnected, the impact of such events grows exponentially. Many of the skills needed to cope with such events, moreover, are much the same as those that government needs in order to manage many of its programs, from welfare reform to health care for the elderly, and from mass transit to environmental protection. We need a government that is linked and limber, capable of joining related organizations and programs together effectively and of learning quickly from experience. These are the lessons of September 11 and Katrina and the economic crisis. It is critical to heed what they teach us, not only for policy lightning cases but for the rest of public policy as well.

How well does government learn? And why, when such a powerful consensus emerges to prevent bad things from happening again and to rebuild bigger and better, are the results so often disappointing? The answers depend critically on how we take advantage of opportunities created when crises open policy windows.

Crises that Open Policy Windows

In his classic *Agendas, Alternatives, and Public Policies*, political scientist John Kingdon theorizes that from time to time "policy windows" open and allow new issues to move onto the nation's agenda. For policy change to occur, Kingdon argues, an issue has to ripen, wait for a policy window to open, and then leap through. "Policy windows open infrequently, and do not stay open long," he explains.[8] The September 11 terrorist attacks did more than pop open a window—they blew down a wall, and through the resulting hole came a raging stream of policy proposals. The same was true for Katrina. In many ways, the 2008 economic meltdown blew down the whole house, since the Fed and the Treasury took unprecedented steps and the financial system will never again be the same.

After September 11, once the window was open, a truly remarkable collection of issues tried to squeeze through under the guise of "homeland security." The Bush administration used the attacks to make its case for war in Iraq. The Patriot Act contained many provisions investigators had wanted for years. Sales at some major retailers slipped, and large corporations invested in new private security systems. Local governments posted guards at power plants and bridges; state governments conducted new bioterrorism drills. Private companies rushed a wide variety of new products to store shelves, and old products like duct tape and plastic sheets unexpectedly found new markets. New consultants provided security advice to corporations and building owners, from how best to screen visitors to how to secure their products against terrorism. A new army of security guards appeared at the front desks of government office buildings and many private companies around the country. Local governments used federal homeland security aid for a vast array of items, including new air-conditioned garbage trucks (justified on the grounds that the air conditioning would help the city cope with a bio-attack). For political players who could fashion their cases into some form of "homeland security," the September 11 attacks provided an unparalleled opportunity to obtain action.

The nature of the homeland security problem multiplied opportunities for action. Terrorism can emerge unexpectedly from any of a considerable number of sources, with a stunning array of consequences. The

huge impact of the terrorist attacks created a demand for strong leadership. But the breadth and ambiguity of the problem made it impossible
to decide *which* action was *most* needed. The airlines quickly won their
bid for financial support. Aid to state and local governments came much
more slowly. The Bush administration implicitly linked September 11
with Saddam Hussein but later backed away from the connection when
evidence failed to materialize. But all these issues—and many more—
tried to crawl through the policy window that Kingdon describes.

So, too, did a vast array of issues following Katrina. Local officials everywhere pleaded for more emergency management support. Manufacturers
of special communications equipment peddled their wares to government
officials. Casino operators in Mississippi capitalized on post–Katrina aid to
reset their businesses, and insurance companies used the storm to press
their case for fundamental changes in insurance underwriting.

The 2008 financial crisis transformed the economic community. This
was not a case where strong interests were standing ready and waiting
for a chance to rush long-planned changes through, but it did radically
change the roles of many players. The Fed had been growing in power

Although much of the Gulf Coast struggled to recover from the ravages of Hurricane
Katrina, the gambling industry quickly got back on its feet. This Isle of Capri casino
in Biloxi, Mississippi, was closed for four months to repair storm damage, but a
Florida tourist was soon happily playing a video slot machine.

as Congress and the president increasingly proved unable to pass budgets. Its role in shaping the money supply became ever more important
as fiscal policy—decisions about how much to spend and tax—became
gridlocked. As major investment banks began to crumble, commercial
banks teetered on the verge of failing, and lending around the world
began to seize up, no player in American government could move far
enough and fast enough to stem the tide. But the Fed didn't fly solo. After
fighting for most of its life for independence from the Treasury, which
Fed officials always worried would create pressure to politicize monetary policy to serve the short-term interests of presidents in fostering low
interest rates and high employment, Fed and Treasury officials worked
quietly but closely in unprecedented coordination of their efforts. Some
critics grumbled about the sudden expansion of the Fed's power, but
no one had a better idea. When the giant insurance company American
International Group faltered in September 2008, the Fed and the Treasury
quickly stepped in to bail out the company in a $182 billion deal. In an
instant, the federal government owned the stock of one of the world's
largest insurance companies. The Fed's balance sheet, with the bailout of
AIG and the incentives to help JPMorgan Chase purchase investment bank
Bear Stearns, doubled to more than $2 *trillion*, all without prior authori-
zation from Congress. AIG eventually repaid the money it borrowed, plus
an additional $22 billion, although the company received tax breaks that
significantly offset the profit. However, these giant financial transactions,
all without congressional oversight, were unprecedented. Not only did the
Fed and the Treasury act aggressively to stem the financial hemorrhage,
but they vastly increased their power in the process.

Policy windows like those opened by the September 11 attacks,
Katrina, and the financial meltdown open rarely. In part this is because
few shocks are likely to be so large, and in part this is due to the nature
of the events themselves. As analyst Robert Kupperman told Congress
twelve years to the day before the September 11 attacks, "The problem
with terrorism is its episodic nature. During the periods of relative calm,
large governments, including our own, view terrorism as a minor annoy-
ance, especially when compared with grander visions of geopolitics,
and it is often difficult to get the policy levels of government focused
on the problem at all. But when an incident occurs, particularly one
dominated by media coverage, terrorism takes on virtual strategic signif-
icance. When terrorists strike, governments go on hold, paralyzed by an
unfolding human drama which is televised for all to see."[9] The same was
certainly true for Katrina and financial regulation as well. New problems
intrude, old ones reemerge, and the political system has to respond to
massive stress.

For students of public policy, a central question is whether big stresses push the system deeper into incremental change or spark something greater and more profound. In the early 1970s, paleontologist Stephen Jay Gould examined just this question in trying to explain the evolution of life. Scientists had long argued, in the tradition of Charles Darwin, that environmental forces pressed plants and animals to adapt to new circumstances. Those that adapted most successfully were those that endured; those that did not slipped away. Evolution was thus a relatively steady course.

Together with his colleague Niles Eldredge, Gould stunned the world of biology by arguing that evolution often took a very different, unanticipated course. Darwinian theory predicted that scientists would find a series of fossils that charted the incremental steps taken by organisms as they evolved. However, when researchers looked for those in-between fossils, they often couldn't find them. Were they looking in the wrong places? Not looking carefully enough? Or could it be, as Gould and Eldredge concluded, that the in-between creatures did not exist? The pair became convinced, in fact, that life changes not so much through *evolution* as through *revolution*—not so much through gradual adaptation as via the effects of catastrophic events, such as meteor strikes. Big forces, they argued, periodically produce big transformations.[10]

If we want to understand the truly important forces shaping life, Gould maintained, we have to understand that life exists in a relatively steady equilibrium most of the time, punctuated occasionally but importantly by radical change: "Punctuational change writes nature's primary signature."[11] From this came his theory of "punctuated equilibrium," which shook paleontology to its core. For Gould, the long tableaus of incremental change are not nearly as interesting or pivotal as the short but hugely important bursts of fundamental change that, in turn, dramatically reshape the evolution of life.

Political scientists Frank R. Baumgartner and Bryan D. Jones have suggested that similar patterns exist for public policy problems. They contend that the political system is relatively stable most of the time, with change occurring incrementally. However, forces tend to build and then to erupt explosively in large, fundamental change when big events roil the political system. "Important political questions are often ignored for years," but sometimes everyone focuses on the same issues in the same way. As attention surges, so does the pressure for policy change. As a result, "external shocks" periodically shift public debate and public policy.[12] "Punctuated equilibrium, rather than stability and immobilism, characterizes the American political system."[13]

The Baumgartner and Jones argument proved just as contentious in political science as Gould's did in paleontology. Just as Gould attacked the dominant idea of his field, Baumgartner and Jones set out to revise the theory of "incrementalism," a time-honored and timeworn orthodoxy of American politics. The theory's foundation lay in work by political scientist Charles E. Lindblom and his famous 1959 article, "The Science of 'Muddling Through.'" The article contended that "incrementalism"— policy change through small steps—described not only the way most things happened most of the time, but also the way they *should* happen. Incrementalism, he argued, provides a self-adjusting process of correcting little mistakes before they become big ones.[14] Political scientist Aaron Wildavsky echoed Lindblom's ideas with his study of the federal budget process. He concluded that policymakers set most agencies' budgets most of the time by making small, "fair-share" incremental adjustments to each agency's existing base. Like Lindblom, he concluded that this provided not only a good description of most budgetary decisions but also a good normative prescription for how things should operate.[15] Together, Wildavsky's and Lindblom's work established the dominant approach to public policy: incrementalism as both description and prescription.

Incrementalism left several important questions unanswered. It did not clearly define how large a change could qualify as "incremental" or how long the system might wait for a "punctuation." In the short term, most changes can appear incremental; over the long run, new equilibriums emerge.

The central issue is how large a change the system can accommodate and how quickly it can move. Does the complexity of political forces break the impetus for change? Can major shocks, such as the September 11 attacks and Hurricane Katrina and the financial crisis, push the system toward deep and fundamental changes? Should we expect to see, as Lindblom suggests, a string of fossils indicating a gradual evolution of the U.S. political system? Or, as Gould suggests, will we discover occasional large breaks in the chain of fossils that signal big shocks that produced big changes?

Results of the Stress Test

When cardiologists assess a patient's stress tests, they carefully examine the tracings produced by the heart monitors, which show how the heart reacted to the stress. They check the heart's rhythms, how much the test's stress accelerated the heart rate, whether the stress produced potentially dangerous reactions, and how well the heart settled back to a normal rhythm when the treadmill slowed down.

What would we see if we had similar tracings to record the performance of the U.S. government in the aftermath of the huge September 11 stress test? Despite the advances in public opinion polling, scientists have not yet figured out a way to hook electrodes up to the body politic and to the nation's political institutions. But we can imagine what the stress test might look like in different models of the U.S. political system, and it shows the nonincremental impact of big system shocks.

Figure 7.1 illustrates the incremental model. It traces the system moving along its normal path—and then being shocked by enormous stress. The stress rocks the system, but all the powerful cross-pressures that make incrementalism such an influential force soon pull the system back to normal. Changes occur—from shifts in airline screening to new cooperation between the FBI and CIA—but the fundamental forces shaping policy in the system ultimately drift back, more or less, to where they previously were.

But is a shock as great as the terrorist attacks likely to leave the system relatively stable? The punctuated equilibrium model argues that this is precisely when big changes in government occur—and it would be hard to imagine a bigger punctuation. The stress shakes up the system. Public officials react by creating a new cabinet department, dramatically shifting priorities, and living the "everything has changed" mantra. As the system recovers from the shock, it moves into a new and very different equilibrium. Figure 7.2 charts what a punctuated equilibrium model for the stress test would look like.

Which model better captures the results of the stress tests to which the system has been subjected? A careful look at the evidence presented in this book suggests that neither model is a good fit. On the one hand, the events and aftermath of September 11 were distinctly nonincremental. The federal government engaged in the largest restructuring since the creation of the Department of Defense in 1947. Indeed, because all the existing agencies maintained their previous missions and took on a new homeland security mission as well, the restructuring might well have been not only the largest but also the most difficult in U.S. history. New security arrangements

Figure 7.1 Incrementalism

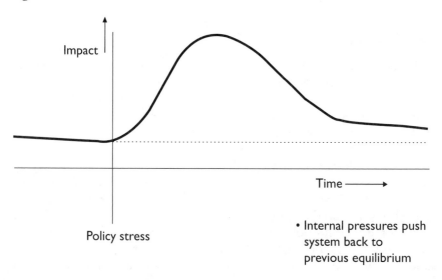

completely transformed the airline industry. Airline passengers encountered new, unprecedented, and permanent levels of screening, both visible and behind the scenes. With each new threat, such as the August 2006 terrorist plot to blow up planes using carry-on liquid explosives, that screening increased. The FBI radically shifted the mission of most of its agents from investigating crimes and arresting criminals after the fact to probing and disrupting possible terrorists before the fact. Enough major changes had irrevocably altered the nation. Never again could it settle back to the policies and practices it had known on September 10, 2001.

On the other hand, equally powerful forces put a brake on some of the changes. Sustaining many of the new policies and practices instituted after the attacks proved difficult. When long lines drove fliers away and increased the edginess of those preparing to fly, airlines soon pressured federal officials for changes in the passenger screening system. In the intelligence arena, the one area where everyone agreed there was a need to connect the dots, the FBI, CIA, and NSA successfully fought to retain their autonomy, even though improved coordination and cooperation was the mandate. Proposals to concentrate all intelligence gathering into a single agency died a quick death. The Department of Homeland Security, designed to be the federal government's center of operations, found itself a weak player in intelligence debates. For its part, Congress reinforced the fragmentation of the nation's homeland security system by failing to make any major change in its own organization and functioning, which guaranteed that much of the fragmentation in executive branch powers and politics would endure.

Therefore, although the terrorist attacks provided a major shock to the system and unquestionably produced permanent changes, there

Figure 7.2 Punctuated Equilibrium

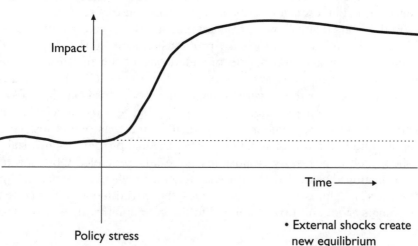

were equally compelling forces that undermined proposals for other important changes. As a result, the U.S. government ended up substantially different from what it had been on September 10, but the new version was not nearly what the post–September 11 days had suggested it would—and should—be.

As so many experts concluded, terrorism on U.S. soil had deep and profound effects. But was it an event that would forever and fundamentally change politics in the United States? Or did it represent a momentary blip in a long-term, relatively stable policy system in which age-old forces resist change? In the immediate aftermath of the attacks, the consensus was that "everything has changed." Had it? How much? And how would we know? When will we know, if ever?

Answering these questions is difficult, but we can pose two scenarios to help us approach some answers. First, on September 10, 2001, what would we have predicted that the policy world would look like in the not-too-distant-future? In the years that followed, big changes emerged that we could not have predicted before the attacks occurred. Security at airports increased dramatically. Foreign policy shifted to a far stronger focus on terrorism. The risks of bioterrorism loomed much larger. Security around public buildings and facilities, from the White House and sports arenas to theme parks and nuclear power plants, increased greatly. These changes were large and seemingly permanent. They had gone far beyond what one would have expected before the terrorist attacks.

Second, on September 12, 2001, in the immediate aftermath of the attacks, what would we have predicted the policy world would look like in the next few years? In the hours, days, and weeks that followed the attacks, grim determination emerged from the nation's shock and grief. Everyone agreed that everything *had* changed, and that the cracks in the system that permitted the attacks to occur *would* be filled. Just what would be done was unclear, but it was impossible to escape the sense of resolve.

In the years that followed, results exceeded what we once may have expected but fell short of the early promises. In early 2003, the TOPOFF exercise in Chicago and Seattle provided one of the first tests of the nation's emergency response system for terrorist attacks. The conclusion, according to the government's own report, was that the nation wasn't much better prepared to deal with a big terrorist attack than it had been before September 11. "Fortunately, this was only a test," the report stated. "If a real incident occurs before final procedures are established, such unnecessary confusion will be unacceptable." Obstacles to coordinating the local response with federal intelligence remained. In the exercise, almost no one could track the government's color-coded warning system and how it applied to the communities. The result, the report found, was widespread disagreement and confusion about who was supposed to do what. One government observer commented, "The criticisms are among the worst I've ever heard."[16]

Thus, several years after September 11, the homeland security system continued to show dangerous vulnerabilities and problems in coordination. Despite the overwhelming consensus for action and the pressure for change, the system had proved surprisingly resistant to the fundamental restructuring that had seemed inevitable in the aftermath of the attacks. When Katrina hit, the nation discovered that many of the TOPOFF lessons, as well as the findings from FEMA's 2004 drill on the impact of a major hurricane in New Orleans, had gone unheeded.

To understand why the political system drifted to this new level— more vigilant than in the past, less transformed than might have been expected—requires charting the forces that produced this in-between response. What shaped the new equilibrium?

Homeland security, like all other important issues, doesn't exist in a vacuum. The war on terror has to fight for policy space, within government agencies and among the public at large, with hurricanes like Katrina. Both must tug against other issues, like war and health care, fires and murders, and education and roads. The system has built-in brakes that make it hard to sustain high-level attention on any one issue, no matter how important, for very long. Some of this is human nature; some is the inevitable flood of other policy problems that demand attention. There is a natural tendency toward backsliding—toward resuming the previous equilibrium. When big stresses jar the system, it is never likely to retreat back completely to where it was, but neither can it maintain a laserlike focus on a single issue.

As a result, the system's stress test results are much more apt to look like Figure 7.3. Faced with a major shock, the system reacts quickly and forcefully, but then it tends to settle back to a new equilibrium—at a significantly different level from before (and thus unlike the incremental model) but not at the level that the punctuated equilibrium model would suggest. It is more a case of *punctuated backsliding*, with a large initial jolt, a big change in policy, and a subsequent slip back toward the previous equilibrium. The result is an enduring pressure toward stasis in the system. That's just what happened, in fact, in the aftermath of the financial crisis.

Pressures for Backsliding

What caused this backsliding? The stress test can help us identify the forces that pulled the system back from the "everything has changed" level. The pressures for backsliding came from four sources, which

Figure 7.3 Punctuated Backsliding

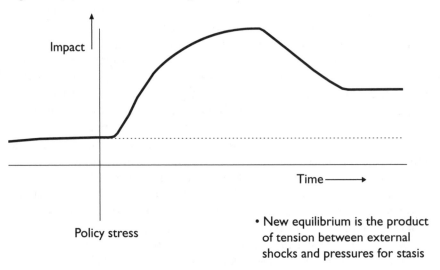

we have explored in earlier chapters: the bureaucracy's reaction to the many post–September 11 changes, the complexities of coordinating the nation's vast system of federalism, the recurring tendencies that bubbled up out of Congress, and the nature of the risk that terrorism presents (see Box 7.1).

The *bureaucracy* demonstrated its enduring instinct for autonomy. Although everyone recognized the need to coordinate more extensively, most agencies resisted the idea of doing so on another agency's terms. Coordination often becomes a matter of turf—where the lines are drawn and who gets to call the shots. Strengthening coordination can mean shifting the bureaucratic balance of power, and this is something agencies quite understandably resist. The job is even harder when the agencies trying to coordinate have different organizational cultures. The *what* of coordination is one thing; the *how* is quite another. Different agencies that approach problems from fundamentally different cultures can clash. For most agencies, including most of those within the Department of Homeland Security, homeland security was not their only mission, as Katrina made painfully clear. Leaders became distracted by competing goals. The more time that passed after September 11, the more the older missions reasserted themselves and presented problems of balance to top officials. All these forces combined to produce powerful pressures for backsliding.

The nation's system of *federalism* also challenges the mission of homeland security. Federal officials, of course, spend most of their time

---

Box 7.1   Forces for Backsliding

Bureaucracy

- Instinct for autonomy
- Different organizational cultures
- Multiple, conflicting missions

Federalism

- Inattention by federal officials to state and local problems
- Difficulties in state-local coordination
- Difficulties in coordination among local governments

Congress

- Multiple, overlapping committee jurisdictions
- Instinct to use homeland security funds for pork

Nature of the policy problem

- Few rewards for preventing crises
- Recurring argument that money and energy are more urgently needed elsewhere
- Tendency for complacency to build over time

---

on federal issues. They certainly understand that the intergovernmental aspects of homeland security are critical, but these often are not their most pressing concerns. It's little wonder, therefore, that state and local officials so often complain that federal officials have little understanding of the problems, both financial and policy, that they face. A Democratic Party task force on homeland security that surveyed 304 local government officials in late 2003 determined that 56 percent of those surveyed considered coordination with federal officials inadequate. Fifty-three percent believed the Department of Homeland Security didn't understand the vulnerabilities local governments faced, 87 percent believed federal funding was inadequate, and 69 percent believed the federal government wasn't doing everything it could to help.[17] (Although the Democrats had been most interested in embarrassing the Bush administration, these findings matched the observations of many experts.) The recurring complaint that the federal government doesn't understand the needs of state and local governments is an old and enduring tension in the intergovernmental system. So, too, is the difficulty state governments have in securing better coordination among local governments and between state homeland security offices and local officials. The September 11 attacks sharpened these old strains and brought them painfully to the surface. We love our system of federalism for the many points of political access it provides. But it can be ungainly and fragmented, both politically and administratively. This adds to the pressures for backsliding.

Congress also complicated coordination. Although Americans view the president as responsible for the bureaucracy's performance, with a role much like a private executive's responsibility for a company, the reality is that the bureaucracy is fundamentally the creature of Congress, not the president. Congress passes the laws, creates the programs, establishes the agencies, and appropriates the money. In the balance-of-power system, the president has a powerful role, but Congress exerts a stronger pull on most federal agencies than the president does. After September 11, even as members of Congress called on these agencies to connect the dots, Congress's own attention to homeland security remained remarkably fragmented. Congressional scholar Norman J. Ornstein counted thirteen House and Senate committees and more than sixty subcommittees with at least some jurisdiction over homeland security—eighty-eight committees and subcommittees in all.[18] Each carefully guarded its own jurisdictions. A new select committee on homeland security wasn't powerful enough to shake the deep congressional tradition of committees' tending their own jurisdictions. And for most members of Congress, the new funding for homeland security was more of an opportunity to bring cash back to their districts than to focus money on the areas of highest risk. The programs became a meaty source of pork. Congress's procedures and operations contained built-in backsliding pressures, and it was impossible for federal agencies to coordinate their efforts if the congressional committees overseeing them did not.

The *nature of the policy issues* adds a final backsliding pressure. There surely are strong incentives in the political system to punish anyone who might open the door to attack. The system reacts strongly to big stories that gain wide publicity—from the shoe bomber to the person who shipped himself as airborne freight—but it provides few rewards for *preventing* attacks. It's impossible to know for sure what attacks the system has prevented and what their consequences might have been. Therefore, it's hard to applaud successes, and success in preventing attacks always gets less publicity than dramatic cases of failure. Moreover, it is certain that resources invested in homeland security could have been invested instead in other policies, such as prescription drug benefits for senior citizens or more aid for college students. Thus, in the absence of attacks, it's easy to argue that other programs need the money more. Homeland security has a built-in imbalance of incentives that makes it hard to sustain a high level of attention over time, and these forces further reinforce the tendency toward backsliding. Success, or at least the absence of attack, can breed complacency, and complacency can make it easier for other issues to push into the policy arena and nudge homeland security aside.

In the years since the September 11 attacks, Katrina, and the 2008 economic meltdown, the system clearly has learned. In late 2003, American troops tracked down Saddam Hussein, the Iraqi dictator who had masterminded the use of biochemical weapons on thousands. He was literally unearthed by American troops from a small "spider hole" along with little more than the clothes on his back. As images of the bedraggled and almost zombielike former dictator were broadcast around the world, proponents of a no-holds-barred, no-tolerance policy on terrorism proclaimed victory. Here was proof that proper coordination among various intelligence agencies, adequate funding for sophisticated technology and highly trained manpower, and ever-present vigilance paid out tremendously high dividends. Then, in late 2011, a team of Navy Seals took out the mastermind behind the September 11 attacks, Osama bin Laden, and aerial drones targeted a large number of al-Qaeda leaders. As President Obama told the nation in announcing the death of bin Laden, "we can say to those families who have lost loved ones to al Qaeda's terror: Justice has been done."[19]

Through luck and skill, the cases showed big advances after September 11, but analysts always worried that no matter how fast the system learned, problems would develop faster. When an al-Qaeda bomber failed to ignite a bomb inside his shoes, another tried an underwear bomb. When protection increased for passenger aviation, terrorists tried to hide devices inside air freight shipments. And as hard as dealing with terrorist threats might be, weather is even more unpredictable. Hurricanes go where nature guides them, and threats from nature extend far beyond hurricanes. When financial stress tests provided good report cards on many banks, financial uncertainty continued to percolate through the system. When the New York financial community seemed to settle, problems spread to London. In the European Union, crises bounced from Greece to Spain to Ireland to Italy. Stress tests helped diagnose the problems but struggled to keep up in devising solutions. With every victory came the same puzzle about whether success would breed complacency and complacency would lead to more backsliding.

CHALLENGES TO THE POLICY SYSTEM

In exploring the political origins of U.S. social policy, political scientist Theda Skocpol observed, "As politics creates policies, policies also remake politics."[20] This is a tale that ripples throughout American history, but it proved explosively true in the 2000s. The triple shock of the September 11 terrorist attacks, Katrina's 2005 assault on the Gulf Coast, and the 2008 financial collapse combined to pose enormous challenges to the policy system.

1. *What should be the balance of public and private power?* In the aftermath of the financial crisis, some observers suggested that the government should simply nationalize large economic institutions, since the government had in effect become the owner of banks, insurance companies, and even auto companies. Within a few years, most of the companies that had received large infusions of government cash were able to dig themselves out and reprivatize themselves, but the balance between public and private power had unquestionably shifted more toward the government. Despite the recovery, some analysts continued to push the point. Economist Gar Aplerovitz, for example, argued that "very large corporations could easily undermine regulatory and antitrust strategies." Wherever there can't be real market competition, he concluded, the government should assume control. He pointed out that the government had nationalized General Motors in 2009 and that in 2012 it still held a controlling share of its stock. Although "it would probably take another financial meltdown to make banking nationalization politically tenable," he admitted, he considered it a strategy we ought to pursue. "Given how the sector has behaved since the last crisis, a repetition seems inevitable, and sooner rather than later." Better to nationalize now than in the midst of another major meltdown, he felt.[21]

Following the September 11 attacks, Americans accepted, perhaps grudgingly, government's growing role in their lives. They took off their shoes when going through airport screening and accepted see-through scanners to detect hidden bombs. They put up with new identification procedures when they opened bank accounts and more intrusions into their privacy from hidden (and sometimes not-so-hidden) surveillance cameras. On many campuses, it's impossible to drive or walk without being captured on video, and in even the smallest government facilities there are more guards and security checkpoints than there used to be. The federal government came to own majority stakes in insurance companies, banks, and car companies, at least until the crisis wound down. So one possible argument is this: a larger, more powerful government is the inevitable result of a world with larger threats with bigger consequences.

2. *What should be the balance of power within the governmental system?* In guarded conversations at the highest levels of government,

senior officials debated what to do if there was another Katrina-like breakdown of government. Some federal officials concluded that their biggest mistake was counting on state and local officials to respond. After local governments teetered on the brink of collapse and federal officials waited for state and local officials to right their operations, progress was slow and the feds had to step in when the crescendo of criticism proved deafening. In the end, the federal government shouldered much of the public blame. In fact, the point at which the "negatives" exceeded the "positives" in public opinion polling on the performance of President Bush—and never recovered—came in the aftermath of the storm. The lesson, many of these federal officials concluded, was that they should never again allow themselves or citizens to be the captives of slow-moving local officials. In cases of emergency, federal officials would ride fast and hit hard. Not everyone agreed with this answer, but it was impossible to escape the fundamental questions. So another possible argument is this: big disasters tend to centralize power within the American intergovernmental system, with the balance shifting away from state and local officials and toward the federal agencies that have the resources to step in with needed help.

3. Do big crises forever reset these balances? In each of these crises, the government stepped in aggressively. Having jumped that gap during the crisis, is it even easier to do so again? Once the government, especially the federal government, aggressively steps in, is it possible to go back? Or do such crises make it inevitable that federal power will ratchet up over time?

4. Are our institutions broken? From the tough debates come an even tougher question: have our governmental institutions, revered for more than 225 years, fallen hopelessly out of sync with the problems they are trying to solve? Our founders quite deliberately designed the American constitutional system to divide power so it could be controlled. They aimed to prevent the rise of another king and cleverly arranged the system with tough limits on what any branch could do without the consent of the others. George Washington took the limits on governmental power so seriously that he insisted on being called simply "Mr. President" instead of a more exalted title. And, despite a steady parade of big crises, the institutions have proven remarkably resilient.

Following the big crises of the 2000s, however, even the most sympathetic observers began to worry that the system that had served America so well for the first two centuries would buckle under the pressures of the third. Two of the nation's most seasoned and insightful observers, Thomas E. Mann and Norman J. Ornstein, sadly concluded in 2012 that "it's even worse than it looks."[22] Another keen political observer, watching from Australia the debacle of Congress's 2011 battle over raising the national debt, shook his head and said, "This is how great empires fall."[23] Have the pressures of political extremism coupled with the truly difficult problems of the 2000s paralyzed our political institutions, especially Congress, to the point that they can't effectively respond to problems, that backsliding is inevitable—and that the nation will fall further and further behind in its efforts to meet twenty-first-century challenges?

5. Can we ever do enough? The effects of the September 11 attacks reached virtually every corner of the American political system in some fashion, and they are unlikely to diminish. Indeed, it's unlikely that the nation can ever truly "win" the war against terrorism. We can never be fully secure, and it's likely that the campaign against terrorism will last decades. It's not a war that the federal government can fight on its own. Rather, this will be a campaign that will require strong and sustained partnerships among the nation's federal, state, and local governments; between government and the private sector; and between the United States and the world community. It will be a war with large and uncertain costs that will compete with other national goals, like good education for children, sound retirement benefits for the elderly, and effective health care for everyone. It's one thing to launch a campaign to change the government of a tyrant, as the United States did in Iraq in 2003; it's quite another to shift national goals, resources, strategies, and tactics to carry on a sustained effort to protect the nation from new, insidious, and clever terrorists. As the Gilmore Commission, a special advisory panel to the president and Congress, concluded in its 2003 report *Forging America's New Normalcy*,

> There will never be an end point in America's readiness. Enemies will change tactics, citizens' attitudes about what adjustments in their lives they are ready to accept will evolve, and leaders will be confronted with legitimate competing priorities that will demand attention. . . . In the end, America's response to the threat of terrorism will be measured in how we manage the risk. There will never be a 100% guarantee of security for our people, the economy, and our society. We must resist the urge to seek total security—it is not achievable and drains our attention from those things that can be accomplished.

The "new normalcy," the report concludes, requires that the nation devise a strategy for pursuing its enduring values, reducing fear, and countering the terrorist threat.[24] It means determining how to do what must be done without being distracted by the pursuit of what cannot be done.

After September 11, the United States found itself embroiled in broad and contentious global issues that it could neither escape nor fully control. Defense analysts in the 1990s wondered how the fall of the Berlin Wall and the end of the Cold War would affect diplomacy and world order. They discovered that ethnic conflicts and terrorism had replaced tensions between the United States and the Soviet Union—that asymmetric conflicts had replaced symmetric ones. President George W. Bush announced a strategy of preemption, which defined a military approach in which the United States stood ready to launch an attack to prevent other forces from striking the nation. His critics contended that the go-it-alone strategy risked alienating the United States from its allies and undermining its ability to build international coalitions in the antiterrorism war. In a host of areas, the nation found itself facing new puzzles, with sweeping implications for policy and politics. Moreover, both political parties came to realize that there is frequently little political gain in *preventing* problems. Citizens take for granted that their officials will try to keep the nation safe. There can be political risk if terrorist attacks or financial crises occur, since the party in power can be blamed for failing to prevent them. At the same time, however, the September 11 attacks demonstrated that shocked citizens often rally around the flag and support a president who promises strong action. Terrorism's effects on the political system have proved deceptively difficult to forecast.

I know several homeland security specialists, both experts on terrorism and experts on natural disasters. Three things strike me about them. One is that they are extraordinarily dedicated. They spend endless amounts of time on some of the nation's most important issues. The second is that they are very, very smart. They have an uncommon ability to sort through the vast noise and confusion of the homeland security debate to bring real clarity to the issues, which is no mean feat. The third is that they spend their time strategizing about events that most of us would gladly not think about. The very nature of asymmetric conflict— the focus on small forces strategically placed to bring maximum damage to large, powerful nations—is that it is uncertain, dangerous, and often aimed at innocents. The rise of new, post–Cold War problems coupled with the rise of asymmetric conflict means that, unfortunately, such experts are unlikely to run out of work. The implications are sobering. Add to that the warnings that climate-based disasters could well increase and that continued economic instability seems a certainty. The coming years will be packed with big challenges that demand response—and where no response is ever likely to be enough.

THE CHALLENGE TO TWENTY-FIRST-CENTURY AMERICAN DEMOCRACY

Can the American system cope with these ongoing challenges? The debate rages. Optimists, like Baumgartner and Jones, believe that the government and its institutions have tremendous flexibility to respond to shocks. Government, they claim, often makes its biggest and most productive changes when big events punctuate the equilibrium, and the system's resiliency gives it the ability to adapt. But other analysts aren't so sure. Political scientists John E. Chubb and Paul E. Peterson argue that government has steadily become less effective. Special interests steer policy away from the public interest. Congress is more fragmented, and the presidency is more politicized. The federal bureaucracy has become more labyrinthine and difficult to control. Efforts to tackle previous problems have often been unsuccessful. The roots of the problem, Chubb and Peterson say, are in the behavior of American political institutions, and they wonder whether government can govern.[25] Todd LaPorte, one of America's best observers of organizational behavior, wonders whether what we have is as good as it gets.[26]

American government has clearly made progress in resolving some of these issues. It is also quite clear, through recurring crises, that many of the promises of reform have fallen far short. We are expecting government to do more things, and more of these things are harder than what we've asked government to do before. The spotlight on performance has become more intense, and debates about the performance of government—not only the coordination of its administrative systems but also the behavior of key political institutions—have become far more heated.

For some problems, such as the budget deficit or the balance of trade, the implications may be huge, but the immediate costs of failure—or even stumbling in dealing with the issues—are not catastrophic (at least in the short run). For homeland security and natural disasters, however, even small errors can have huge and punishing costs. We won't accept the possibility that terrorists can again kill thousands of Americans on a single day, or that Americans will stand up to their waists in water wondering where their government is, or that their financial system will collapse and take their life's savings with it. As these issues become more important, the fundamental question becomes sharper.

As cardiologists always tell patients after stress tests, it's important to learn from the tracings and improve. There are countless distractions for patients trying to eat right and exercise well. It's easy to imagine that government will do no better. But these are issues for which that answer is unacceptable. Devising new strategies for effective governance— adapting our historic institutions to new and unforgiving challenges— stands as the largest challenge to democracy in the twenty-first century.

There is reason for optimism. Government agencies have become *far more effective in linking their operations*—in "connecting the dots." American officials have developed new, sophisticated partnerships with colleagues abroad. We have come to take for granted the enormous change in grassroots governance brought by the welfare reform strategy of the 1990s: the new service networks bringing together local governmental officials and nongovernmental partners in moving people from welfare to work. Much of the health care senior citizens receive is delivered through a government-financed partnership among a vast array of service providers. Some analysts believe that even the biggest problems can be solved, "not by a single, seismic event, but by a slow shift in politics." In fact, according to Matt Bennett and Jonathan Cowan of the Washington think tank Third Way, "virtually nothing is impossible in American politics. Even mountains will eventually be moved, but it will take the work of years, not a moment of shock or pain."[27] In short, incrementalism might just triumph in the end.

Moreover, *a new generation of leaders*, including retired Coast Guard Admiral Thad Allen, who helped mobilize government resources in aid of those mired in Katrina's muck, has helped identify and solve the central paradox: increasingly complex problems and growing organizational complexity require even stronger individual leadership. These leaders—meta-leaders, as some theorists call them—can serve as bridge builders to link related organizations who share a piece of important, interconnected missions.[28] It's unlikely that we will be able to reform our institutions quickly enough to match the pace of shifting problems. It's even more unlikely, even if we succeeded in doing so, that such reforms could stabilize those institutions for long, before new challenges overwhelmed them yet again. If that's the dark side of the issue, the bright side is that, when leaders lead, they can provide the energy and insight needed to build the critical bridges required to arrive at networked solutions to complex problems. This, in turn, is the opportunity facing those who care about the nation's future. Never before has leadership been as important, and never before has leadership across organizational boundaries been such a critical component. As Allen explained, "It's [about] how you work across government and large complex organizations to create unity of effort . . . and how you understand the event and inspire the people around you to create what the public would expect as a whole of government response. That is a real premium in my view on leadership these days."[29]

Nevertheless, government has been undergoing *governance climate change*, which exacerbates policy lightning. Public problems increasingly arise from sources beyond the immediate boundaries of individual government agencies. As the world becomes more complex and interconnected, more problems diffuse across organizational boundaries, intergovernmental boundaries, public-private boundaries, national boundaries, and indeed continental boundaries. In 2009, the deadly H1N1 virus spread around China. A single airplane passenger was infected in a Hong Kong hotel (perhaps without ever having been in physical contact with the person who first became ill), flew home to Toronto, and sparked an outbreak that within days virtually shut the city down. It's very hard for bureaucracies to be resilient in the face of problems launched so far away and that ripple so quickly through such complex and unpredictable chains.

That creates an *accountability dilemma.* When policy lightning strikes, the media and the public typically call for the heads of the responsible officials. Because the climate change producing policy lightning is so complex, however, it's often very difficult—if not impossible—to identify and remove the officials responsible for the problem. The September 11 terrorist attacks led to a wrenching examination of the American governance system and a 585-page report detailing fundamental problems. In the end, no one was fired. There was wide consensus that government had failed during the response to Katrina, but despite catastrophic collapses throughout the system, only one person was fired (the head of the federal emergency relief agency, Michael Brown) and New Orleans's mayor, Ray Nagin, soon won reelection. The 2008 financial collapse cost the jobs of countless workers around the world, but critics argued that many of the financial organizations responsible for the crisis bounced back quickly—with governments' help.

When problems come from so many sources; when an effective response requires a carefully integrated network of public, private, and nongovernmental organizations; and when such networks are tremendously difficult to build and sustain, it's often hard to identify individuals who are responsible and who can be punished. Indeed, given the complexity of both problems and responses, rarely is anyone fully in charge of anything. As a result, there is an accountability dilemma—it's hard to identify who is responsible for big problems, and the bigger the problem the harder it often is to hold anyone accountable.

This underlines the *mismatch of governance structures and policy problems.* Government officials and citizens alike, as I've noted elsewhere, tend to view government as a vending machine: insert tax dollars, pull the lever, and wait for the desired result to emerge from the governance machine.[30] If a problem occurs, then the solution is to climb inside the machine and restructure it—by abolishing an agency here, creating a new agency there, centralizing some decisions, or decentralizing others. But since so many policy lightning problems require integrated cross-sector solutions, no amount of tinkering inside any one machine can equip the system to attack problems that require coordination across machines.

The result is a *governance gap.* Effective solutions to policy lightning and governance climate-change problems demand coordinated action across multiple bureaucracies within individual governments, multiple layers of government, multiple sectors of society, and multiple societies across nations. With more practice, the world's governments have unquestionably become much better at attacking these issues. But the problems outlined above raise big concerns: we need to worry that the problems are spreading and becoming more complicated faster than we are learning and adapting. In sum,

1. More problems have become public problems.

2. More of these public problems are spreading more quickly.

3. The failure to act instantly can pose serious consequences.

4. More of these problems are unknown unknowns.

5. Unknown unknowns are especially difficult to resolve because they lie outside established governmental routines.

6. Many of these problems are evolving more quickly than governments' abilities to solve them, especially because our political institutions poorly match the problems they're trying to solve.

7. It's little wonder that failures result.

8. We're not likely to do better unless we learn how to learn faster.

9. Unless our rate of learning increases, the rate of failure could accelerate.

10. There's good news: There are solutions, but they tend to lie beyond bureaucracy and traditional governance.

Unless we learn how to learn much more quickly, the combination of policy lightning and governance climate-change risks widening the gap between the problems governments face and their capacity to solve them. This, in turn, is likely only to increase the severity of policy lightning storms and the consequences they produce. We risk falling further and further behind. That's the biggest challenge to twenty-first-century American democracy.

Notes

Chapter 1

1. Jeffrey L. Pressman and Aaron Wildavsky, *Implementation: How Great Expectations in Washington Are Dashed in Oakland; or, Why It's Amazing That Federal Programs Work at All, This Being a Saga of the Economic Development Administration as Told by Two Sympathetic Observers Who Seek to Build Morals on a Foundation of Ruined Hopes.* (Berkeley: University of California Press, 1973).

2. Ellen Frielich, "JP Morgan Houston Janitor Wants Jamie Dimon to Walk in Her Shoes," *Reuters* (June 19, 2012), http://blogs.reuters.com/macroscope/2012/06/20/jp-morgan-houston-janitor-wants-jamie-dimon-to-walk-in-her-shoes/.

3. James B. Stewart, "Volcker Rule, Once Simple, Now Boggles," *New York Times* (October 21, 2011), http://www.nytimes.com/2011/10/22/business/volcker-rule-grows-from-simple-to-complex.html?pagewanted=all.

4. Fawn Johnson, "Romney Campaign Says He Wouldn't Abolish FEMA" (October 30, 2012), http://www.govexec.com/management/2012/10/romney-campaign-says-he-wouldnt-abolish-fema/59111/?oref=river.

5. U.S. Department of Defense, Office of the Assistant Secretary of Defense (Public Affairs), *DoD News Briefing—Secretary Rumsfeld and Gen. Myers,* presented by Donald H. Rumsfeld and Richard Myers (February 12, 2002), http://www.defense.gov/transcripts/transcript.aspx?transcriptid=2636.

6. Social Security Administration, *Summary of Performance and Financial Information: Fiscal Year 2011,* 4, http://www.ssa.gov/pgm/FY_2011_Summary_PAR.pdf.

7. Federal Aviation Administration, *FAA's Fiscal Year 2011 Summary of Performance and Financial Information* (2011), http://www.faa.gov/about/plans_reports/media/FY11FAASum.pdf.

8. Walter Isaacson, *Benjamin Franklin: An American Life* (New York: Simon & Schuster, 2003).

9. CNN.com, "Forests of Columns Kept Building Standing" (January 24, 2003), http://www.cnn.com/2003/US/01/24/attacks.pentagon/index.html.

10. "The Story of 'Let's Roll'" (2000–2001), http://www.letsrollheroes.com/thestory.shtml.

11. "The War against America: An Unfathomable Attack," *New York Times* (September 12, 2001): A26.

12. Indira A. R. Lakshmanan, "Attack on America/Nations Respond," *Boston Globe* (September 12, 2001): A20.

13. The White House, "Governor Ridge Sworn In to Lead Homeland Security" (October 8, 2001), http://www.whitehouse.gov/news/releases/2001/10/20011008–3.html.

14. Johns Hopkins Center for Civilian Biodefense, Center for Strategic and International Studies, ANSER, and Memorial Institute for the Prevention of Terrorism, *Dark Winter: Final Script* (June 22–23, 2001), http://www.hopkins-biodefense.org/DARK%20WINTER.pdf.

15. Tara O'Toole, Michael Mair, and Thomas V. Inglesby, "Shining Light on 'Dark Winter,'" *Clinical Infectious Diseases* 34 (February 19, 2002): 972–983, http://www.journals.uchicago.edu/CID/journal/issues/v34n7/020165/020165.html.

16. NTI, "U.S. Not Prepared for Biological Weapons Attack" (July 23, 2001), http://www.nti.org/newsroom/news/not-prepared-biological-weapons-attack/.

17. Eric V. Larson and John E. Peters, *Preparing the U.S. Army for Homeland Security: Concepts, Issues, and Options* (Santa Monica, CA: RAND, 2001), 1–2, http://www.rand.org/publications/MR/MR1251/.

18. CNN.com, "Transcript of Radio Interview with Mayor Nagin" (September 2, 2005), http://www.cnn.com/2005/US/09/02/nagin.transcript/.

19. CNN.com, "American Morning" (September 2, 2005), http://www.transcripts.cnn.com/TRANSCRIPTS/0509/02/ltm.03.html.

20. Michael Lewis and David Einhorn, "The End of the Financial World as We Knew It," *New York Times* (January 3, 2009), http://www.nytimes.com/2009/01/04/opinion/04einhorn.html?_r=1&sq=einhorn&st=cse&scp=1&pagewanted=all.

21. Roger Lowenstein, "Jamie Dimon: America's Least-Hated Banker," *New York Times* (December 1, 2010), http://www.nytimes.com/2010/12/05/magazine/05Dimon-t.html?pagewanted=all.

22. Nathan Vardi, "The Real Loss for Jamie Dimon and JPMorgan Chase: Their Integrity," *Forbes* (July 13, 2012), http://www.forbes.com/sites/nathanvardi/2012/07/13/jamie-dimon-and-jpmorgan-chase-lose-their-integrity/.

23. Fareed Zakaria, "The Politics of Rage: Why Do They Hate Us?" *Newsweek* 22 (October 15, 2001), http://www.thedailybeast.com/newsweek/2001/10/14/the-politics-of-rage-why-do-they-hate-us.html.

24. CNN.com, "Harrowing Tales of Loss Emerge in Katrina's Wake" (August 31, 2005), http://www.cnn.com/2005/WEATHER/08/31/katrina.people/index.html.

25. Vikas Bajaj, "Financial Crisis Enters New Phase," *New York Times* (September 17, 2008), http://www.nytimes.com/2008/09/18/business/18markets.html?_r=1&hp.

26. National Commission on the Causes of the Financial and Economic Crisis in the United States, *The Financial Crisis Inquiry Report* (2011), http://www.gpo.gov/fdsys/pkg/GPO-FCIC/pdf/GPO-FCIC.pdf.

Chapter 2

1. ABCNEWS.com, "The Cell," August 16, 2002, http://www.abcnews.go.com/sections/2020/DailyNews/wtc_yearTheCell_excerpt.html.

2. CBSNEWS.com, "From the Doomed Cockpits," October 16, 2001, http://www.cbsnews.com/stories/2001/10/16/archive/main314846.shtml.

3. Ricardo Alonso-Zaldivar, "Policy of Knives on Airplanes Being Re-examined," *Los Angeles Times* (September 15, 2001): A20.

4. Ibid.

4. Susan Candiotti, "Pakistani Officials Question Two Top al Qaeda Operatives," *CNN Sunday Morning* (September 15, 2002), http://www.cnn.com/TRANSCRIPTS/0209/15/sm.07.html.

5. CNN.com, "Maryland Police Release Hijacker Traffic Stop Video" (January 8, 2002), http://transcripts.cnn.com/TRANSCRIPTS/0201/08/se.01.html

6. CBSNEWS.com, "Hijackers Remain Mysterious" (September 11, 2002), http://www.cbsnews.com/stories/2002/09/11/september11/main521523.shtml.

7. Described in a memo from FBI agent Colleen Rowley to FBI director Robert Mueller, May 21, 2002, http://www.time.com/time/covers/1101020603/memo.html.

8. Chuck Grassley, "Fixing the FBI" (June 7, 2002), http://www.grassley.senate.gov/cgl/2002/cg02–06–7.htm.

9. Joint Inquiry Staff, Joint Committee on Intelligence, Congress of the United States, "Joint Inquiry Staff Statement—Part I," 107th Cong., 2nd sess. (September 18, 2002), http://www.i.cnn.qnet/cnn/2002/ALLPOLITICS/09/18/intelligence.hearings/intel.911.report.pdf.

10. Brian Friel, "State Department Official Blasts Intelligence Agencies" (October 12, 2001), http://www.govexec.com/dailyfed/1001/101201b2.htm.

11. Federation for American Immigration Reform, "World Trade Center and Pentagon Terrorists' Identity and Immigration Status" (April 2003), http://www.fairus.org/html/04178101.htm.

12. U.S. General Accounting Office, *Information Technology: Terrorist Watch Lists Should Be Consolidated to Promote Better Integration and Sharing,* Report GAO-03–322 (April 23, 2003), "Highlights" page.

13. CNN.com, "Senators: 9/11 Report to Detail Intelligence Failures" (July 24, 2003), http://www.cnn.com/2003/ALLPOLITICS/07/24/9.11.report/index.html.

14. U.S. Postal Service, "Message to Customers" (October 17, 2001), http://www.usps.com/news/2001/press/pr01_1010tips.htm.

15. Marie McCullough, "Anthrax Hoaxes, False Alarms Taxing Authorities Nationwide," *Seattle Times* (November 10, 2001), http://www.seattletimes .nwsource.com/html/nationworld/134364704_angst10.html.

16. ABC News, "*Nightline* Biowar Series" (October 1, 1999), http://www .abcnews.go.com/onair/Nightline/n1991001_biowar.html.

17. CNN.com, "One Year Later: Security Tighter, Cities Stretched" (September 12, 2002), http://www.cnn.com/2002/US/09/06/prepared.cities .overview/index.html.

18. "The Shoe Bomber's World," *Time* (February 16, 2002), http://www .time.com/time/world/article/0,8599,203478,00.html.

19. Susan Stellin, "There's No Tiptoeing Past Shoe Policy," *New York Times* (July 20, 2003): section 5, p. 8.

20. Tony Karon, "The 'Dirty Bomb' Scenario," *Time* (June 10, 2002), http://www.time.com/time/nation/article/0,8599,182637,00.html.

21. Harold Seidman, *Politics, Position, and Power: The Dynamics of Federal Organization,* 5th ed. (New York: Oxford University Press, 1998), 142. Portions of the material that follows originally appeared in "Contingent Coordination: Practical and Theoretical Problems for Homeland Security," *American Review of Public Administration* 33 (September 2003): 253–277.

22. Titan Systems Corporation, *Arlington County: After-Action Report on the Response to the September 11 Terrorist Attack on the Pentagon* (2002): A-4–A-7, http://www.co.arlington.va.us/fire/edu/about/pdf/after_report.pdf.

23. Ibid., A-10.

24. Ibid., A-9.

25. Ibid., A-10.

26. Ibid., A-12–A-13.

27. Ibid., A-10.

28. See McKinsey and Company, *Increasing FDNY's Preparedness* (2002), http://www.nyc.gov/html/fdny/html/mck_report/toc.html.

29. Ibid., 13.

Chapter 3

1. National Commission on Terrorist Attacks upon the United States (9/11 Commission), *Final Report* (New York: Norton, 2004), 339.

2. Alison Mitchell, "Joint Congress Transformed into a United Showcase of Courage and Resolve," *New York Times* (September 21, 2001): B5.

3. "President Bush's Address on Terrorism before a Joint Meeting of Congress," *New York Times* (September 21, 2001): B4.

4. Michael Taylor, "New Defense Office Takes Shape," *San Francisco Chronicle* (September 30, 2001): A21.

5. Chester I. Barnard, *The Functions of the Executive* (Cambridge, MA: Harvard University Press, 1938), 94.

6. Sydney H. Freedberg Jr., "Homeland Defense Effort Breaks Down Walls of Government" (October 19, 2001), http://www.govexec.com/daily fed/1001/101901nj1.htm.

7. Ibid.

8. Herbert Emmerich, *Federal Organization and Administrative Management* (University: University of Alabama Press, 1971), 17.

9. For an exploration of this issue, see Robert Axelrod, *The Evolution of Cooperation* (New York: Basic Books, 1984), esp. 6–7; Joel D. Aberbach and Bert A. Rockman, "Mandates or Mandarins? Control and Discretion in the Modern Administrative State," *Public Administration Review* 48 (1988): 606–612; B. Dan Wood and Richard W. Waterman, "The Dynamics of Political Control of the Bureaucracy," *American Political Science Review* 85 (1991): 801–828; and Richard W. Waterman, Amelia Rouse, and Robert Wright, "The Venues of Influence: A New Theory of Political Control of the Bureaucracy," *Journal of Public Administration Research and Theory* 8 (January 1998): 13–38.

10. House Committee on Appropriations, Subcommittee on Commerce, State, Justice, the Judiciary, and Related Agencies, testimony of Dick Thornburgh, chairman, National Academy of Public Administration Panel on FBI Reorganization, 108th Cong., 1st sess. (June 18, 2003).

11. Gregory F. Treverton, "Set Up to Fail" (September 1, 2002), http://www.govexec.com/features/0902/0902s6.htm.

12. Michael Fuoco, "Coast Guard Profile Higher on Rivers," *Pittsburgh Post-Gazette* (May 3, 2003): A1.

13. Statement of JayEtta Z. Hecker, General Accounting Office, *Coast Guard: Challenges during the Transition to the Department of Homeland Security,* Report GAO-03–594T (April 1, 2002), 2.

14. Anne M. Khademian, *Working with Culture: The Way the Job Gets Done in Public Programs* (Washington, DC: CQ Press, 2002), 3.

15. Interview with Michael O'Hanlon (October 18, 2001), http://www.govexec.com/dailyfed/1001/101801njcom1.htm.

16. Robert Pear, "Traces of Terror: The New Department; Lawmakers Asking If Plan on Terror Goes Far Enough," *New York Times* (June 8, 2002): A1.

17. U.S. Department of Health and Human Services, *Accountability Report: Fiscal Year 2001* (Washington, DC: Government Printing Office, 2002), http://www.hhs.gov/of/reports/account/acct01/pdf/intro.pdf, p. viii.

18. Richard B. Schmitt, "FBI's Computer Upgrade Develops Its Own Glitches," *New York Times* (January 28, 2003): 1.

19. Shane Harris, "Rebooting the Bureau" (August 1, 2002), http://www.govexec.com/features/0802/0802s3.htm.

20. Schmitt, "FBI's Computer Upgrade."

21. Harris, "Rebooting the Bureau."

22. Government Accountability Office, *Weak Controls over Trilogy Project Led to Payment of Questionable Contractor Costs and Missing Assets,* Report GAO-06–306 (February 2006).

23. Kenneth A. Shepsle and Mark S. Bonchek, *Analyzing Politics: Rationality, Behavior, and Institutions* (New York: Norton, 1997), 359.

24. Geoff Earle and Mark Wegner, "Reorganization Plan Gains Bipartisan Support on Hill" (June 6, 2002), http://www.govexec.com/dailyfed/0602/060602cd1.htm.

25. Beryl A. Radin, *The Accountable Juggler: The Art of Leadership in a Federal Agency* (Washington, DC: CQ Press, 2002), 70.

26. James L. Sundquist, "Congress as Public Administrator," in *A Centennial History of the American Administrative State,* ed. Ralph C. Chandler (New York: Free Press, 1987), 285.

27. John Arquilla and David Ronfeldt, *Networks and Netwars: The Future of Terror, Crime, and Militancy* (Santa Monica, CA: RAND, 2001), ix.

28. Ibid., 364–365.

29. Brody Mullins and Pamela Barnett, "Move Underway to Authorize Homeland Security Office" (October 5, 2001), http://www.govexec.com/dailyfed/1001/100501cd1.htm.

30. Executive Order (October 8, 2001), http://www.whitehouse.gov/news/releases/2001/10/20011008–2.html.

31. Freedberg, "Homeland Defense Effort Breaks Down Walls of Government."

32. Patty Davis, "Critics Fault Airport Security System," CNN.com (September 18, 2001), http://www.edition.cnn.com/2001/TRAVEL/NEWS/09/18/rec.airport.security/.

33. George W. Bush, "Radio Address of the President to the Nation" (October 27, 2001), http://www.whitehouse.gov/news/releases/2001/10/20011027.html.

34. April Fulton and Keith Koffler, "Senators Press House to Federalize Airport Security" (October 23, 2001), http://www.govexec.com/dailyfed/1001/102301cd2.htm.

35. CNN.com, "Daschle Joins Call for Independent 9/11 Probe" (May 22, 2002), http://www.cnn.com/2002/ALLPOLITICS/05/22/probe.daschle/.

36. David Johnston and Neil A. Lewis, "Whistle-Blower Recounts Faults within the FBI," *New York Times* (June 7, 2002): A1.

37. National Commission on Terrorist Attacks, *Final Report,* 276.

38. Transcript of speech by President George W. Bush, *New York Times* (June 7, 2002): A20.

39. Ibid.

40. Kellie Lunney, "Administration Already Has Homeland Security Flexibility, Union Says" (August 28, 2002), http://www.govexec.com/dailyfed/0802/082802m1.htm.

41. Remarks by the president on signing of Homeland Security Act, November 25, 2002, http://www.whitehouse.gov/news/releases/2002/11/20021125–6.html.

42. Siobhan Gorman, "FBI, CIA Remain Worlds Apart" (August 1, 2003), http://www.govexec.com/dailyfed/0803/080103nj1.htm.

43. John Gray, *Men Are from Mars, Women Are from Venus: A Practical Guide for Improving Communication and Getting What You Want in Your Relationships* (New York: HarperCollins, 1993); for the comparison, see Gorman, "FBI, CIA Remain Worlds Apart."

44. Gorman, "FBI, CIA Remain Worlds Apart."

45. "Homeland Security Department Targets Child Sex Abuse," *Washington Post* (July 10, 2003): A8.

Chapter 4

1. Unless otherwise cited, quotations in this chapter come from the *New Orleans Times-Picayune*'s Pulitzer Prize–winning coverage of the storm, http://www.nola.com/katrina/updates/index.ssf?/mtlogs/nola_Times-Picayune/archives/2005_08_29.html.

2. PBS, "The Storm," *Frontline* (2005), http://www.pbs.org/wgbh/pages/frontline/storm/etc/script.html.

3. This account comes from interviews by the author and from an extended newspaper account by Christopher Rhoads, "After Katrina, City Officials Struggled to Keep Order," *Wall Street Journal* (September 9, 2005): A1.

4. Senate Committee on Homeland Security and Governmental Affairs, *A Nation Still Unprepared,* 109th Cong., 2nd sess. (2006), 15–3, http://www.hsgac.senate.gov/index.cfm?Fuseaction=Links.KatAdd.

5. Ibid., 15–6.

6. PBS, "The Storm."

7. Ibid.

8. White House, "President Arrives in Alabama, Briefed on Hurricane Katrina" (September 2, 2005), http://www.whitehouse.gov/news/releases/2005/09/20050902–2.html.

9. "An Open Letter to the President," *New Orleans Times-Picayune* (September 4, 2005): A15.

10. Senate Committee on Homeland Security, *A Nation Still Unprepared,* 6.

11. House Select Bipartisan Committee to Investigate the Preparation for and Response to Hurricane Katrina, *A Failure of Initiative,* 109th Cong., 1st sess. (2005), x, http://katrina.house.gov/.

12. White House, "Introduction to *The Federal Response to Hurricane Katrina: Lessons Learned*" (2005), http://www.whitehouse.gov/reports/katrina-lessons-learned/.

13. Quoted in Senate Committee on Homeland Security, *A Nation Still Unprepared,* 27–5.

14. National Commission on Terrorist Attacks upon the United States, *The 9/11 Commission Report* (New York: Norton, 2004), 344, 350.

15. Interviews with the author. Sources remained off the record.

16. Senate Committee on Homeland Security, *A Nation Still Unprepared,* 12–10.

17. U.S. Government Accountability Office, *FEMA's Control Weaknesses Exposed the Government to Significant Fraud and Abuse,* Report GAO-06–655 (June 2006).

18. Senate Committee on Homeland Security, *A Nation Still Unprepared,* 11–1.

19. Ann Scott Tyson, "Strain of Iraq War Means the Relief Burden Will Have to Be Shared," *Washington Post* (August 31, 2005): A14.

20. Mary-Rose Abraham, "Police Fired Shots to Prevent Katrina Evacuees from Crossing Bridge, Officials Confirm," *Columbia Journalist* (September 12, 2005), http://www.columbiajournalist.org/rw1_dinges/2005/article.asp?subj=national& course=rw1_dinges&id=572.

21. Senate Committee on Homeland Security, *A Nation Still Unprepared,* 10–3.

22. Ibid., 10–5.

23. Ibid., 10–15.

24. Bill Nichols and Richard Benedetto, "Govs to Bush: Relief Our Job," *USA Today* (October 2, 2005), http://www.usatoday.com/news/washington/2005–10–02-gov-survey_x.htm.

25. Henry B. Hogue and Keith Bea, *Federal Emergency Management and Homeland Security Organization: Historical Development and Legislative Options,* Report RL33369 (Washington, DC: Congressional Research Service, 2006).

26. National Response Team, *Final Report: Exercise TOPOFF 2000 and National Capital Region After-Action Report* (2001).

27. Senate Committee on Homeland Security, *A Nation Still Unprepared,* "Recommendations," 5.

28. Peter Eisinger, "Imperfect Federalism: The Intergovernmental Partnership for Homeland Security," *Public Administration Review* 66 (July/August 2006): 537–545.

29. Interview with the author.

30. James Kitfield, "New Coast Guard Chief Discusses Lessons Learned from Katrina" (June 2, 2006), http://www.govexec.com/story_page.cfm?articleid=34234&dcn=todaysnews.

Chapter 5

1. Railroad Commission of Texas, "Highway-Rail Grade Crossing Safety," http://www.rrc.state.tx.us/divisions/rail/gxovervw.html.

2. Martin Landau, "Redundancy, Duplication, and the Problem of Duplication and Overlap," *Public Administration Review* 29 (July/August, 1969): 346–358.

3. See Todd LaPorte, "High Reliability Organizations: Unlikely, Demanding and At Risk," *Journal of Crisis and Contingency Management* 4 (1996): 55–59; Todd LaPorte and Craig Thomas, "Regulatory Compliance and the Ethos of Quality Enhancement: Surprises in Nuclear Power Plant Operations," *Journal of Public Administration Research and Theory* 5 (1996): 111–139; Todd LaPorte and Paula Consolini, "Working in Practice but Not in Theory: Theoretical Challenges of High-Reliability Organizations," *Journal of Public Administration Research and Theory* 1 (1991): 19–47; and H. George Frederickson and Todd LaPorte, "Airport Security, High Reliability, and the Problem of Rationality," *Public Administration Review* 62 (September 2002): 33–43.

4. Susan Stellin, "There's No Tiptoeing Past Shoe Policy," *New York Times* (July 20, 2003): section 5, p. 8.

5. Frederickson and LaPorte, "Airport Security, High Reliability, and the Problem of Rationality," 41.

6. Columbia Accident Investigation Board, *Report,* vol. 1 (Washington, DC: Government Printing Office, 2003).

7. David Ropeik and George Gray, *Risk: A Practical Guide for Deciding What's Really Safe and What's Really Dangerous in the World around You* (New York: Mariner Books, 2002).

8. Paul Slovic and Elike U. Weber, "Perception of Risk Posed by Extreme Events" (paper presented at the conference "Risk Management Strategies in an Uncertain World," Palisades, NY, April 12–13, 2002), http://www.ldeo .columbia.edu/CHRR/ Roundtable/slovic_wp.pdf.

9. Baruch Fischhoff, "Behaviorally Realistic Management," in *On Risk and Disaster: Lessons from Hurricane Katrina,* ed. Ronald J. Daniels, Donald F. Kettl, and Howard Kunreuther (Philadelphia: University of Pennsylvania Press, 2006), 77, 87.

10. See http://www.biz.uiowa.edu/iem/markets/.

11. MSNBC News, "Pentagon Kills 'Terror Futures Market'" (July 29, 2003), http://www.msnbc.com/news/945269.asp.

12. See, for example, Charles E. Lindblom, *Politics and Markets: The World's Political Economic Systems* (New York: Basic Books, 1977).

13. Lloyd Dixon, Noreen Clancy, Seth A. Seabury, and Adrian Overton, "The National Flood Insurance Program's Market Penetration Rate: Estimates and Policy Implications" (RAND Corporation, 2006), http://www.rand.org/ pubs/technical_ reports/TR300/.

14. Wayne Perry, "Hurricane Sandy: A Glimpse at New York's Scary Future" (November 2, 2012), http://www.livescience.com/24496-hurricane-sandy-new-york-future-superstorms.html.

15. For an analysis of these issues, see Howard Kunreuther, "Has the Time Come for Comprehensive Natural Disaster Insurance?" in *On Risk and*

Disaster: Lessons from Hurricane Katrina, ed. Ronald J. Daniels, Donald F. Kettl, and Howard Kunreuther (Philadelphia: University of Pennsylvania Press, 2006), 175–201.

16. Government Accountability Office, "National Flood Insurance Program: Actions to Address Repetitive Loss Properties," Report GAO-04–401T (March 25, 2004), http://www.gao.gov/highlights/d04401thigh.pdf.

17. FOXNews.com, "Insurance Disputes Delaying Gulf Coast Rebuilding" (June 11, 2006), http://www.foxnews.com/story/0,2933,199057,00.html.

18. Jan Glidewell, "Terrorism Shield Takes on New Hue," *St. Petersburg Times* (March 15, 2002), http://www.sptimes.com/2002/03/15/news_pf/Columns/Terrorism _shield_take.shtml.

19. Jay Leno, quoted in "Political Humor with Daniel Kurtzman," http://www.politicalhumor.about.com/library/blterrorhumor.htm.

20. Linda Hales, "This Year's Gridiron Dinner: Funny, but Not Ha-Ha Funny," *Washington Post* (March 10, 2003): C1.

21. Elisabeth Bumiller, "In Case of Emergency, Cupboards May Be Bare," *New York Times* (February 17, 2003): A9.

22. Matthew Engel, "The Terror of Duct Tape," (London) *Guardian* (February 18, 2003): 17.

23. John Tierney, "Ridge Gets the Joke, but He Hasn't Lost His Focus," *New York Times* (March 17, 2003): A20.

24. Shawn Reese, *Homeland Security Advisory System: Possible Issues for Congressional Oversight,* Report RL32023 (Washington, DC: Congressional Research Service, 2003), 8; and Shawn Reese, *Federal Emergency Warning Systems: An Overview,* Report RS21377 (Washington, DC: Congressional Research Service, 2003).

25. CNN.com, "U.S, U.K. Discuss United Anti-terrorism Front" (April 3, 2003), http://www.cnn.com/2003/US/04/03/blunkett.cnna/.

26. Home Office, "Terrorism: Frequently Asked Questions," http://www.homeoffice.gov.uk/terrorism/threat/faq/index.html#10.

27. Ibid.

28. CNN.com, "Color-Coded Threat System to Be Replaced in April" (January 26, 2011), http://www.cnn.com/2011/POLITICS/01/26/threat.level.system.change/index.html.

29. U.S. Department of Homeland Security, "DHS Discontinues Color-Coded Alert System" (January 27, 2011), http://www.dhs.gov/news/2011/01/27/secretary-napolitano-announces-new-national-terrorism-advisory-system-more.

30. Jennifer Barrett, "Newsweek Poll: Bin Laden to Blame for Anthrax" (October 20, 2001), http://www.msnbc.com/news/645354.asp.

31. "Post-ABC Poll: Financial Regulations," *Washington Post* (February 11, 2010), http://voices.washingtonpost.com/behind-the-numbers/2010/02/post-abc_poll_financial_regula.html.

32. Harris Poll no. 46, "Special 9/11 Poll" (September 10, 2002), http://www.harrisinteractive.com/harris_poll/index.asp?PID=325.

33. "Post-ABC Poll: Financial Regulations," *Washington Post*.

34. Robert C. Tucker, *Politics as Leadership* (Columbia: University of Missouri Press, 1981), 18–19.

35. Judith Miller, Jeff Gerth, and Don Van Natta Jr., "Planning for Terror but Failing to Act," *New York Times* (December 30, 2001): A1.

Chapter 6

1. House Permanent Select Committee on Intelligence and Senate Select Committee on Intelligence, *Report of the Joint Inquiry into the Terrorist Attacks of September 11, 2001,* Senate Report 107–351, House Report 107–792, 107th Cong., 2nd sess. (2002).

2. Ibid., xv.

3. Thomas Farragher and Alice Dembner, "America Prepares Law and Politics," *Boston Globe* (September 30, 2001): A1.

4. Peter Slevin and Mary Beth Sheridan, "Suspects Entered U.S. on Legal Visas; Men Blended In; Officials Say 49 Have Been Detained on Immigration Violations," *Washington Post* (September 18, 2001): A6.

5. Farragher and Dembner, "America Prepares Law and Politics," A1.

6. Martin Wolf, "Guarding the Home Front," *Financial Times* (London), September 17, 2001, 24.

7. Farragher and Dembner, "America Prepares Law and Politics."

8. Robert O'Harrow Jr., "Six Weeks in Autumn," *Washington Post* (October 27, 2002): W6.

9. Philip Shenon, "Ashcroft Wants Quick Action on Broader Wiretapping Plan," *New York Times* (September 18, 2001): B4.

10. Ibid.

11. Philip Shenon and Robin Toner, "U.S. Widens Policy on Detaining Suspects," *New York Times* (September 19, 2001): B4.

12. American Civil Liberties Union, "In Defense of Freedom at a Time of Crisis" (September 20, 2001), http://www.aclu.org/NationalSecurity/NationalSecurity.cfm?ID= 9137&c=111.

13. White House, "Remarks by the President at Signing of the Patriot Act, Anti-Terrorism Legislation" (October 26, 2001), http://www.whitehouse.gov/news/releases/2001/10/20011026-5.html.

14. Charles Doyle, "The USA PATRIOT Act: A Sketch," Congressional Research Service (April 18, 2002), http://www.fas.org/irp/crs/RS21203.pdf.

15. Michael R. Zimmerman, "Ashcroft Stumps for Patriot Act in Boston," *eWeek* (September 10, 2003), http://www.eweek.com/article2/0,4149,1259935,00.asp.

16. George W. Bush, "Address to a Joint Session of Congress and the American People" (September 20, 2001), http://www.whitehouse.gov/news/releases/2001/09/20010920-8.html.

17. Human Rights Watch, "September 11: One Year On" (September 9, 2002), http://www.hrw.org/press/2002/09/sept11.htm.

18. Dana Priest and Barton Gellman, "U.S. Decries but Defends Interrogations," *Washington Post* (December 26, 2002): A1.

19. Ibid.

20. Seymour M. Hersh, "Torture at Abu Ghraib," *New Yorker* (May 10, 2004), http://www.newyorker.com/fact/content/?040510fa_fact.

21. Dean Schabner, "Northern Revolt: Alaska Passes Anti–Patriot Act Resolution" (May 23, 2003), http://www.abcnews.go.com/sections/us/DailyNews/alaska_ patriot030523.html.

22. Robert A. Levy, "The USA Patriot Act: We Deserve Better" (Washington, DC: Cato Institute), http://www.cato.org/current/terrorism/pubs/levy-martial-law.html.

23. "CCR Files Constitutional Challenge to Patriot Act" (2003), http://www.ccr-ny.org/v2/reports/report.asp?ObjID=FjMAeaTxLu&Content=278.

24. American Library Association, "Resolution on the USA Patriot Act and Related Measures that Infringe on the Rights of Library Users" (January 29, 2003), http://www.ala.org/Content/NavigationMenu/Our_Association/Offices/ALA_Washington/Issues2/Civil_Liberties,_Intellectual_Freedom,_Privacy/The_USA_Patriot_Act_and_Libraries/ALA_Resolution_on_PATRIOT_Act.htm.

25. Eric Lichtblau, "Ashcroft Mocks Librarians and Others Who Oppose Parts of Counterterrorism Law," *New York Times* (September 16, 2003): A23.

26. Eric Lichtblau, "Government Says It Has Yet to Use New Power to Check Library Records," *New York Times* (September 19, 2003): A16.

27. Richard B. Schmitt, "Planned Sequel to Patriot Act Losing Audience," *Los Angeles Times* (July 29, 2003): part 1, p. 14.

28. Philip Shenon, "Report on USA Patriot Act Alleges Civil Rights Violations," *New York Times* (July 21, 2003): A1.

29. Dana Blanton, "Americans Say Saudis Should Do More to Fight Terror" (August 1, 2003), http://www.foxnews.net/story/0,2933,93549,00.html.

30. Will Lester, "Poll: Freedom's a Concern," *Wisconsin State Journal* (September 11, 2003): A3.

31. Toni Locy, "Patriot Act Blurred in the Public Mind," *USA Today* (February 25, 2004), http://www.usatoday.com/news/washington/2004–02–25-patriot-main_x.htm.

32. Gary Langer, "Poll: Support Seen for Patriot Act," *ABC News* (June 9, 2005), http://www.abcnews.go.com/US/PollVault/story?id=833703.

33. Dahlia Lithwick and Julia Turner, "A Guide to the Patriot Act: Part 1" (September 8, 2003), http://www.slate.msn.com/id/2087984.

34. Quoted by Attorney General John Ashcroft, speech given on April 2, 2003, http://www.usdoj.gov/ag/speeches/2003/040203agremarks.htm.

35. U.S. Department of Justice, "Preserving Life and Liberty" (2003), http:// lifeandliberty.gov.

36. Ibid.

37. Dana Milbank, "President Asks for Expanded Patriot Act," *Washington Post* (September 11, 2003): A1.

38. David E. Sanger, "President Urging Wider U.S. Powers in Terrorism Law," *New York Times* (September 11, 2003): A1.

39. Milbank, "President Asks for Expanded Patriot Act," B4.

40. Eric Lichtblau, "Counterterror Proposals Are a Hard Sell," *New York Times* (September 11, 2003): A19.

41. Charles Babbington, "Congress Votes to Renew Patriot Act, with Changes," *Washington Post* (March 8, 2006): A3.

42. White House, "President Signs USA PATRIOT Improvement and Reauthorization Act" (March 9, 2006), http://www.whitehouse.gov/news/releases/2006/03/ 20060309-4.html.

43. Paul Kane and Felicia Somnez, "Patriot Act Extension Signed into Law Despite Bipartisan Resistance in Congress," *Washington Post* (May 27, 2011), http://www.washingtonpost.com/politics/patriot-act-extension-signed-into-law-despite-bipartisan-resistance-in-congress/2011/05/27/AGbVlsCH_story.html.

44. CNN.com, "Homesick Man Who Flew as Cargo Recounts Journey" (September 10, 2003), http://www.cnn.com/2003/US/Southwest/09/10/stowaway.flight.ap/index.html.

45. Patty Davis and Beth Lewandowski, "Airport Screeners Find Loaded Gun in Teddy Bear" (July 17, 2003), http://www.cnn.com/2003/TRAVEL/07/17/gun.teddy.bear/.

46. "Police Believe Domestic Dispute Led to Gun in Stuffed Animal at RI Airport," *CBS Local* (May 8, 2012), http://boston.cbslocal.com/2012/05/08/gun-ammo-found-inside-childs-stuffed-animals-at-ri-airport/.

47. Jim Puzzanghera, "California Law on Driver's Licenses Spurs National Security Concerns," *SunHerald.com* (September 9, 2003), http://www.sun-herald.com/mld/sunherald/news/politics/6731576.htm.

48. U.S. Government Accountability Office, Statement of Robert J. Cramer before the Senate Committee on Finance, *Security: Counterfeit Identification and Identification Fraud Raise Security Concerns,* Report GAO-03–1147T (September 9, 2003).

49. *CBS Evening News,* "Airport Security Lax at Back Door" (September 8, 2003), http://www.cbsnews.com/stories/2003/09/08/eveningnews/main572208.shtml.

50. "Man Sneaked aboard Commuter Plane," *Holland* (Michigan) *Sentinel Online* (May 29, 2003), http://www.hollandsentinel.com/stories/052903/new_05290 3034.shtml; "Airport Has No Answers for Security Breach,"

ThePittsburghChannel.com (May 28, 2003), http://www.thepittsburgh channel.com/news/2232715/detail.html.

51. Philip Shenon, "Airline Gave Defense Firm Passenger Files," *New York Times* (September 20, 2003): A1.

52. Quoted by Declan McCullagh, "Anger Grows over NSA Surveillance Report," *CNETNews.com* (May 11, 2006), http://www.news.com.com/Anger+ grows+over+Bush+surveillance+report/2100–1028_3–6071525.html.

53. "White House Backs Sale of Ports," *Washington Times* (February 17, 2006), http://www.washingtontimes.com/business/20060216–103648– 2842r.htm.

54. American Bar Association, "Task Force on Presidential Signing Statements and the Separation of Powers Doctrine" (2006), http://www .abanet.org/op/signingstatements/aba_final_signing_statements_recom mendation-report_7–24–06.pdf.

55. CNN.com, "ABA: Bush Violating Constitution" (July 24, 2006), http:// www.cnn.com/2006/POLITICS/07/24/lawyers.bush.ap/index.html.

56. Stuart Taylor Jr., "Rights, Liberties, and Security: Recalibrating the Balance after September 11," *Brookings Review* 21 (Winter 2003): 25–31, http://www.brook.edu/press/review/winter2003/taylor.htm.

57. Peter Finn and Anne E. Kornblut, "Guantanamo Bay: Why Obama Hasn't Fulfilled His Promise to Close the Facility," *Washington Post* (April 23, 2011), http://www.washingtonpost.com/world/guantanamo-bay-how- the-white-house-lost-the-fight-to-close-it/2011/04/14/AFtxR5XE_story.html.

58. CNN.com, "Feds: Chicago-Area Man Charged over Attempted Terrorist Attack" (September 16, 2012), http://www.cnn.com/2012/09/15/ justice/illinois-terrorism-arrest/index.html.

59. U.S. Senate, Committee on Homeland Security and Governmental Affairs, Permanent Subcommittee on Investigations, *Federal Support for and Involvement in State and Local Fusion Centers* (October 3, 2012), 1, http://www.hsgac.senate.gov/download/?id=49139e81–1dd7–4788-a3bb- d6e7d97dde04.

Chapter 7

1. Anna Hipsley, "Goldfish Three-Second Memory Myth Busted," *ABC News* (Australian Broadcasting Corporation, February 19, 2008), http:// www.abc.net.au/news/2008–02–19/goldfish-three-second-memory-myth- busted/1046710.

2. See Discovery, "Goldfish Memory MiniMyth" [video], http://dsc .discovery.com/tv-shows/mythbusters/videos/goldfish-memory-minimyth .htm.

3. Federal Deposit Insurance Corporation, "Failed Bank List," http:// www.fdic.gov/bank/individual/failed/banklist.html.

4. Paul Krugman, "Financial Reform 101," *New York Times* (April 1, 2010), http://www.nytimes.com/2010/04/02/opinion/02krugman.html?r=1.

5. Michael McKee and Scott Lanma, "Greenspan Says U.S. Should Consider Breaking Up Large Banks," *Bloomberg* (October 15, 2009), http://www.bloomberg.com/apps/news?pid=newsarchive&sid=aJ8HPmNUfchg.

6. CNBC.com, "Squawkbox" (July 25, 2012), http://www.cnbc.com/id/48315170.

7. Dan Fitzpatrick, Robin Sidel, and Victoria McGrane, "Bank Breakups: Not So Fast," *Wall Street Journal* (July 29, 2012), http://online.wsj.com/article/SB10000872396390444130304577557183028589736.html?mod=WSJ_hps_LEFTTopStories.

8. John F. Kingdon, *Agendas, Alternatives, and Public Policies,* 2nd ed. (New York: Longman, 1995), 166.

9. Senate Committee on Governmental Affairs, testimony of Robert Kupperman, Center for Strategic and International Studies, 100th Cong., 2nd sess., *Federal News Service* (September 11, 1989).

10. See Niles Eldredge and Stephen Jay Gould, "Punctuated Equilibria: An Alternative to Phyletic Gradualism," in *Models in Paleobiology,* ed. Thomas J. M. Schopf (San Francisco: Freeman, Cooper, 1972), 82–115.

11. Stephen Jay Gould, *Dinosaur in a Haystack: Reflections in Natural History* (New York: Three Rivers Press, 1996), 136.

12. Frank R. Baumgartner and Bryan D. Jones, *Agendas and Instability in American Politics* (Chicago: University of Chicago Press, 1993), 20–21.

13. Ibid., 236.

14. Charles E. Lindblom, "The Science of 'Muddling Through,'" *Public Administration Review* 19 (1959): 79–88.

15. Aaron Wildavsky and Naomi Caiden, *The New Politics of the Budgetary Process,* 5th ed. (New York: Longman, 2004).

16. Robert Block, "FEMA Points to Flaws, Flubs in Terror Drill," *Wall Street Journal* (October 31, 2003). Excerpts from the government report come from this article. The federal agency, FEMA, did not release the report, and the reporter relied on a leaked copy. In fact, this muddy trail further underlines the difficulty of getting good information about the nation's preparedness.

17. Democratic Task Force on Homeland Security, "Federal Homeland Security Assistance to America's Hometowns: A Survey and Report from the Democratic Task Force on Homeland Security" (October 29, 2003), http://www.house.gov/maloney/issues/Homeland/Survey.pdf.

18. House Select Committee on Homeland Security, Subcommittee on Rules, testimony of Norman J. Ornstein, "Perspectives on House Reform of Homeland Security," 108th Cong., 1st sess. (May 19, 2003), http://www.aei.org/news/newsID.175 14/news_detail.asp.

19. White House, "Remarks by the President on Osama bin Laden" (May 2, 2011), http://www.whitehouse.gov/the-press-office/2011/05/02/remarks-president-osama-bin-laden.

20. Theda Skocpol, *Protecting Soldiers and Mothers: The Political Origins of Social Policy in the United States* (Cambridge, MA: Harvard University Press, 1992), 58.

21. Gar Alperovitz, "Wall Street Is Too Big to Regulate," *New York Times* (July 22, 2012), http://www.nytimes.com/2012/07/23/opinion/banks-that-are-too-big-to-regulate-should-be-nationalized.html.

22. Thomas E. Mann and Norman J. Ornstein, *It's Even Worse Than It Looks: How the American Constitutional System Collided with the New Politics of Extremism* (New York: Basic Books, 2012).

23. Interview with the author.

24. Advisory Panel to Assess Domestic Response Capabilities for Terrorism Involving Weapons of Mass Destruction, *Forging America's New Normalcy: Securing Our Homeland, Protecting Our Liberty* (Santa Monica, CA: RAND, 2003), 2, http://www.rand.org/nsrd/terrpanel/volume_v/volume_v.pdf.

25. John E. Chubb and Paul E. Peterson, eds., *Can the Government Govern?* (Washington, DC: Brookings Institution Press, 1989).

26. Interview with the author.

27. Matt Bennett and Jonathan Cowan, "Why Gun Control Isn't a Lost Cause," *Washington Post* (July 27, 2012), http://www.washingtonpost.com/opinions/gun-control-wont-go-anywhere-in-congress-right/2012/07/27/gJQAt8dwDXstory.html.

28. Leonard J. Marcus, Barry C. Dorn, and Joseph M. Henderson, "Meta-Leadership and National Emergency Preparedness: A Model to Build Government Connectivity," *Biosecurity and Bioterrorism: Biodefense Strategy, Practice, and Science* 4 (2006): 128–134; Leonard J. Marcus, Isaac Ashkenazi, Barry Dorn, and Joseph Henderson, "The Five Dimensions of Meta-Leadership" (Cambridge, MA: National Preparedness Leadership Initiative, Harvard School of Public Health, November 2007), http://www.asph.org/userfiles/Competencies-Resources/24_Harvard5D.pdf.

29. Dan Verton, "Adm. Thad Allen: Changing Government Requires Flexible, Learning Leaders," *AOL Government* (December 1, 2011), http://gov.aol.com/2011/12/01/adm-thad-allen-changing-government-requires-flexible-learning/.

30. Donald F. Kettl, *The Next Government of the United States: Why Our Institutions Fail Us and How to Fix Them* (New York: Norton, 2009), pp. 109–113.

Photo Credits

Index

CQ Press, an imprint of SAGE, is the leading publisher of books, periodicals, and electronic products on American government and international affairs. CQ Press consistently ranks among the top commercial publishers in terms of quality, as evidenced by the numerous awards its products have won over the years. CQ Press owes its existence to Nelson Poynter, former publisher of the *St. Petersburg Times,* and his wife Henrietta, with whom he founded Congressional Quarterly in 1945. Poynter established CQ with the mission of promoting democracy through education and in 1975 founded the Modern Media Institute, renamed The Poynter Institute for Media Studies after his death. The Poynter Institute (*www.poynter.org*) is a nonprofit organization dedicated to training journalists and media leaders.

In 2008, CQ Press was acquired by SAGE, a leading international publisher of journals, books, and electronic media for academic, educational, and professional markets. Since 1965, SAGE has helped inform and educate a global community of scholars, practitioners, researchers, and students spanning a wide range of subject areas, including business, humanities, social sciences, and science, technology, and medicine. A privately owned corporation, SAGE has offices in Los Angeles, London, New Delhi, and Singapore, in addition to the Washington DC office of CQ Press.

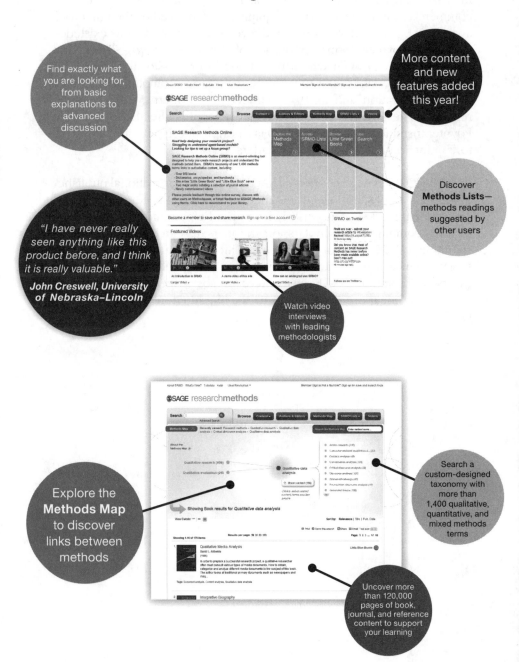

SAGE researchmethods

The essential online tool for researchers from the world's leading methods publisher

More content and new features added this year!

Find exactly what you are looking for, from basic explanations to advanced discussion

Discover Methods Lists—methods readings suggested by other users

"I have never really seen anything like this product before, and I think it is really valuable."
John Creswell, University of Nebraska–Lincoln

Watch video interviews with leading methodologists

Explore the Methods Map to discover links between methods

Search a custom-designed taxonomy with more than 1,400 qualitative, quantitative, and mixed methods terms

Uncover more than 120,000 pages of book, journal, and reference content to support your learning

Find out more at
www.sageresearchmethods.com